THE COUNTRY CLERGY

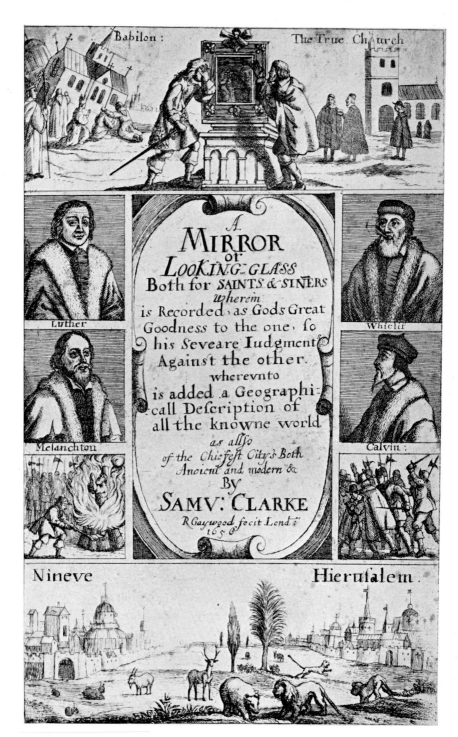

A Mirror for Saints and Sinners, 1656

The COUNTRY CLERGY

In Elizabethan & Stuart Times
1558 - 1660

A. TINDAL HART
M.A, D.D

PHOENIX HOUSE LTD
LONDON

TO

My Grandfather

Horace Fuller Rackham, M.A

VICAR OF HIGH WYCH
FROM 1886 TO 1928

In Memory

© A. TINDAL-HART 1958

Printed in Great Britain
in 11 point Monotype Fournier by
C. Tinling & Co., Ltd., Liverpool, London and Prescot
for Phoenix House Ltd, 38 William IV Street,
Charing Cross, W.C.2

FIRST PUBLISHED 1958

CONTENTS

ILLUSTRATIONS

*The illustrations are reproduced by
permission of the British Museum*

PREFACE

LET ME BEGIN by clearing away a possible misunderstanding. The sharp modern distinction between the town clergy in their swarming industrial parishes and their more slow-moving brethren of the English countryside cannot be applied to the sixteenth and seventeenth centuries. For in that unspecialized age all the parochial clergy, outside possibly London itself and the Universities of Oxford and Cambridge, were thoroughly countrified in their fundamental habits and instincts. One man, indeed, might happen to be the puritanical vicar of a largish market town and another the Laudian rector of a tiny isolated village, yet nothing could permanently disguise the fact that both were also countrymen with identical social and economic interests, pursuing similar pastoral activities, indulging in similar pastimes and recreations, and sometimes alas succumbing to common temptations. That at any rate is the assumption here.

Comparisons are odious; but the intelligent reader of these pages will be quick to notice some startling parallels with our own time. Here are the same dilapidated churches, unkempt churchyards, and decaying parsonages; and here too, owing to the shortage of clergy and their difficulties in making both ends meet on an inflated currency, are those twin necessary evils: pluralities and lay-readers. The quarrels between high and low churchmen over ceremonies, vestments, and ritual strike a familiar note, along with the perennial argument concerning the respective values of the Preaching of the Word and the Sacrament of the Altar; and the unquenchable itch of the episcopate to discipline the clergy. In connection with this last the enthusiastic upholders of the new Canons at present before Convocation might well take warning from the fate that befell their predecessors in 1640.

The period covered by this book, equally with our own, was essentially an age of revolution in every walk of life: social, economic, political, and religious; a time when in the words of one seventeenth-century cleric, 'wee reckon our expenses but not our sins; we account what wee expend but not where wee offend'; and in those of another, Tom Fuller, 'we pray with the saints, but play with the sinners'.

I should like to take this opportunity of thanking my wife for undertaking the arduous work of compiling the index.

A. TINDAL HART

December 1957

FIRST CHAPTER

Background

IN THAT FIRST INSTALMENT of sixteenth century nationalization, the Dissolution of the Monasteries, and despite the legend carefully fostered in certain quarters that the monks had been turned adrift to starve and helped to swell the numbers of the beggars on the roads or the sturdy rogues and vagabonds in the greenwood, generous compensation was in fact actually paid. The Public Record Office contains the full and strictly kept accounts of the three thousand or more pensions regularly and punctually paid out to the ex-religious, first from the Court of Augmentations and then from its successor, the Exchequer. Ex-abbots and priors drew pensions ranging from £160 per annum to about £40, which for those times represented very comfortable incomes indeed if we trouble to translate them into the highly inflated currency of our own day. These they enjoyed for the rest of their lives, practically regardless of any other emoluments they might earn in other capacities.

When, however, we turn to the fate of the rank and file we find that there are four different classes of ex-monks to be considered. First, there were those whose Houses had been attached to cathedral churches. Generally speaking in such cases the senior monks remained as prebendaries and their juniors as minor canons. Secondly, the monks who at the Dissolution were already holding livings by dispensation from either Rome or Canterbury; these men could hardly expect pensions since they were already provided for. Thirdly, the religious who, under the Act of 1536 suppressing the smaller monasteries, had opted for the world, had been absolved from their vows, and had become incumbents; they, too, were not pensioned. Finally there were those who surrendered between 1537 and 1540, all of whom received pensions. What exactly did they get?

Arrears of wages were scrupulously paid up and a bonus of something like £100 in terms of present day currency given to each man, who also received on an average a pension of £5, equivalent to about £350 to £400 today. No doubt the older and more decepit monks retired on this very comfortable income for a single man, and settled down to end their days in the vicinity of their old abbey. But the younger men, who were not content to idle away the rest of their lives, set about securing benefices as fast as they could. They had been dispensed from their vows; and a careful modern investigation has shown that practically all the evicted monks, excluding the old and sick, quickly became incumbents. This was certainly in the interest of the Crown or the individual to whom the King had sold a particular abbey, since if they could provide the pensioned religious with livings of an equivalent value to their pensions, then these last might be extinguished. We therefore find, for instance, the Duke of Norfolk busily ridding himself of the pensions he had to pay the monks of Castleacre, Thetford, and Sibton by giving them rich benefices in Norfolk and Suffolk. Other church patrons, however, with no axe to grind in this way, were usually indifferent as to whether the clergy they appointed were pensioned or not, which meant of course that many of the ex-religious were very much better off than their secular brethren, being in receipt of two or more incomes. Monks had a reputation for greediness that did not desert them in their misfortunes; and there are well substantiated stories of pension-holders' relations who suppressed the news of their deaths and went on drawing the money for themselves. A good example of the kind of thing which was happening to these ex-monks up and down the country is to be found in the person of one Christopher Cartwright, a former canon of the priory of Catley in Lincolnshire. The report of the Pension Commissioners for 1554 stated that he was now Vicar of Dorrington and in receipt of a pension of £2 a year; and that he had married Joan Astley, a former nun of Sempringham, who also had a pension of £2 6s. 8d. This devoted and most religious couple could hardly be said to lack the necessities of life.[1]

What effect had all this on religious life in rural parishes? Undoubtedly the impact of the Reformation as a whole and the Dissolution of the Monasteries in particular caused much dislocation and unrest. The ex-monks accepting country livings were certainly far from popular with their secular brethren[2]; while the passing into private hands of the numerous monastic advowsons and appropriated tithes, together with the breaking down of images by the royal commissioners in accordance with the Injunctions of 1547 and the Orders in Council of 1548, occasioned considerable resentment. Then the compulsory submission of the secular clergy to the Royal Supremacy; the attacks of the reformers on the Pope and the Mass; the translation of the Bible into English and the launching of the two Prayer Books of 1549 and 1552; and above all the pillage of the chantries, 'witnesses in nearly every church of the ever-present solicitude of the living for the dead, of the religious bond in every gild and fraternity'[3], had further greatly troubled the waters of clerical life. These innovations, in fact, did not pass without violent protest: Henry VIII faced and overcame the formidable Pilgrimage of Grace; and his son Edward had to deal with a a similar insurrection in the west country. But the Marian reaction, when it arrived, was neither popular nor successful; for it became irretrievably linked with the Protestant Martyrs and the foreign domination of Spain, with the ejection of the married clergy and the wholesale intrusion into orders of unlearned and ignorant men.

The sum total of all this added up to the undisputed fact that at the beginning of Queen Elizabeth's reign religious life in the parishes was at a low ebb, with ruinous churches and a largely ignorant, poverty-stricken, and often absentee clergy, who either clung obstinately to the old traditions or had been carried away on the full flood of Calvinist iconoclasm.

The advent of the Elizabethan Age with its wise ecclesiastical compromise that came in time to be accepted by the bulk of the nation, brought about an eventual and much needed stability; although, of course, the extremes of left and right continued to oppose it.

The older Marian clergy, although they might outwardly accept the Elizabethan Settlement, could in practice hardly be persuaded to use public prayers and read the scriptures in English; but as they died out and the bulk of the younger men adapted themselves to the *status quo*, the hard core of Roman Catholic recusants became increasingly associated with treasonable conspiracy and the attempted overthrow of the national monarchy in the interests of a foreign power; and hence forfeited any popularity they might otherwise have possessed. The Rising of the North in 1569, the successive conspiracies hatched round the person of Mary Queen of Scots, the infiltration of the Jesuits, and finally the Bye and Gunpowder plots ruined their cause; a cause that the later Stuart kings, Charles II and James II, were powerless to restore.

It has been argued[4] that a majority of the people under Elizabeth remained Catholic until the Armada, after which they rapidly declined in numbers. In 1586 a secret estimate of Catholic strength was made by Spanish agents, who informed Philip II that its numbers in practically every county were considerable. This may have encouraged him in his invasion schemes. Certainly throughout the reign the Catholics remained strong in the north, where in Yorkshire and Durham at least the latin Mass continued to be said in secret for a considerable time; and some of their clergy were described as 'imps of Antichrist, and for the most part very ignorant and stubborn, past measure false and soothly only fear maketh them obedient'[5]. The invasion of England in the fifteen-eighties, first by the seminary priests from Douai and later by the Jesuits, led to savage reprisals: imprisonments, fines, and even executions; although it was always clearly understood that these last were imposed for treason rather than religion. Sandys, Archbishop of York, reported of his Yorkshire recusants in 1571: 'They will not say Amen to the prayer for the Queen, they glory in their ignorance of the Bible, they prefer prison to conference with the archbishop'[6]. Priests who returned again after banishment were liable to be hanged; and in 1588, the year of the Armada, more than thirty paid the supreme penalty. Undoubtedly the penal laws became fiercer as the struggle with Spain reached its climax. It was decreed, for example, that every recusant who denied the royal authority, seduced others, or attended unlawful assemblies was subject to imprisonment, banishment, or fine. But in point of fact the last was the favourite form of punishment; since, the papists being often men of substance, it paid the State well to keep them under observation. This was frequently all that was done; the ruinous fines imposed never actually being enforced.

At the opposite end of the scale the Puritans were a different kettle of fish altogether. For the Protestant extremists, returning from their Marian exile after drinking at the pure fountain-head in Geneva, proved themselves much more doughty opponents of the Elizabethan compromise than the Catholics. Remaining, apart from insignificant exceptions, within the Establishment, they sought continually to mould it to their will; and faced by the united hostility of the Crown, the bulk of the episcopate, and Convocation, turned to Parliament and laid the foundations of an alliance that was eventually to overturn monarch and Church alike. Generally speaking the Anglican had followed Luther in affirming that the Bible, although it contained all things necessary for salvation, did not legislate in matters of church worship and government; but the Puritan supported Calvin's contention that the Word of God was the sole authority for Church and State alike, and declared that since man by his fall was corrupt, his works must be equally evil[7].

All the reformers were opposed to the Mass as continually offering anew a sacrifice made once and for all on Calvary; to the priesthood as the indispensable instrument of mediation between God and man; and to the invocation of those Saints, whom the Catholics believed could help mitigate an individual's pains and penalties in purgatory. They likewise agreed on the need to restore the pure worship of the Primitive Church; but differed on the important question of what exactly that worship should consist of. Luther had always regarded the traditions of the Church to be of value where they did not contradict the Scriptures; but Calvin would have none of them. He was interested only in the four doctrines of The Word of God, Original Sin, The Work of the Holy Spirit, and Election. Consequently the English Puritans were bitterly hostile to the whole of the Elizabethan Settlement, which was based on what they contended to be the unscriptural ministerial Orders of bishops, priests, and deacons. Apart from apostles and prophets, ministers were alone recognized in the New Testament, where elders and deacons were simply lay officials, the one concerned with the spiritual, the other with the temporal needs of the Church.

Secondly, they insisted on the two Sacraments of Baptism and the Lord's Supper being closely copied from the Bible. In the former case they objected to private baptism, baptism by women, questions put to the child, and godparents other than the real parents. In the latter they criticized the manner of Anglican administration as being individual rather than corporate, and demanded an examination of all would-be communicants in order to prevent an unworthy reception. 'They [the Anglicans]', the Puritans said scornfully, 'eate not the Lordes Supper but playe a pageant of theire owne, to make the sillie soules beleeve they have an Englishe Masse, and so putt no difference betwixt Christe and Antichriste, betwixt God and the devill'[8]. Confirmation most of them condemned 'whollye', since in their opinion it merely added a third and superfluous sacrament, which, unlike the other two, required the administration of a bishop. Thirdly the Puritans violently objected to all vestments, including the cassock, as Aaronical or idolatrous. The early nonconformists did not even wear gowns, but simply officiated in lay attire. 'What reason is there', one of their spokesmen asked, 'that the fashion and forme of Ministers' attire should be different from other men's?'[9] 'Unedifying' ceremonies such as the crossing in baptism, the ring in marriage, and kneeling for communion, were presumptuous human inventions or unnecessary additions. The last, indeed, savoured too much of transubstantiation and the adoration of the elements. 'They are carnall', affirmed the precisian, 'beggarlie, Antichristian, Pompes, rytes, Lawes, garmentes and traditions . . . they are worse than lowsye: for they are sibbed to ye sarke of Hercules, that made him teare his owne bowells asunder'[10]. Saints' days and other church festivals should be abolished in order to emphasize the uniqueness of the scriptural sabbath; the reading of the Apocrypha in public worship should be omitted, for it was not part of the Canonical Scriptures; auricular confession was anathema since it was both priestly and popish; and 'pistling and gospelling' or other 'shredding' of scripture must not be tolerated, any more than 'short-cut' prayers and 'vain repetitions'. Puritan worship itself was strictly biblical and embraced the six ordinances of Prayer, Praise, the Proclamation of the Word, the administration of the Sacraments of Baptism and the Lord's Supper, Catechizing, and the exercise of Discipline. Their prayers were long and usually extempore: the minister praying in a loud voice and the people assenting with an even louder Amen. Praise consisted of the congregational singing of the Psalms;[11] and a psalm invariably concluded the Communion service as it had done after the Last Supper. Preaching meant simply the proclamation of God's Word; and sermons were long, at least of an hour's duration, while two were expected to be delivered each sabbath. The Puritans used notes, but strenuously resisted reading the homilies, which they regarded as unprofitable moral essays. The sermon in fact, they felt, represented the most important part of the service, far out-weighing the efficacy of praise, prayer, and even the Lord's Supper, since its aim was to win souls by hammering home biblical teaching with urgent and vehement gestures. At the administration of the Lord's Supper the elements were given to the people sitting; and it was the general policy of the Presbyterians at least to celebrate quar-terly communions. Catechizing, especially of young people and ser-vants, was universally practised in nonconformist circles. It was, however, in the exercise of discipline that the puritanical system met with the severest criticism[12]. Had the individual minister, asked the Anglican, the right to exclude his parishioners from communion or the regular Sunday services? But in Puritan eyes the object of such ex-communication was always corrective rather than vindictive, scrip-tural not arbitrary, and repentance immediately led to the restoration of spiritual privileges. There were three well-defined stages in an act of discipline: the culprit was first admonished, then excommunicated, and finally, if impenitent, rejected. Nevertheless excommunications were often imposed for quite trivial offences such as gossiping or laziness.

Puritan churches were noted for their plainness and simplicity; with whitewashed walls, whose only decoration were scriptural texts. A high pulpit stood in a central position in the nave, the Bible resting on its cushion; and immediately below it was the communion table. On the whole, Puritan worship, although it ignored the ceremonial and pictorial and largely concentrated on ear-gate, did much by its rever-ence for scripture, its purity, simplicity, and spontaneity, its relevance to the life of its worshippers and protection of the Holy Communion against unworthy receivers, to raise the standards of morals and re-ligion among the laity. Its defects lay in its often narrow-minded fanaticism and exaggerated fears of Roman Catholicism. 'In their enthusiasm to root out the errors of antiquity, they ignore the wisdom of antiquity. They would have been less iconoclastic if they had heeded Luther's principle, that "abusus non tollit usum".'[13] The name 'Puritan' was used to cover all those protestant reformers who in any way opposed the Elizabethan Settlement; and in no sense denoted a compact homogeneous Church. It embraced separatists like the Brown-ists besides the great majority who remained within the Establishment, the moderate reformers as well as the root and branch men. Neverthe-less, as the reign went on a greater sense of discipline and unity of purpose began to prevail among the leaders; their demands hardened and crystallized; their strategy began to operate on a national rather than a regional basis; and they found in the House of Commons rather than in the Crown or Convocation their best hopes for the future.

Taking advantage of the reaction against all things Marian, and the fact that the Government had its hands full in coping with the Roman Catholics, the Puritans began their attacks on the externals of worship before the end of 1558; and by the summer of 1559 the Royal Visitors found that many parish churches had already been drastically cleansed.[14] At first, indeed, the bishops made little or no attempt to enforce the Injunctions; and Archbishop Parker's Metropolitical Visitation of 1560/61 was only very partially successful in restoring order out of confusion. Emboldened by this practical immunity and the support of some of the bishops, the Puritans made their famous attack on the Prayer Book in 1563, when the demands of the moderate nonconformists were very nearly successful, and were in fact only finally defeated in the Lower House of Convocation by a single vote.[15] Narrow as was this majority it marked the turn of the tide. The Puritans, although still volubly hostile to vestments and the other externals of worship, now began to concentrate their forces against the Prayer Book in general and the episcopal form of church government in particular; while the scene of battle shifted away from Convocation and into the House of Commons. Henceforth the adoption of the Presbyterian system was the avowed ultimate objective; together of course with the destruction of the episcopate. However, many of their suggested moderate reforms had episcopal and even archiepiscopal support, as for example the need for a more learned, i.e. preaching, ministry, the abolition of pluralities, the equalization of endowments, the restoration of the impropriate tithes, and the reconstruction of the universities in order to produce a better type of clergyman. From about 1570 it became a custom of the clergy in the more puritanical districts to meet once a week for 'prophesyings'.[16] These aimed at producing efficient 'right-minded' ministers; but also provided opportunities for the puritans to get to know one another better and to co-ordinate their actions. William Harrison wrote approvingly of them: 'in manie of our archdeaconries we have an exercise latelie begun, which for the most part is called a prophesie or conference, and erected onelie for the examination or triall of the diligence of the cleargie in their studie of the scriptures'.[17] He thought they would act as 'a notable spurre unto all ministers' and keep them from 'hawking, hunting, tables, cards, dice, tipling at the alehouse, shooting and other like vanities'.[18] Thomas Fuller thus described the procedure:

'The junior divine went first into the pulpit, and for half an hour, more or less, as he could with clearness contract his meditations, treated upon a portion of scripture, formerly by a joint agreement assigned unto him. After him, four or five more, observing their seniority, successively dilated on the same text. At last a grave divine, appointed on purpose, as father of the Act, made the closing sermon, somewhat larger than the rest, praising the pains and performance of such as deserved it; meekly and mildly reproving the mistakes and failings of such of those if any were found in their sermons'.[19]

Many of the gentry, although never actively participating, used to attend these exercises, which flourished particularly in Essex, Norfolk, and Northamptonshire. They were approved by Archbishop Grindal and Bishop Parkhurst of Norwich; but resisted by the Queen, who had been warned by Archbishop Parker that 'they were no better than seminaries of Puritanism'.[20] Eventually, much to the indignation of Harrison,[21] she suppressed them; and likewise strongly and successfully resisted all attempts by the Puritans to legislate through Parliament.

The Puritans now began to find the authorities in Church and State solidly allied against them. They had failed in Convocation in 1563 and in Parliament during the debates of 1571/72;[22] while the Queen and the majority of the bishops were openly hostile. The likelihood of an internal and constitutional reform of the Church and Prayer Book became increasingly remote; and from the fifteen-eighties onward the nonconformists began to organize themselves in open opposition to both. The 'prophesyings' had helped like-minded ministers to get to know one another; and these meetings continued in secret after their suppression. The leaders of the various groupings commenced a correspondence; and about 1584 they began tentatively, especially in the east, London, and the midlands, to put into operation Walter Travers's *Book of Discipline*. This denied that church government by bishops was scriptural and declared that church discipline must be vested in ministers, congregational elderships, the classes, and synods both provincial and national.[23] Travers's work was carefully revised and accepted by such leaders as Field and Wilcox in London, Snape of Northampton, Chaderton of Cambridge, Knewstubbs of Suffolk, and Reynolds of Oxford, who quietly and gradually began, with their followers, to substitute it in their parishes for the Book of Common Prayer. 'All ecclesiastical government in the parishes was vested in a pastor, elders, deacons, and widows. The ministers of twelve parishes combined to form a classis to handle matters common to the parish. Delegates from the ministers and elders of twenty-four classes formed a provincial synod or council, and the delegates from these synods formed the national synod or general assembly'.[24] In the individual parishes the ministers remained supreme; and although, like Snape of Northampton, they might be chosen by the classis, they would also be elected by their own congregations. The minister, with his body of elders, alone decided what ceremonies or portions of the Prayer

Book were to be omitted in his parish, and exercised discipline there. 'Mr Lewis', it was recorded in the Dedham Classis minute book, 'moved his brethren to have theire handes set to a writinge for confirmation of that which they had already set downe, that a Pastor should have his owne people'.[25] Assistant curates were renamed 'doctors'; churchwardens were transformed over-night into 'deacons'; episcopal ordination and institution were submitted to merely as civil and legal requirements; and extempore prayers and preaching from notes constituted the bulk of the worship. This movement, fortunately, never struck very deep roots, it was only supported by a limited number of ministers and parishes, and disappeared rapidly after 1592. National synods were held at Cambridge and in London during the years 1586 to 1587; and Fuller describes at length the resolutions adopted by a provincial synod which was convened at Coventry in 1588. These declared that private baptism was unlawful; the homilies must not be read; the sign of the cross must not be used; the calling of bishops was illegal and no minister need be ordained by them; the bishops themselves had no power either to excommunicate or deprive, and ought not to be acknowledged 'either for doctors, elders or deacons'; and that *The Book of Discipline* was 'a draught essential and necessary for all time'.[26]

The strength of the Puritan movement at this stage can be gauged by the flood of petitions from all over the country that poured into the Government between 1584 and 1586, complaining of the lack of learned ministers, the deprivation and persecution of 'godly and peaceable men', and such abuses as pluralism and non-residence.[27] Certainly they did not fail to impress the Queen and her Privy Council. From then onwards the party made marked progress. The number of known puritanical ministers with university degrees grew rapidly; and were to be found equally thickly in the south as well as in the east and midlands. Sussex became, for example, as great a centre of Puritan influence as Norfolk or Northamptonshire. As regards the laity: Molin, the Venetian ambassador, was under the impression that about a third of England had become Puritan by 1603. This was undoubtedly a gross exaggeration; since, judging from the number of ministers presented by their parishioners for not wearing the surplice or omitting portions of the Prayer Book, many of their nominal congregations were in reality far from sympathetic towards their opinions. Probably where the gentry or corporations showed a marked puritanical turn of mind the people acquiesced readily enough in their choice of a minister; but the number of the enthusiastic laity in any one parish must have been strictly limited. It has, indeed, been estimated that at the end of Elizabeth's reign about 2 per cent of the population was ardently Puritan, 5 per cent Roman Catholic, 18 per cent zealous followers of the Establishment, and 75 per cent dull peasants utterly indifferent to any form of church government, provided it did not interfere too drastically with their old customs and superstitions. The Puritans certainly benefited from the new order of affairs that had accumulated large numbers of advowsons in the hands of a few great landlords. Lord Rich, Lady Bacon, Lord Grey of Wilton, Sir Richard Knightly, Sir Edward Montague, Sir Francis Hastings, Sir Robert Wroth, Sir Robert Jermyn, and Drew Drury were, for instance, mainly responsible for the strength of nonconformity in counties like Warwickshire, Leicestershire, Northamptonshire, Norfolk, Suffolk, Essex, Hertfordshire, and Buckinghamshire. Where the puritanical gentry had no livings in their gift, they sometimes acquired them by purchase; while other Puritan ministers were employed as chaplains in the homes of the great.[28] These patrons, too, protected them against the attentions of a too zealous bishop. On the whole, however, the Puritans in Queen Elizabeth's reign were not seriously or systematically persecuted; some of the bishops and archdeacons themselves had puritanical leanings; the slowness of communications and the dilatory processes of the courts, both civil and ecclesiastical, told in their favour; and above all the Queen herself was not anxious to push doctrinal or ceremonial definitions too far. The Elizabethan Settlement was essentially a political rather than an ecclesiastical one; and her idea was to make it as wide and loose as possible in order to include the maximum number of Protestants for the fight against Rome and Spain. The clergy, but not the laity, had merely to subscribe to the Royal Supremacy, the Prayer Book, and the thirty-nine Articles of Religion.

When Elizabeth died the Puritan party within the Establishment probably consisted at the most of three-hundred and fifty ministers, supported by a substantial number of the gentry, the town corporations, and the laity in the eastern counties, London, the midlands, and the south. Their avowed object was still the transformation of the church government into Presbyterianism, in accordance with the directions of *The Book of Discipline*.

Anglicanism as we know it today was born in the Elizabethan Age, that inherited a chaotic situation, but slowly and surely moulded the foundations of the present Church of England. For this the Queen herself, some of her ministers like Cecil, and her two great archbishops, Parker and Whitgift, were largely responsible. Another Elizabethan Bishop, Richard Bancroft, later himself Archbishop of Canterbury, was to carry the reconstruction a further long step forward in the reign of James I. The Supremacy and Uniformity Acts, together with the Royal Injunctions of 1559, which were collated with those of Edward VI, formed the basis of the Settlement; but many of the last were so loosely worded that they could be and were interpreted in different ways, while no great diligence was used either by the Royal Visitors in 1559 or during the Metropolitical Visitation of 1560/61 to enforce subscription. It is noteworthy that the number of ministers deprived for all causes between 17 November 1558 and 17 November 1564 was probably not more than 200 out of a possible 8,000 beneficed clergy.[29]

The Injunctions of 1559,[30] while renewing the old prohibitions against images, relics, miracles, and processions (apart from Rogationtide perambulations), sought to enforce the use of the Prayer Book, to compel the clergy either to preach their quarterly sermons (if licensed) or else to read the homilies,[31] to catechize and to study. Careful regulations were laid down for clerical marriage: 'It is thought', Injunction 29 declared, 'very necessary that no manner of priest or deacon shall hereafter take to his wife any manner of woman without the advice and allowance first had upon good examination by the bishop of the diocese, and two justices of the peace of the same shire'.[32] In the matter of dress the clergy were expected, according to Injunction 30, to 'use such seemly habits, garments, and such square caps,[33] as were most comonly and orderly received in the latter year of the reign of King Edward VI'.[34] These would have included cassocks, gowns, and tippets, to all of which of course the Puritans took the strongest possible exception. Ignorant priests were no longer to be instituted to livings; and all incumbents were expected to avoid alehouses, cards, dice, etc. Every able-bodied person was expected to attend the Sunday services, and overseers were appointed in each parish 'diligently to see that all the parishioners duly resort to their church upon all Sundays and holy days, and there to continue the whole time of the godly service'.[35] When in church worshippers were expected to behave themselves, to kneel for prayer and to receive the communion, to bow at the name of Jesus, and to observe other 'old customs of reverence'. Music and singing were to be encouraged. Altars must be taken down and tables erected in their place, which were to be brought into the chancel for the celebration of the Holy Communion, 'at which time the same shall be so placed . . . as whereby the minister may be more conveniently heard of the communicants in his prayer and ministracion, and the communicants also more conveniently and in more number communicate with the said minister'.[36] These words were purposely vague. In theory the table was normally to stand altarwise at the east end of the chancel; but must be moved to the west end for communion. After the service it was to be replaced. In practice, however, the majority of churches retained it permanently at the lower end of the chancel or even in the nave, where it occupied a table-wise position. The celebrant took his stand at the north end, with his assistant opposite, and the communicants kneeling on mats or rushes round about them.[37] Again, the demand of the Injunctions for wafer-bread of a plain sort[38] was at variance with the Prayer Book rubric which spoke of ordinary bread. In point of fact this Injunction was never strictly enforced and the bishops were content to tolerate the use of ordinary bread.[39]

The same ambiguity existed in the case of the Ornaments rubric in the 1549 Prayer Book and how far it had been superseded by Archbishop Parker's *Advertisements* of 1566. Once more the bishops refrained from pressing the matter of Eucharistic vestments, and satisfied themselves with insisting upon the wearing of the surplice.[40]

The Metropolitical Visitation of 1560/61, reinforced by the bishops' *Interpretations and Further Considerations* that were based on the 1559 Articles of Inquiry, had as their primary objective the need to test the working of the Uniformity Act, to assess roughly the clergy's obedience to the Royal Injunctions, and to correct moral offences. For the churchwardens' returns had disclosed a sad state in the parishes: decayed and desecrated churches, a shortage of clergy, few services, the non-keeping of registers, and a refusal in many instances, particularly in the north, to destroy images or read the prayers and scriptures in the vernacular. Many parishes had no clergy at all, pluralities abounded since endowments were pitiably small, and parishioners were often behaving in a most irreverent and unseemly manner in both church and churchyard. Consequently the Ecclesiastical Commissioners in 1561 laid down some firm rulings for the guidance of the parochial clergy, which were to form a solid foundation for the future. In the first place indiscriminate destruction was to be stopped immediately. There were to be no more 'open decays and ruins of coverings, walls and windows' or 'unseemly tables with foul cloths for the communion of the sacrament' or churches 'desolate of all cleanliness of meet ornaments'.[41] The wholesale defacing of monuments, breaking of glass, wrecking of windows, and melting down of bells in which the returned Marian exiles had freely indulged themselves, were now sternly forbidden. The table of the ten commandments must be set up in all the churches; the old rood loft altered to form a screen between nave and chancel; and the holy table commonly covered, i.e. out of service time, with 'silk buckram or other such like'.[42] At communion a fair linen cloth was to be used. The clergy were ordered to say the daily services with their parishioners according to the Prayer Book rubric, the clerks to sing 'their modest and distinct song', the churchwardens to fine absentees from church and to prevent brawling, trading, or games in the churchyard during service time; and the laity to put away their week-day business of a Sunday and attend their parish churches. The Prayer Book of 1559 had ordered that Morning and Evening Prayer should be said 'in the accustomed place of the church, chapel or chancel, except it shall otherwise be determined by the ordinary of the place'; and this was commonly interpreted to mean a desk at the upper end of the nave, or even further down the church, so that the minister faced his people and enabled them to hear and follow the prayers. Bishop Parkhurst, the puritanically-minded Bishop of Norwich, actually issued instructions in 1569, 'that in great churches, where all the people cannot conveniently hear their minister, the churchwardens and other, to whom that charge belongeth, shall provide and appoint a decent convenient seat in the body of the church, where the minister may sit or stand, and say the divine service, that the congregation may hear and be edified therewith. And in smaller churches there be some convenient seat without the chancel door for that purpose'.[43] The minister was also expected to say the Litany every Wednesday and Friday; to observe the authorized fasts[44] and festivals; and to wear the proper vestments, i.e. in practice the surplice and university hood (if any). The loose phrases and ambiguities in the Elizabethan rubrics, injunctions, and visitation articles appear to have been taken full advantage of, judging from the following reported utterance of Bishop Grindal in 1565:

'Some say the service and prayers in the chancel, others in the body of the church; some say the same in a seat made in the church, some in the pulpit with their faces to the people; some keep precisely to the order of the book, others intermeddle psalms in metre; some say in a surplice, others without a surplice; the Table standeth in the body of the church in some places, in others it standeth in the chancel; in some places the Table standeth altarwise, distant from the wall a yard, in some others in the middle of the chancel, north and south; in some places the Table is joined, in others it standeth upon trestles; in some places the Table hath a carpet, in others it hath not; administration of the Communion is done by some with surplice and cap, some with surplice alone, others with none; some with chalice, some with a communion cup, others with a common cup; some with unleavened bread, some with leavened; some receive kneeling, others standing, others sitting; some baptize in a font, others in a basin; some sign with the sign of the cross, others sign not; some with a square cap, some with a round cap, some with a button cap, some with a hat.'[45]

This variety continued throughout the reign; for as late as 1581 John Aylmer, Bishop of London, declared that out of the three hundred and fifty parishes in Essex, only seven performed their services identically.[46] Such in broad outline was the picture of the Elizabethan Settlement. But now let us turn from the general to the particular, to individual parsons and parishes in order to see how these injunctions and regulations worked out in practice; and to glimpse something of the life of the ordinary parish priest: his learning, religious services, social and economic status, and personal relationships with his parishioners.

NOTES

[1] G. Baskerville, *English Monks and the Suppression of the Monasteries*, p. 258.

[2] F. M. Powicke, *The Reformation in England*, p. 29.

[3] Powicke, *Reformation in England*, p. 86.

[4] Brian Magee, *The English Recusants*, pp. 27–8, & 205.

[5] W. H. Frere, *The English Church in the Reigns of Elizabeth and James I*, p. 67.

[6] Frere, *The English Church*, p. 214.

[7] See H. F. Woodhouse, *The Doctrine of the Church in Anglican Theology*, *1547–1603*, p. 35.

[8] *Tracts Ascribed to Richard Bancroft*, ed. A. Peel, p. 25.

[9] Ormerod, *The Picture of a Puritan*, London, 1605, p. 3.

[10] *Tracts Ascribed to Richard Bancroft*, pp. 26–7.
Some even of the bishops were opposed to vestments. Bishop Jewel of Salisbury called them: 'the habits of the stage, the relics of the Amorites'. D. Neal, *The History of the Puritans*, Vol. I, p. 159.

[11] Organs, much used in parish churches during the Middle Ages, were anathema to the Puritan, who cast them out. Anthony Hoggett, the puritanical incumbent of Northill, Beds., sold his in 1590 for 40s. Bedfordshire Record Society, Vol. 33, *Elizabethan Churchwardens' Accounts*, p. 48.
A proposal to abolish organs altogether was narrowly rejected by Convocation in 1562/3.

[12] Woodhouse, *Doctrine of the Church*, pp. 108–11.

[13] Horton Davies, *The Worship of the English Puritans*, p. 275.

[14] See 'The Queen's proclamation against defacers of monuments in churches', issued in 1560. E. Cardwell, *Documentary Annals*, Vol. I, pp. 257–60.

[15] W. H. Frere and C. E. Douglas, *Puritan Manifestoes*, ix.

[16] Based on I.Cor.XIV.31. An outstanding example of the fruit of such 'prophesyings' was seen in the *Northampton Sunday* of 1571, which is described by J. Strype, *Annals of the Reformation*, Vol. II, Part I, pp. 133–4; and by Neal, *History of the Puritans*, Vol. I, pp. 221–2.

[17] *Harrison's Description of England in Shakespeare's Youth*, ed. F. J. Furnival, Vol. I, p. 17.

[18] *Harrison's Description of England*, Vol. I, p. 18.

[19] T. Fuller, *The Church History of Britain*, Vol. III, pp. 6 and 7.

[20] J. Strype, *The Life and Acts of Matthew Parker*, p. 461.

[21] *Harrison's Description of England*, Vol. I, p. 19.

[22] This failure led to the publication of *An Admonition to the Parliament*, by Field and Wilcox, and an acrimonious pamphlet warfare followed with the bishops. See, Frere and Douglas, *Puritan Manifestoes*, pp. xiii–xxxi.

[23] R. G. Usher, *The Reconstruction of the English Church*, Vol. I, p. 42.

[24] *Presbyterian Movement in the Reign of Queen Elizabeth as Illustrated by the Minute Book of the Dedham Classis*, ed. R. G. Usher, (Camden Society) p. xvii.

[25] *Presbyterian Movement in the Reign of Queen Elizabeth*, p. 62.

[26] Fuller, *Church History*, Vol. III, pp. 111-12.

[27] Lincolnshire Record Society, Vol. 23, *The State of the Church in the Reigns of Elizabeth and James I*, ed. C. W. Foster, p. xxxviii.

[28] See Neal, *History of the Puritans*, Vol. I, p. 306.

[29] G. M. Trevelyan, *English Social History*, p. 174.

[30] For the Royal Injunctions of 1559 see, H. Gee, *The Elizabethan Clergy*, pp. 46-65.
See also Cardwell, *Documentary Annals*, Vol. I, pp. 178-209; W. H. Frere and W. M. Kennedy, *Visitation Articles and Injunctions of the Period of the Reformation*, Vol. III, pp. 8-29.

[31] All preaching had previously been forbidden by a proclamation of 27 December, 1558, in view of Puritan excesses. See Frere and Kennedy, *Visitation Articles and Injunctions*, Vol. III, p. 9.

[32] Frere and Kennedy, *Visitation Articles and Injunctions*, Vol. III, p. 19.

[33] When Bucer was asked why he did not wear the square cap he replied, because his head was not square. See Neal, *History of the Puritans*, Vol. I, p. 158.

[34] Frere and Kennedy, *Visitation Articles and Injunctions*, Vol. III, p. 20.

[35] Frere and Kennedy, *Visitation Articles and Injunctions*, Vol. III, p. 22.

[36] Frere and Kennedy, *Visitation Articles and Injunctions*, Vol. III, p. 28. See also Somerset Record Society, Vol. 43, *Collectanea, II*, p. 180; and Cardwell, *Documentary Annals*, Vol. I, p. 202.

[37] See G. W. O. Addleshaw and F. Etchells *The Architectural Setting of Anglican Worship*, p. 113.

[38] Frere and Kennedy, *Visitation Articles and Injunctions*, Vol. III, p. 28.

[39] Frere and Douglas, *Puritan Manifestoes*, xxvii.

[40] See W. K. Lowther Clarke, *Liturgy and Worship*, pp. 851-4.
The use of copes, however, appears to have survived in some parish churches as late as 1586. W. P. M. Kennedy, *Elizabethan Episcopal Administration*, Vol. I, cxiii.

[41] Frere, *The English Church*, p. 68.

[42] Addleshaw and Etchells, *The Architectural Setting*, p. 33.

[43] Frere and Kennedy, *Visitation Articles and Injunctions*, Vol. III, pp. 208-9.

[44] The laws passed for political rather than religious purposes about fish days decreed that no meat was to be eaten during Lent or on Wednesdays and Fridays. See Trevelyan, *English Social History*, p. 189.

[45] H. Gee, *The Elizabethan Prayer Book*, p. 164.

[46] Strype, *The Life and Acts of John Aylmer*, p. 133. Nevertheless all but three used the Prayer Book.
Robert Kitchen, Rector of Stisted in Essex, informed his patron, Archbishop Parker, in the fifteen-sixties that there was 'great liberty used among the clergy' of his neighbourhood 'in varying from the appointments of the church; that some conferred baptism in basins, some in dishes, rejecting the use of the font; some held there must be seven godfathers; some would that every father should christen his own child . . . some detested the surplice in ministracion; and that in Bocking it had been laid-a-water.' *Annals of Evangelical Nonconformity in the County of Essex*, ed. T. W. Davids, p. 64. Essex was, of course, a hot-bed of Puritanism.

SECOND CHAPTER

The Elizabethan Clergy

AT THE BEGINNING of Queen Elizabeth's reign the number of parochial clergy was not only inadequate; but the majority of those already serving were grossly deficient in learning. 'As for the inferior clergy under them [the bishops]', wrote Fuller, 'the best that could be gotten were placed in pastoral charges. Alas! tolerability was eminency in that age. A rush candle seemed a torch where no brighter light was ever seen before.' And he referred his readers to the remark of a Mr Tavernour, High Sheriff of Oxfordshire, who compared the ministers in his part of the country with 'the chickens of the Church, the sparrows of the Spirit';[1] while William Harrison bitterly complained that many lay patrons 'doo bestow advowsons of benefices upon their bakers, butlers, cookes, good archers, and horsekeepers, insted of other recompense, for their long and faithful service which they imploie afterward unto their most advantage. . . . The very cause weavers, pedlars and glovers have been made ministers . . . for a glover or a tayler will be glad of an augmentation of 8 or 10 pound by the yere, and well contented that his patron shall have all the rest, so he may be sure of this pension.'[2] Archbishop Parker himself admitted as much; for writing to Bishop Grindal of London in 1560 he remarked wryly: 'Whereas, occasioned by the great want of ministers, we and you both, for tolerable supply thereof, have heretofore admitted into the ministry sundry artificers and others, not traded and brought up in learning, and, as it happened in a multitude some that were of base occupations.'[3] Fulke spoke of 'our Ministers, which are come out of the shop into the clergy, without gifts sufficient for that calling';[4] and Whitgift declared that some of the clergy were of 'the basest of the people'.[5] These criticisms are certainly borne out by diocesan records. At Lincoln the ordination lists between 1555 and 1585, together with the *Liber Cleri* of 1585, show that many of the non-graduate clergy were drawn from 'base callings'. There were day-labourers, serving men, ostlers, husbandmen, parish-clerks, poor-clerks, ex-monks, carpenters, glovers, drapers, tallow-chandlers, shoemakers, soldiers, fishermen, clothiers, and even a bestiarius.[6] 'A Survey of Sixteene Hundreds in the County of Essex, containing benefices 335' which was undertaken as late as the fifteen-eighties, revealed a large number of clergy of servile origin. Here are a few examples: 'Mr Whiting, parson of Toppesfield, sometime a serving man; Mr Potts, parson of Tolleshunt Darcie, sometime a tailor; Mr Hickson of Munden, sometime a serving man; Mr Washer, parson of Upminster, sometime a grocer; Mr Hewet, parson of Copford, sometime an apothecary; Mr Ellis, curate of Abberton, sometime a linen draper; Mr Perkins, parson of South Hanningfield, sometime a fishmonger, now a button maker, a very careless and insufficient minister, an alehouse haunter'.[7]

The *Liber Cleri* of 1576 recording Bishop Cooper's Visitation of the Leicester, Lincoln, and Stowe archdeaconries, noted that whereas 167 of the clergy were Latinists and 207 sufficiently qualified in sacred learning, 226 were ignorant of Latin and 206 others deficient in any sort of knowledge. The Leicester *Liber* further stated that 'only one clergyman is somewhat learned in Greek'; while, alas, very many were described as 'utterlie ignorant'.[8] In 1573 Bishop Cooper ordained Thomas Morley as priest 'upon necessitie, although in the holy scriptures unacquainted'; but would not issue his letters of Orders until he had shown that he had profited by a study of the Bible. In 1576 Morley was presented to the rectory of Wyberton, but the Bishop refused to institute him because on examination he still appeared ignorant. He was told 'to apply his study' for six months; but at the end of that period again failed to satisfy the Bishop, and the rectory was given to another clerk. Eventually, a year later, Morley was instituted to the vicarage of Heckington instead.[9]

The Royal Injunctions of 1559 and Parker's *Advertisements* had directed the bishops and archdeacons to examine all their clergy below the degree of M.A. at their visitations in order to find out 'how they have profited in the Study of the Holy Scripture'.[10] In Essex, for instance, the Archdeacon of Colchester demanded of his incumbents in 1586 that they should obtain certain theological books, pursue a definite course of theological study, and compose specimen sermons under the supervision of a special clerical tutor appointed by himself. Furthermore, unless the clergy concerned could secure a satis certificate from their supervisor to produce at the next visitation they were liable to be punished by suspension from their ministry. In September 1587 the rector of Little Sampford and the vicars of Rickling, Manuden, and Elsenham were actually so suspended, while others were severely reprimanded; and the same policy was followed in succeeding years.[11] In the diocese of Lincoln only D.D.s and B.D.s escaped such an examination, which seems to have been of a formidable nature, judging from the fact that in 1576 the incumbent of Ingoldmells and Panton 'withdrew before the examination in spite of being admonished to undergo it'; similarly William Brown of Careby also 'withdrew before his examination'.[12] In his Injunctions of 1577 Bishop Cooper of Lincoln demanded 'that the ministers bend themselves diligently to the study of the Holy Scriptures and Word of God ... every day in the week ... to read over one chapter at the least of the Bible, taking some notes in a paper book of such wholesome sentences and good matter as he shall observe in the reading of the Bible as the *Decades*[13] . . . that he may show the same when he shall be thereunto called'.[14] The archdeacons were then instructed at their next visitation to see that these orders had been carried out. In his own Injunctions of 1571 Archbishop Grindal insisted upon a strict and thorough examination of his clergy after ordination: 'Ye shall daylie reade', he told them, 'at least one chapter of the oulde Testament and another of the New with good advisement, and such of you as be under the degree of a maister of arts shall provide and have of your owne, accordinge to the quenes majesties injunctions, at least the New Testament both in latine and englishe, conferringe the one with the other everye day one chapter thereof at the leaste, so that upon examination of the Archdeacon commissary or their officers in synodes and visitations or at other appointed tymes it may appeare how ye profit in the studye of holye scripture'.[15]

The rapid growth of the Tudor grammar schools, where the clever boy from any rank of society could pick up a good Latin education before going on to the revived and flourishing Universities of Oxford and Cambridge, greatly helped in raising the standard of clerical learning in the latter half of the reign. It is of interest therefore to note the remarkable increase in the number of clerical graduates as the years went by.[16] Institutions to benefices in the diocese of Lincoln between 1540 and 1570 show that there were: five D.D.s, two B.D.s, nineteen M.A.s, six B.A.s, one LL.B, and one 'literate', as against 298 with no kind of qualification.[17] Turning to the Ordination lists we find that between 1578 and 1584 out of 252 men ordained, 128 possessed university degrees.[18] Moreover the *Liber Cleri* of 1585 disclosed that there were 399 graduates out of a total of 1,285 clergy; and that of 1603 gave 646 men with degrees as against 538 without any. The standard was in fact steadily rising in the diocese of Lincoln;[19] while in the neighbouring diocese of Norwich, judging from a list of the Norfolk clergy drawn up in 1592–3, conditions were very similar. For out of the 484 clergy named therein 198 were graduates, i.e. 2 D.D.s, 3 LL.D.s, 22 B.D.s, 108 M.A.s, 59 B.A.s, 3 LL.B.s, and 1 Mus.B.[20] Finally, it should be noted that the overall Bishops' Report of 1603 announced that 3,352 out of 8,179 clergymen in the Province of Canterbury and 454 out of 1,065 in the Province of York held degrees of one kind or another.[21]

Some of the clergy, particularly at the beginning of the reign, were not only unsatisfactory scholars, but what learning they possessed was infected with Romanism. Thomas Briggs, Vicar of Pateley in Yorkshire, was said 'to be himselfe backward in matters of religion and to seduce others by his synister whisperinge in their eares. And being wylled before the assemblie then and ther presente to yield his opynion upon these two texts of scripture viz. Tu es Petrus and Hoc est corpus meum for their satisfaction who stode in doubt of his zeale in God's truthe, he partely refused to do it publiquelie and shewed himselfe very unwillinge to do yt and at last spoke somethinge thereof verie absurdely. Wherefore and for other causes the Commissioners movinge the said Bryggs was comyted to the Castell of York ther to remayne.'[22] Briggs was no isolated case in Yorkshire; and in the north as a whole there must have been many such men. And not only in the north. From puritanical Essex came similar reports in 1580: 'Mr Woodthorpe, parson of Lamershe, sometime a popish priest . . . Mr Housmann, vicar of Canewdon, sometime a town broach, made a mass priest. A persecutor in Queen Mary's days, now he hath two benefices. A very careless man, and one that cannot preach sincerely the truth.'[23]

As a temporary measure, owing to the alarming shortage of clergy and in order to fill the vacant parishes,[24] a special class of 'Readers' were appointed, who were commissioned by the bishops to read the service and homily, but forbidden to administer the sacraments or marry. These readers were especially useful in supplying those cures that were held in plurality, and where the incumbent himself was non-resident. For it was now illegal—although the law was sometimes evaded—for students at the universities to be instituted to livings unless they had been ordained into the diaconate and were at least twenty-three years of age.[25] A reader was not licensed like a curate, but 'tolerated' and entered into a bond to pay the bishop's officer £20, if he violated the terms of his contract, in which he promised that 'he the above-bounded N.N. being tolerated and admitted to read prayers in the church or chapel of N. . . . according to the Book of Common Prayer, together with the chapters and suffrages appointed by the same, do not in any thing or things touching his said office contrary or otherwise than in the said book specified and allowed, then this present obligation to be void and of none effect, or else to stand and remain in full force.'[26] Curates, too, were sometimes only 'tolerated'. The Lincoln *Liber Cleri* of 1580 mentioned several by name;[27] while Bishop Cooper's Register referred on 8 September 1575 to a certain Henry Berde, curate of Asgarby, as being 'not in orders. Serveth by tollerance';[28] and the *Liber Cleri* of 1576 described John Dee, Rector of Leadenham, in the following terms: 'does not reside; neither is he in holy orders; vehemently suspected in religion; an astronomer not a theologian'.[29]

At the beginning of Elizabeth's reign laymen were sometimes presented to benefices or even made prebendaries. Archbishop Parker wrote to Bishop Grindal in November 1560 that many of his clergy 'as well of your cathedral church as of others beneficed in your diocese, be

neither priests nor deacons';[30] and a year later was asking his archdeacons 'how many of them [the clergy] be neither priests nor deacons'.
The answers were evidently unsatisfactory for the question was repeated in 1567.[31] A good example of the lay ecclesiastic was Archdeacon Wendon of Suffolk who went about in 1565 'in a cloak with a
Spanish cape, and a rapier by his side'.[32] In June 1561 Archbishop
Parker had been asked by Thomas Seckford 'to subscribe your name
to his [Wendon's] bill of presentation' to a vacant prebend in Norwich
Cathedral and Parker obligingly 'subscribed'.[33] Suffolk parishes were
certainly being served by laymen as late as 1597 when Nicholas Curtys
of Farnham was presented because 'he serveth the Cure and hath done
a quarter of a yeare being a mere Laye man';[34] and a similar complaint
was made of John Packard of Earl Stonham, who 'is a lay man, and
sometymes in the absence of the minister doth read dyvyne servyce in
the parishe Church'.[35] In neither of these cases was there any suggestion that they were authorized 'Readers'. However, the bishops in
their *Interpretations and Further Considerations* had demanded that the
clergy should be 'well scanned first, and if their character and biblical
knowledge are satisfactory, they may be tolerated in the office of deacon;
but they are to be promoted to the priesthood only after a good time of
probation';[36] while episcopal visitation articles, charges, and injunctions
throughout the reign reinforced this early determination to secure at
all costs a regular and learned clergy. Edwin Sandys, Bishop of Worcester, declared in 1562, 'That no bishop shall admit into any ministry,
who hath not good testimony of his conversation; who is not learned
fit to teach the people; and who hath not presently some appointed
place, cure and living to serve. And that he do not admit the same
without the consent of six learned ministers; who shall all lay their hands
upon his head';[37] and Archbishop Grindal asked the churchwardens
in his Metropolitical Visitation of 1576 whether their incumbents
'leave their cures to a rude and unlearned person', or 'whether there be
any lay or temporal man, not being within orders, or any child, that
hath or enjoyeth any benefice or spiritual promotion?'[38]

The clergy were expected to stick to their own calling and not 'to
use themselves as laymen'. Bishop Redman of Norwich's Visitation of
1597 led to a number of incumbents being presented on this account:
some of them had farmed too vigorously, and others practised physic
or taught at a private school. Thomas Cheshier, Rector of Nacton,
'useth all kinde of husbandrye, as plowe, harrowe and Carte';[39]
Edward Ketle, Rector of Semer, 'stamped crabbs for the ladie Heigham.
. . . He worketh in harvest tyme in byndinge of oats without anie hatt
on his head, or dublett on his back, but onelie in his hose and shirte';[40]
Robert Wattkinson, curate of Dunwich, All Saints, 'practizeth
physicke';[41] and Thomas Mondaye, Vicar of Cromer, 'teacheth a

schole'.[42] Some of the 'Readers', on the other hand, who were trades-men, were not obliged 'wholly to forbear their callinge'.[43] This latter experiment was not, however, an unqualified success and gradually came to an end as more clergy were ordained.

The Royal Injunctions of 1559 had instructed the clergy to 'preach in their own persons, once every quarter of the year at least one sermon, being licensed especially thereunto . . . or shall read some homily pre-scribed to be used by the queen's authority every Sunday at the least, unless some other preacher, sufficiently licensed . . . chance to come to the parish for the purpose of preaching'.[44] Actually the licensed preachers, who were strictly limited in number, were expected to deliver monthly sermons, 'wherein they shall purely and sincerely declare the Word of God';[45] while the non-licensed were obliged to provide a preacher once a quarter. This last order was all too frequently ignored. At Thorp-Arch in Yorkshire it was reported: 'They have had no sermon in their churche these XXty yeres'. Pluralists were par-ticularly remiss in that respect: John Holme, Vicar of North Clifton, Notts., was presented for being non-resident and not preaching 'any of his ordinary sermons within theise thre yeres'; and Christopher Parker, Vicar of Mansfield, Notts., and also of Tattershall in Lincoln-shire, 'haithe been absent from his benefice this two yeares duringe which tyme they have had no quarterly sermons'.[46] In the Norwich diocese there was also wide-spread neglect of this injunction. Bishop Redman's Visitation in 1597 disclosed that 8 churches in Norfolk had no quarterly sermons, 88 no monthly sermons, and in 17 no homilies were read either. In Suffolk the position was no better since 42 churches had neither monthly nor quarterly sermons and some of them none at all. The homilies were omitted in 6 others. James Venables, Rector of Iken in Suffolk, was one such offender. 'They have seldom any ser-monses', it was stated. 'He redith the homilies seldome';[47] and at Freethorpe and Ormesby St Michael in Norfolk their incumbents were equally reprehensible. 'They have had not above one sermon this fower yeares', the churchwardens alleged of the first, while it was said of the second: 'There have been noe sermon preached there by the space of two yeares last past, but one about Easter last past. He readeth not the homilies'.[48] The Vicar of Wiggenhall St Peter in-geniously refuted the charge 'they have but twoe sermondes in the yeare' by explaining, 'he have a smale parishe and have requested manie prechers to preche in his churche, but the auditie [i.e. the congregation] is so smale he cannot get one'.[49] Evidently preaching parsons in this part of the country were choosey!

In other dioceses the position was much better. The Act Book of the Archdeacon of Oxford's Court for 1584 could produce only one case of neglected quarterly sermons, that of John Wright, curate of Stanton

Harcourt, who was presented by his churchwardens because no sermons had been preached in South Leigh chapel. Wright, however, explained that the quarterly sermons were delivered in the parish church and not at the chapel, although one such address had been given 'before Midsomer last, namelie by Mr Emmott'.[50] The non-preachers had to read, Sunday by Sunday, one or other of the authorized twenty-one homilies; but were not allowed to indulge in any kind of glossing or exposition of either these or the Scriptures. So not unnaturally they were jealous of their preaching brethren; and we hear, for example, of Mr Stubs, Rector of Wath, 'hindering the preacher in the pulpitt and bidding him go to his text'. Sometimes unlicensed preachers were invited to speak to a congregation. Such a man was Robert Blackwood, a Scotsman, who spoke at Kirton; and whose preaching was described as 'the roaringe of an Oxe in the toppe of an ashe tree'.[51] Several of these unlicensed preachers were presented after Bishop Redman's Visitation of Suffolk in 1597: John Keale, curate of Bromeswell, 'preacheth not licensed'; and Robert Swett, Vicar of Weybread, 'preacheth and not licensed'; but the worst case of all was that of a lay schoolmaster of Bradfield, who 'dyd preache at Bradfield the Xth of October, 1596, not licensed'.[52] The Metropolitical Visitation of 1561/2 found some 15 licensed preachers out of 129 clergymen in the archdeaconry of Leicester; while the *Liber Cleri* of 1576 recorded only 57 qualified preachers and 17 others who preached without a licence, in the whole diocese of Lincoln.[53] But by 1592 the numbers were very much larger everywhere. Out of 484 Norfolk ministers listed in 1592/3 there were 106 preachers of one sort or another, and variously described as 'licensed', 'preacher', 'preacher in his owne cure', 'able to preach', and 'public preacher';[54] then on taking four other dioceses at random, we find that Gloucester had 84 preachers as against 169 non-preachers; Chester 172 against 213; Ely 79 against 38; and York 207 against 372.[55] Bishop Redman's Visitation had revealed only 50 clergymen qualified to deliver any kind of sermon;[56] but a return made six years later gave the number of licensed preachers for the Norwich diocese as 396; and in the same year the large Lincoln and Stowe archdeaconry boasted 228 preachers and only 292 'dumb-dogs'.[57] In contrast to all this the vast and backward diocese of Coventry and Lichfield could only muster 51 preachers.[58] In Bishop Cooper of Lincoln's Register, folio 35d, appears 'An Order to be Subscribed unto of Preachers'. In this document the subscriber promised: 'to teache the wourde of god soberly sincerely and trulie accordinge to the fourme of doctrine publiquelie established in this Realme', and 'I shall not suffer any person to use my licence being so required by that aucthorytie from whom I had yt'.[59] Before his admission to any clerical office a Lincolnshire clergyman had also to declare: 'I shall not preache or publiquelie interprete, but only read that which is appointed by publique aucthorytie without speciall licence of the bishop under his seale'.[60]

'The evil that men do lives after them, the good is oft interred with their bones'; so possibly it may have been with the Elizabethan clergy. Certainly we hear a great deal about their misdemeanours. The Darlington Articles, 19.Eliz., asked some very pertinent questions of the Yorkshire clergy. Article 10 demanded to know, 'whether there be any parsons vicars curates or other person ecclesiasticall that wear laie apparall great ruffes great bumbasted breches, skalings or scabulonious clokes or gownes after the laie fashion and contrarie to the Advertisements and Injunctions'.[61] The answer was often in the affirmative both in Yorkshire and elsewhere: John Birkbie, Rector of Moor-Monkton, was reported in the visitation returns of 1567 to be 'of verie dissolute lieffe and lewd conversacion and usethe verie undecent apparell namelie great britches cut and drawn oute with sarcenet and taffite, and great ruffes laid on with laceis of gold and silk'.[62] However, William Harrison stood up for them: 'The apparell . . . of our clergie', he declared, 'is comlie', and a great improvement on the old popish days, when 'to meet a priest in those daies was to behold a peacocke that spreadethe his taile when he danseth before the henne'.[63] In some dioceses at any rate the clergy had to subscribe to the following declaration before being admitted to office: 'I shall use sobrietie in apparell and especiallie in the Church at common praiers accordinge to order appointed'.[64]

Clerical haunters of taverns, players at cards or dice, fornicators and adulterers, dancers and brawlers were, alas, all too common in most dioceses: Mr Tampion, Rector of Normanton in Rutland, instead of doing his duty of a Sunday was found 'playing at the tables with the scholemaster of Hambleton';[65] John Wainhouse, Rector of Kirk-Smeaton, Yorks, 'haithe been suspected to lyve incontinently with one Perkins wif of the saide towne and with certeyne other light women comers and goers thyther. And moreover kepeth in his howse one Francis Lancaster a woman of evill Conversacion and an incontinent lyver';[66] while the incorrigible John Birkbie was accused of being a fornicator and drunkard, and moreover dancing 'verie offensivelie at alehouses and marriages in the presence of common people'.[67] The Rector of Sherington, Bucks, on 26 May 1576, 'wolde have taken away a mans wief from him by the high waie and used such filthy speech that they banished him out of their company';[68] and the Vicar of Stickford in Lincolnshire 'beat his wife in the churchyard, and is a common sower of discord amongst his neighbours; and he has two wives'.[69]

Turning to the dioceses of Oxford and Norwich we find the position no better: five of the Oxfordshire clergy are accused of

Clerical corruption in Tudor times (1569)

incontinence before the Archdeacon's Court in 1584; and one of them, Henry Wise, curate of Horton, is also charged with being a tables player, dice player, and a ribald talker;[70] while drunkenness, gambling, swearing, and immorality were rife amongst the clergy of Norfolk and Suffolk in 1597. At Cantley the Rector, William Phillippes, was 'often overtaken with drincke',[71] and his example was followed by his brethren of Freethorpe,[72] Hanworth and Saxlingham;[73] William Wilson of Fulmodeston 'playeth at cardes and tables manie tymes in the towne and out of the towne, to the offence of the parishe'[74]; and Thomas Cheshier, Rector of Nacton, added to his many other sins by being 'a swearer, Curser and brawler makeing debate amonge his neighbours'.[75] There were, moreover, two cases of suspected immorality, at Great Plumstead and Great Bircham.[76] Essex, too, possessed unsatisfactory parsons: 'Mr Levitt', it was alleged in 1580, 'parson of Leaden Roding, a notorious swearer, a dicer, a carder, a hawker and hunter, a very careless person. . . . He is a quarreller and fighter for he quarrelled and fought with the parson of Stoke in a common Inn in Chelmsford'; and Mr Vaux, Vicar of High Easter, was also declared to be 'a very negligent man, and one that spendeth much time at the bowls, cards and tables, and one very careless for his family, for his wife and children want at home, while he spendeth abroad'.[77]

The Elizabethan parson, in fact, unless he likewise happened to be a Puritan, was a very human sort of person, who enjoyed a glass of ale, a day's hunting, dancing on the green, the society of pretty women, and even an occasional round of fisticuffs. The vicarage ale-house was no uncommon institution in country districts. It was kept partly for profit and partly as a means of refreshing parishioners who had a long way to come to church. At Skipton, for example, it was noted that 'the vicar's brother doth dwell with him in the vicaredge howse and some-times breweth ale and selleth to his friends'; or that John Cockerell, vicar of Burton-Fleming, 'suffereth a vittaling house to be kept in the vicarage'.[78] Such means of increasing their meagre stipends were usually frowned upon, and wherever possible suppressed by the bishops. At the Metropolitical Visitation of 1576 it was asked, 'whether they [the clergy] or any of them, do keep or suffer to be kept in their parsonage or vicarage-houses any ale-houses, tipling-houses or taverns, or do sell ale, beer, wine or any victual?'[79] And the Lincolnshire clergy were obliged to promise not to 'intermeddle with any artificers' occupations, as Covetouslie to seke a gaine therebie'.[80] Nor was the hunting parson any more popular. Humphrey Hall, Rector of Patring-ton in Yorkshire, and Evan Ryecroft, Rector of Coddington in Cheshire, were famous huntsmen; but their churchwardens did not approve and 'hold it offensive'.[81] A certain Essex clergyman, at the beginning of the seventeenth century, arrived one Sunday morning on horseback at his church door; and, on being asked by the wardens whether he intended to take a service and preach, 'swore, so God should judge his soule, he muste and would go seeke his dogge which, as he said, was stolne, which he would not loose as he said for a sermon'.[82] Nevertheless it was considered an even graver offence to dance on a Sunday. Tristram Tildesley, the minister at Rufford and Marsden, 'upon Sondaies and hollidaies hath daunced emongest light and youthful companie both men and women at weddings, drynkings and rish-bearings'; and 'in his dauncing and after wantonlye and dissolutely he kissed a mayd . . . wherat divers person were offended and so sore grieved that ther was weapons drawn and great dissension arose'.[83]

In 1591 the notorious William Rae, Vicar of Oundle, was summoned with both his churchwardens before Bishop Howland of Peterborough and excommunicated in absentia for his relations with one Alice Hayes, who was evidently not his wife.[84] But the whole question of clerical marriage was still very much in the melting pot. The parson's wife had, indeed, been recognized by Convocation as early as 1549; but it was not until 1604 that her position was confirmed in law; and

C

in the meanwhile her status was to say the least of it highly controversial. Queen Mary's reactionary zeal had driven her helter-skelter
out of the parsonage; and although Queen Elizabeth, grudgingly
enough, allowed her to come creeping back again, she never really
approved of parsons' wives; and most of them were kept discreetly in
the background of their husbands' lives. Hence, not unnaturally, much
spiteful gossip circulated round the heads of these dim pathetic ladies.
It was reported of Melchior Smith, Vicar of Hessle, Yorks, that 'he
kepe a woman in his house at Hull as his wife boothe at bedd and at
board . . . she haithe bene forced what with feare and sorow to rone
from him toward the great water of Hull and to lepe over the stayth
there into the Water'.[85] The Vicar of Stickford was not the only
clergyman to be a reputed bigamist; for William Hutchinson, curate of
Felmersham, Bedfordshire, was presented in June, 1576, 'touchinge
his marryeing two wyves'.[86] William Lynche, the unsatisfactory
Rector of Beauchamp Roding in Essex, who was presented in 1564
for being drunk and made to do penance with a white sheet and wand
in the market place at Chelmsford, had a wife who not only drank herself and danced 'at the common alehouse'; but was kissed there by her
partners. And, on being examined, confessed, 'that she hath herd herself accused of yvill fame'.[87] Another obstreperous wife was Margaret,
the far-from-loving spouse of the Rector of Little Wenham in Suffolk,
'who', or so it was alleged in 1597, 'keepeth her husband in prison
uppon an execution at her suite. They have not lived together theise
ix years'.[88]

The Royal Injunctions of 1559 had laid down some strict rules concerning clerical matrimony; and these were firmly enforced. The
churchwardens of Pickering, Yorkshire, presented their vicar because,
as they said, 'they ar uncerteyne whether his Wif was commended unto
him by justices of the peace, nor whether he was licensed to marrye hir
according to hir maiestie's iniunctions'.[89] A marriage licence granted
to William Yomans, Rector of Stoke-Goldington, Bucks, and Joan
Piggot of Bayford, London, in the year 1570/71 declared: 'which
marriage, the consent and assent of the ordinary of the place and of
others required in that behalf being had, they intend to solemnize in
the face of the Church with all convenient speed, We, being by faithful
witness informed of the laudable conversation, morals, honesty and
uprightness of the said Joan Piggot, have given our consent and
assent'.[90] The clergy who failed to comply with these regulations
were penalized. At Lincoln on 26 June 1599, before his father-in-law
Thomas Randes, archdeacon's commissary, George Merton, clerk,
'confessed that he had procured matrimony to be celebrated in the
face of the Church between himself and Mary Randes . . . within the
archdeaconry of Lincoln, without having observed all things pre-

scribed in the twenty-ninth injunction of the year 1559 and submitted himself to the correction of the said master Thomas.' Not unnaturally the commissary was merciful: 'thinking that a case of confession should be dealt with more leniently than a case of conviction'; and Merton was dismissed 'with an admonition'.[91] The prejudice against parsons' wives died hard. In 1610 at King's Sutton in Northamptonshire, a certain Hugo Holland and his wife Deanes spoke of 'Mr Smeth our Minister uncharitably . . . and saithe the World was never merrie since preasts wear married. And sainge Mrs Smith wiffe to the said Mr Smith the first night she was married to him gave hir selffe to the divell'.[92]

The Elizabethan clergy were frequently involved in brawls. The scandalous Melchoir Smith was said 'within the church' on All Saints' eve 1564 to have pulled Nicholas Laborn, a seaman, 'by the beerd. and also gave him such a strooke upon the face with his fist that Laborn brast out of blood at the mouthe and at the nose'.[93] In the Lincolnshire deanery of Bolingbroke a rector was reported to have struck one Francis Clarke on the mouth in the chancel, 'wherefrom there came blood and teeth';[94] and the Rector of Worlingham in Suffolk, Mr Knight, was excommunicated 'for striking and drawing blood in the Churchyard of Wyrlingham on Easter Eve anno domini 1594'.[95] Sometimes it was the clergyman himself who was assaulted: Mr Lammynge, Rector of Caenby and Vicar of Glentham, was attacked by a fishmonger named Henry Cooke at Burton Stather on 20 June 1575, over a quarrel about some cattle. Cooke called the rector 'a foole, a doltish fool and a knave, a doty-pole priest and a knave priest'; he then struck him in the face with his staff and said: 'He cared for never a knave preest in Lincolnshire and he flew upon him and closed with him and bett him, saying that he wold have killed him'.[96] At Halton, Bucks, a curious scene took place in 1584: John Cadburye of Wheatley 'was ringing at Halton upon the birtheday of our Soveraigne Ladie the Queen in memoriall of her matie and thereupon the parson came into the churche and tooke the respondentes hatt lying upon the ffont and threwe yt owte of the doeres, and thereupon this respondent sayed unto the parson yf that he wolde serve him so in another place he wolde give him a boxe on the eare'.[97] Certainly many Elizabethan parsons were not popular with their flocks; and there are stories of clergymen being dragged from the pulpit, having their gowns torn off, and receiving a sound beating, because what they had to say did not please the more fanatical members of their congregations.[98]

At the beginning of the reign the Church Authorities were chiefly concerned with the fight against superstition and the conservatism of the Marian clergy; but later on more interest and energy were displayed in resisting Puritan innovations and omissions. Bishop Parkhurst of Norwich in 1562 had commanded his clergy, 'That they neither suffer the Lord's Table to be hanged and decked like an aulter, neyther use any gestures of the popish masse in ye time of ministration of the communion, as shifting of ye boke, washing, breathing, crossing, or such like'. Furthermore did they 'to the uttermost of their wit, power, knowledge and learning . . . without colour or dissimulation, declare four tymes yearelye in their severall sermons or exhortations that the power of the Bishop of Rome and all other forreign powers are justlie taken away'.[99] The Darlington Articles had also been careful to ask whether the clergy, 'say any communions or commemorations for the dead or at burialls of the dead, whether they say service upon any abrogated holidaies or suffer anie ringing on All Saints daie at night'; and 'whether they be known or suspected to have or kepe any vestments tunicles mass books grailes images crucifixes pixes paxes or any other such cursed and execrated and abominable monuments or supersticion poperie and idolatrie; whether there be anie that use to make curtesy or do reverence to anie crosse of wood or stone or to bow there knees to suche, or in passing by to leave them on there right handes of purpose and for reverence sake'.[100]

Undoubtedly in many parts of the country, notably for example in Worcestershire, Essex, Yorkshire, and Durham, there was a widespread and tenacious clinging to the customs and rites of the old religion, while proscribed 'monuments of superstition' and church furnishings were often cunningly concealed against what was hoped would be yet another turn in the religious tide. At Churchill, as late as 1584, various parishioners were presented 'for kepinge coopes', 'kepinge relickes', and 'for deleying relicques'. The indictment went on; 'there was abowt a vi or vii yeares agoe in the custodie of one Wm Kerrie three copes or vestments, one of velvit and ii of silke and too crosses, of wch they tooke one of the crosses and put it to the belfounders in Oxford to make there sauncebell withall, wch said reliques have remaynid in the custodie of this respondent ever synce undefaced untill they by chaunce came to light of late'.[101] The Archdeaconry of Essex Visitation Book for 1565 recorded the reluctance of many incumbents and their flocks to carry out the terms of the Elizabethan Settlement: at Maldon St Peter an altar was 'standing still in the Spital to the offence of the people'; South Ockendon had 'certain vestments and other church goods, used in the time of popery, undefaced'; and in Little Warley church there was 'a beam whereon was wont to stand a light before an image called Our Lady, which Mr Tyrell will not suffer to be pulled down'.[102] Yorkshire was just as bad. The visitation returns of 1567 accused a number of the clergy of such practices as making wafers for Holy Communion with pictures of the crucifix upon them, of keeping holy water stoops, or preserving images and tabernacles. Nicholas Coke, Rector of Roos, had preserved his rood aloft with its images and

paintings; similarly the orders of the ecclesiastical commissioners had
been resisted at Waghen and Skirlaugh, where paintings could still be
seen on the church walls. The curate and churchwardens at Askrigg,
who had kept both images and vestments, were compelled to carry
them to the fire 'with their own hands'. Moreover the clergy were
admonished to put the communion wafer into the hand instead of the
mouth, to refrain from crossing or breathing over the elements, and
not to 'lifte upp the same to the people to be by them worshipped and
adored'.[103] Archbishop Grindal's Injunctions of 1571 forbade the
ringing of bells for superstitious purposes, the holding of any prohibited fast or festival, the burning of candles at Candlemas, auricular
confession, the worship of images, and many other popish practices.[104]
Nevertheless they persisted; and in particular the old medieval religious
customs died a hard death. On 3 August 1576 Richard Hackney,
Rector of Cranoe, Leics., was ordered by his bishop that 'upon
sondaie next in the pulpitt before his congregation he shall openly
acknowledge that he hath ben convented before the Bisshop his
Ordinarie upon Complaint that he suffered the Churche of God and
howse of praier to be prophanely abused with Poppet plaies and that
this offence he doth acknowledge and is sorie for yt and requireth his
parishioners not to take anie ensample to doe or suffer the like hereafter and in consideration of his repentance shall give unto the poor of
the parish iiis and iiiid . . . and in no wise hereafter shall suffer any such
order eyther by morris daunce or otherwise to be in his Churche. . . .
And upon the performance hereof he ys restored unto the celebration of
ecclesiastical functions'.[105] Edmund Clement of Combe appeared
before the Archdeacon of Oxford's Court in 1584 charged with being
one of those who 'upon All Hallon daye last . . . rang a peale after
service was done'. His ingenious defence was, 'they did yt because
there was a brydalle the same daye and not in anie superstition'.[106]

But by this date it was usually the extreme Puritan who was getting
himself into trouble rather than the traditionalist. The principal
offences of the Protestant non-conforming clergy were the refusal to
baptize with the sign of the cross or marry with the ring, to perambu-
late in rogation week, to church women, and above all to wear the
surplice. Mr Johns, Vicar of Easington, Yorks., a late Tudor visitation
book for 1595/6 informs us: 'dothe not signe children in baptisme with
the signe of the cros. He useth not the perambulacion in the rogation
week . . . he dothe not wear a surples usuallye'.[107] Many clergy of this
kind were to be found in the eastern counties and the midlands. Their
name was indeed legion; but here are a few examples taken out of the
dioceses of Lincoln, Norwich, and London. The episcopal visitation
returns of 1588 record the presentments of numerous Lincolnshire
puritanical clergy and for a variety of reasons. At Brant Broughton

and Swineshead the curates were accused of not 'wearing the surplice'; at Sutton-le-Marsh there was no Easter communion; and at Freston and East Kirkby neither incumbent said the prayers 'according to the Book of Common Prayer'. There was a peck of troubles at Grantham. Thomas Yardley was presented 'for denying the laudable ceremonies of the church'; and both he and Richard Morley had to do penance for refusing to allow their wives to be churched. The Vicar of Sleaford would only baptize on Sundays and neglected to use the sign of the cross. As a result, or so it was affirmed, 'certain infants have died without baptism'.[108]

The archdeaconries of Norfolk and Suffolk possessed sixty-four churches in 1597 where the surplice was never worn, and sixty-seven more where its use was only occasional. In the latter cases there were some interesting variations. At Binham and Great Yarmouth in Norfolk the incumbents would willingly don the surplice for every service *except* Holy Communion, when they flatly declined to do so. On the other hand, in churches like Longham, Aldringham, Falkenham, Little Glemham, and Tatingstone it would be worn at communion, but on no other occasion. Sometimes, admittedly, the parson had a perfectly legitimate excuse for refusing to wear it. The Vicar of East Tuddenham said 'he have and doe use to weare the surples excepte when yt is in washing and not dried'; Robert Boothe of Salhouse explained that 'he wore it not for that it was so rent that yt was not decent to be worne'; and the Rector of Great Ryburgh complained 'that the suples is verie litle'. It must be remembered, of course, that the surplice, usually a large affair with sleeves, was supplied by the parish and the churchwardens were responsible for its condition.[109] As regards the perambulations, the two archdeaconries could muster fifty-two parishes that had not 'walked'; in some cases for as long as five or even seven years. The puritanical clergy were also active or inactive in other ways: John Trendle, Rector of Ovington, was accused in 1592 of catechizing every Sunday, 'but not the Catechism articulate but with Mr More's. He publisheth not holly dayes by their speciall names nor fastinge dayes at all. He have often in the pulpitt prayed for elders and trewer discipline to be in this Church of Englande, and they never hard him give her Majestie the titles Articulate; in his sermons he have usuallie termed such ministers as cannot preache domme dogges, as evill as devills. He hath divers tymes persueaded many to leave their owne churches in service tyme when ther minister cannot preach and to resort to such as can preache . . . he havinge private contention with John Withers dyd of his owne authoritie suspend him from Churche . . . he have heretofore repelled from the Communion divers parishioners uppon frevelous causes . . . he hav been very unquiett and troublesom amonge his parishioners in sutes'.[110]

Turning to those further strongholds of puritanism, the home counties of Herts and Essex, we find many of the clergy in serious trouble. In 1583 three ministers, John Coppin, Elias Thacker, and Thomas Gibson were hanged for 'dispensing Browne's books and Harrison's books'; and large numbers were suspended or deprived for a variety of reasons, such as not wearing the surplice, nor crossing in baptism, or preaching without a licence. One of these last was the famous Mr Ward of Writtle, of whom Fuller wrote:

> Grant, some of knowledge, greater store,
> More learned some in teaching,
> Yet few in life did lighten more,
> None thundered more in preaching.

A petition signed by some two hundred prominent men in the Hundred of Dunmow was presented to Lord Rich on their behalf. This declared: 'The greatest number of our ministers are utterly without learning, or very idle, or otherwise of very scandalous life . . . and those few at whose hands we reaped comfort are from time to time molested, threatened, and put to silence. May it, therefore, please your Honour . . . to make known our lamentable case . . . that . . . our grievance be redressed'.[111] Neither did the nonconformists scruple by ridicule and abuse to carry the war into the enemy's country. At Hatfield Peverel in 1585 a Puritan named John Sharpe 'sayd when he did se ye minister were ye surplice that the fole had gotton on his fooles cote, and did axe the minister yf he wolde have yt to keepe him warme'.[112] Here is a final example of a Puritan parson from Hertfordshire, Anthony Watson of Watford, who besides committing all the usual offences, added to his sins by administering 'the communion to the people standing'.[113]

'As we still use the Prayer Book', writes G. M. Trevelyan, 'it is not very hard to reconstruct in our minds an Elizabethan service. There was no intoning either of prayers or psalms. The prayers were said and the psalms were sung. Congregational singing was a great part of the appeal of Protestant worship. But instead of the modern hymns now sung in Church, the psalms appointed for the day were sung in the rhymed metrical version of Sternhold and Hopkins . . . the music of viols and wind instruments might or might not accompany the psalm-singing of the congregation'.[114] William Harrison described the church services of his time at some length: At Sunday Morning Prayer the psalms for the day were read by 'the minister with a lowd voice' (if they were not sung) and then the two lessons, one probably by the Parish Clerk.[115] These were followed by 'the litanie and suffrages, an innovation in mine opinion not devised without the great assistance of the spirit of God'; by the ante-communion, which was derisively called 'the drie communion'; a psalm; homily or sermon; another psalm; and finally, baptism. 'In the afternoon likewise we meet againe, and after the psalmes and lessons ended, we have commonlie a sermon, or at leastwise our youth catechized by the space of an hour'.[116] The parson, indeed, was obliged by law to say or sing Morning and Evening Prayer every Sunday, 'standinge in a pulpitt or seate appointed for that purpose and so turninge your face towardes the people as they may best heare the same'.[117] The Litany was likewise to be said every Wednesday and Friday; Evening Prayer every Saturday and Holy Day[118]; communion celebrated at least four times in the year; and baptism administered as required. The saying of the daily offices was tacitly left to the conscience of the individual priest, and at one period during the reign almost entirely disappeared. However, by the beginning of the seventeenth century it was being steadily revived. The puritans, of course, deliberately ignored holy days, and all too often used a basin for baptism instead of the font.[119] Four communions a year, too, was an ideal not always observed; and an Easter celebration was sometimes the only one, with possibly the addition of others at Christmas and Whitsunday.[120]

The progressive decay of village churches during the greater part of the Elizabethan Age is only too apparent from the numerous visitation returns from all over the country dealing with their ruinous condition. For this state of affairs a number of causes can be cited: the iconoclasm of the Marian exiles returning from Geneva; want of money and energy on the part of churchwardens and clergy; and the sheer indifference or greed of lay impropriators and farmers of the rectory. Certainly the last were particularly blameworthy. The consequences of all this destruction and neglect were, only too often, damp green walls, rotting earth floors, and gaping windows. Some of the puritanically-minded Norfolk gentry were accustomed at the beginning of the reign to use their churches as cart-houses and stables, while keeping pigeons in the belfreys. Gradually matters improved as the Church authorities vigorously intervened. A beginning was made with the clergy, who were ordered to 'bestow . . . a fifth part of that their benefice till they [chancels] be fully repaired, and, being repaired, shall maintain the same in good estate and order'.[121] Parsons who failed to carry out these instructions were presented. In 1567 John Holme, Vicar of North Clifton, Notts, was reported to be non-resident and letting his chancel 'fall into utter ruin and decay'; and the same criticism applied to Leonard Mitchell, Rector of Epperstone, whose 'chancel of the churche the parsonage and howses belonginge the same ar in great decay'. Many other clerics too were named in the same visitation: William Green, Vicar of Arnold, Richard Brand, Rector of Screveton, and John Normavel, Rector of Clifton.[122] John Jennor, Rector of Great Bardfield, Essex, was told in 1587 to repair 'the church windows and decays of the chancell';[123] and ten years later Paul Berbeck of Aldeburgh, Suffolk, was indicted because his 'Chauncell is utterlye ruinated'.[124] These few examples taken from the mass of evidence available indicate that the clergy at any rate were being kept up to the scratch.

It was not so easy to deal with the lay impropriators or farmers of the rectory. The Earl of Lincoln was a particularly notorious offender, who neglected his responsibilities at many Lincolnshire churches. It was said, for instance, of Billingborough in 1602 that 'the Chauncell ys ruinous by the default of the Erle of Lincoln proprietory of this parsonage'. Ecclesiastical impropriators could be just as bad: 'The chauncell of Hallywell a chapell belonging to this parsonage [Bytham Magna] ys in decay; the parsonage ys impropriate to the deane and Chapter of Lincoln to whom or their farmer the repaire belongethe; the church ys well repayred and kept decently'.[125]

It is important to note this contrast between the neglect of the chancel and the repair of the nave, for that is a consistent feature of the 1602 Report. At Swarby again, 'the churche ys well kept in repayre and decencie. The chauncell roofe ys fallen doowne and taken away longe sence. The proprietarie there is one George Fairefax gent' who shuld repayre or reedifie the same'.[126] The nave, of course, was the responsibility of the churchwardens and parishioners, and once the first wave of destruction and neglect was passed, some at least appear to have been active in restoration, judging from parish accounts and visitation returns.[127] In Bishop Scrambler's Visitation of the Archdeaconry of Norwich in 1593, out of 268 churches visited there were only 19 cases of structural defects in the fabric of the nave, but 35 ruinous chancels. Some of the latter were very serious: at Thurning it was stated, 'the chauncell is in verie great decaie of the Roffe and glaszinge; also the seates therein are decayed, so that yt lyeth like a downehouse'.[128] The trouble was sometimes caused not by man but by nature or birds: the damage at Skegness, for example, was wrought by tempest; and that at Mablethorpe by the sea. Hundleby church, which 'ys defectyve in the glase windowes' had been 'defiled with owles and pigeons'.[129] However, churchwardens were often no better repairers than their ministers. Bishop Redman's visitation of the whole of the Norwich diocese, five years after Bishop Scrambler's, revealed glaring cases of neglect: Lakenham church was declared to be 'very ruinous and much decayed for want of reparacions'; at Earlham, 'the churche and steeple be greatly decayed'; at Barmer, 'their church defaced and almost downe'; and at Culpho, 'the Church is in greate Ruine and decaye both in tymber and tyleinge, in such sort as £20 will not repayre the same'.[130] In June 1602 Archbishop Whitgift sent a letter to the bishops asking for a report on the state of the churches.

Their returns showed that much still needed doing, and although there was an oft repeated promise of 'a speedy reformation', church repair and re-beautification were to provide many an episcopal headache for the rest of the period covered by this book.

The interior of most Elizabethan churches displayed a Protestant simplicity. 'As for our churches', wrote William Harrison, 'belles . . . remaine as in time past'; but 'all images, shrines, tabernacles, rood-lofts, and monuments of idolatrie are removed, taken down and defaced; onelie the stories in glasse windowes excepted, which for want of sufficient store of new stuffe . . . are not altogither abolished in most places at once, but by little and little suffered to decaie, that white glasse may be provided and set up in their roomes'.[131] The church walls had been white-washed in order to obliterate the medieval paintings; and the earth floor strewn with straw or rushes to enable the congregation to kneel properly. The want of such a floor covering was sometimes made an excuse for absenteeism.

The number of private pews in church had greatly increased since the Reformation; for many of the old side-chapels, now in ruins, had been seized upon by the local squires and converted into family pews. Various village worthies, too, quite apart from the lord of the manor himself, laid claim to a pew by right of certain properties held by them in the parish or because they paid parochial rates or occupied parochial offices. A pew had become, in fact, a symbol of privilege; and in an age notorious for its violence, its want of stabilizing traditions, and its disputed social claims, not infrequently led to fierce arguments and bitter quarrels. Edward Lethome of Pannal 'dyd misuse Tho. Warde-man in his owne seate in the church att service tyme and thrust him furth of his seate by violence'; and Robert Harrison of Thorner pulled Christopher Austroppe 'out of his stall before prayer time on the Saboth day'. A particularly celebrated case was that of the Kayes of Wetherby. Richard and Robert Kaye, representing the one side to the feud, found Thomas Kaye of the other comfortably seated in the family stall at the 'tyme of divine prayers'. Whereupon they set upon him forthwith: 'twitchinge of him and thrusting pinnes into his armes and buttocks or into one of them . . . and did give Thomas Kaye a blowe upon his head eare or face, not only to the disturbance of the divine service then in hand and disquietinge of the Congregation there assembled but also to the evell example of others beinge there'.[132]

It was part of the churchwardens' duties to allocate the free seating according to the social status of each parishioner. The sexes were generally separated and people were expected to sit in the seat assigned to them by authority and nowhere else. This was often a ticklish problem particularly in the case of the fair sex, since the ladies were obliged to sit strictly according to social standing, age or condition i.e. married or unmarried. There was a distressing scene at St Ebbe's church, Oxford in 1584 when Margery Hopkins, a freeman's wife, was put into a seat that Barbara Nicholles had occupied for the last five years. Margery declared: 'that upon Twelfe daye at night last past after evening prayer was donne this respondent and Barbara Nicholles fell at woordes together in the churche for theire seates, and because that Nicholles is not a freman the churchwardens there placed this respondent being a freman's wiffe in the seate wth the said Barbara Nicholles and upon the better hand in the seate, and because this respondent offered to take her seate at the beginning of evening prayer the sayed Barabara iostled ffurther into the seate and wolde not lett her come into her owne place there, whereupon this respondent sayed unto her, yf yowe will not lett me come into mye owne seat I will sitt upon yor lappe the nexte daye, and thereupon grewe ffurther woordes of inconvenience betwene theime, as whore and basterd and suche lyke as hereafter bye order of lawe shall appeare'.[133]

The churchwardens were expected to provide their parish with a Prayer Book, bread and wine for communion, a calendar and psalter, the English Bible and 'discourage no man from reading of any part of the Bible'[134], two tomes of the homilies, a table of the ten commandments, 'a convenient pulpitt well-placed', the Paraphrases of Erasmus on the Gospels, a holy communion table covered at the celebration with 'a faire linen clothe' or 'commonly' with 'some coveringe of silke buckram or other such like', a silver cup and cover 'which may serve also for the ministracion of the Communion breade', a large surplice with sleeves, 'one book of register, wherin they shall write the day and year of every wedding, christening, and burial',[135] and finally two chests, each with two locks and keys, to house the registers and alms. They were likewise commissioned to prevent any drinking or feasting in the church itself; to keep the churchyard clean and fenced, and free from dancers, pedlars, gamesters and idlers; and to remove and destroy the relics of superstition. Furthermore they were ordered to present the following classes of people: those who absented themselves from church or arrived there late; did not pay their poor and church rates; blasphemers, swearers, drunkards, scolds, and usurers; married couples who had neglected to put up their banns or were within the prohibited degrees of affinity; absconding husbands or wives; and 'favourers of the Romishe and forreyne power'. In addition they must keep an eye on their parson and see that he behaved himself and conducted the services aright.[136] Certainly their duties were manifold and onerous; and although there must undoubtedly have been many poor, ignorant and inefficient wardens about,[137] it was yet on the whole a coveted post and the majority of those who held it were zealous and active men.

The Parish Clerk, who was appointed by the incumbent, donned a surplice and performed such tasks as reading the lessons, epistles, and psalms; besides being responsible for seeing that the whole of the church, its furniture and ornaments, were kept 'faire and cleane . . . againste service tyme'. He might also be asked to teach the younger children to read, 'if he be able to do so'.[138] But the parson himself was expected to catechize 'upon every holy day and every second Sunday in the year, to hear and instruct all the youth of the parish for half an hour at the least before evening prayer, in the Ten Commandments, the Articles of Belief, and in the Lord's Prayer, diligently examine them, and teach the Catechism set forth in the book of Public Prayer'.[139] These instructions were repeated and enlarged by Archbishop Grindal in 1571; for he now demanded that the clergy should catechize 'every Sondaye and Holye day', while besides the youth of the parish 'servaunts both menkynde and womenkynde' were to be instructed. They were also warned to take careful note of parents or masters who did not send their children or servants, and to denounce them 'to the Ordinarye'. Neither was the priest to communicate, marry, or accept as godparents any who 'can not saye by heart at leaste the ten commandments, the articles of the faithe and the Lordes prayer in Englishe'; and, of course, the Catechism.[140]

In pre-Reformation times Sunday had been very laxly kept. Once he had attended Mass the villager was free to spend the rest of the day enjoying himself at fair, wake or church-ale, in the tavern or on the village green. Queen Elizabeth herself was not opposed to such an arrangement; and provided the people first attended their parish churches and forbore to work or play during the hours of divine service, she had no objection to their passing the rest of Sunday as they pleased. The reformers held different views. Only necessary work like harvesting should be permitted on the sabbath; and all amusements must cease. The day ought to be devoted entirely to such religious activities as church attendance, visitation of the sick, or the giving and receiving of religious instruction at home. The Royal Injunctions of 1559 had been purposely vague on the question of the profanation of Sunday; and, while fining absentees from church 12d. for every week they stopped away, gave definite permission for work in the harvest field. All attempts by Parliament to pass legislation for a stricter regulation of Sunday were steadily and successfully resisted by the Queen. Nevertheless, in practice, much was done by the more protestant clergy, churchwardens, and justices of the peace locally to enforce a more reverent and restful sabbath; although, naturally enough, these attempts met with the violent opposition of a conservative peasantry. Despite the permission of the Injunctions we find in 1597 that William Foiston of Rougham, Norfolk, was presented because

'He did mowe corne in harvest last a whole Sabbothe daie'; and Nicholas Lynstead of Honing in the same county for the same offence, namely 'cartin on the Saboth daie in harvest time last'.[141] In a York Visitation Book of 1595 mention is made of a maypole which had been 'sett uppe upon Lawton grene upon a Sabbothe or Holly day where a pyper and dyvers youthe were playing and dancing'. This was suppressed together with a 'faire kepte in the churchyarde' at Hollym, which had been held 'once a year . . . tyme oute of mynde'.[142] Dancing, football, playing, or lying on the grass in the churchyard were all frowned upon. As far as possible, too, Sunday work and trade were stopped: Cuthbert Atkinson defended himself before the Archdeacon of Oxford's Court in 1584 by declaring 'that in the winter season he doethe use to sett his racke upon Sondayes in the morning before morning prayer, and so doethe moste of the fullers in Englande use to doe, because otherwyse they cannott kepe promise wth theire custmers for that there is somtymes scarce one fayre daye in a whole weeke, and otherwyse he denieth the defecte to be trewe'.[143] Other members of the woollen and brewing trades appeared before this Court charged with similar misdeeds. In the north Gilbert Dickson of Otley was found ploughing and sowing on the Sabbath 'to the evell example of others';[144] while in Norfolk Robert Bey of Freethorpe 'spread mucke in the feild' on the Sabbath; and Mrs Joan Large of Sloley was actually excommunicated 'for washing cloathes on the holyday'.[145] Travelling on a Sunday for business purposes was especially reprehensible: a baker, for example, was presented for journeying to Hull in order to sell bread.[146]

The parson and his churchwardens were, of course, legally within their rights in enforcing church attendance, reverence, and order during service-time, and the cessation of work or games in hours of worship. When, for instance, the innkeeper at Saxmundham 'did suffer musitians to playe and singe and Company to daunce in his howse in tyme of evening prayers'; or when George Ebbes and Elizabeth his wife were discovered at Necton to be 'selling victualls and suffering strangers to be eating and drincking in their house in servyce tyme',[147] then the authorities had every justification in acting; but the wholesale closure of ale houses and shops on a Sunday was a very different matter. Excessive strictness, in fact, frequently led to ugly scenes. At Norwich in 1572 'three or four lewd boys, set on by some lewder persons . . . came into the church, and as the said minister began to read "My soul doth magnify the Lord", they burst out into singing of psalms suddenly and unlooked for; and being commanded by the minister to cease, they continued singing, and he reading; so all was out of order, and the godly, well-disposed auditors there disquieted, and much grieved'.[148] Simon Tanfield 'a dronkarde drue his knife and porred with it at Ambrose Jackson in Acaster church'; while Robert Fubarn and Christopher Hudson, who were bowling in Deighton Churchyard, attacked the curate when he rebuked them 'and bett him grevowslie'.[149] For such offences heavy penalties could be imposed, as to be 'sett in the Stocks at the churche side upon Sunday nexte at nine of the clock before nowne and ther to sit in the stocke by the space of one hole hour and at the houre ende to be tayken furthe and laid over the stock and have six yerts with a byrchen rod upon his buttocke'.[150] The parson himself was not slow to read the homily for 'the Place and Time of Prayer', wherein he castigated his parishioners who worked or traded on Sunday, but reserved his especial wrath for those that 'rest in ungodliness and filthiness, prancing in their pride, pranking and pricking, pointing and painting themselves, to be gorgeous and gay; they rest in excess and superfluity, in gluttony and drunkenness, like rats and swine; they rest in brawling and railing, in quarrelling and fighting: they rest in wantonness, in toyish talking, in filthy fleshliness; so that it doth too evidently appear that God is more dishonoured, and the devil better served on the Sunday than upon all the days in the week beside'.[151] But by the end of the reign the nation at large was becoming more conscious of the 'apartness' of the sabbath; and its special claim to be treated as holy unto the Lord.

'It is permitted', wrote William Harrison, 'that a sufficient man may (by dispensation from the prince) hold two livings not distant either from other above thirtie miles'.[152] This system of pluralities, he went on to explain, had become necessary owing to the shortage of learned clergy with university degrees; and also because 'one most commonlie of these small livings is of so little value, that it is not able to maintaine a meane scholar, much lesse a learned man'.[153] Since the Reformation there had been a good deal of legislation seeking to control, regulate, and if possible reduce pluralities; but the steadily rising cost of living defeated them all. These facts were so self-evident in the Elizabethan age that even the Puritans, who attacked pluralities, were often only too glad to make use of them to secure a bare living. In the Lincoln *Liber Cleri* for 1588 we read of Robert Hanson, Vicar of Rasen Drax, 'of which the fruits do not exceed the sum of eight pounds a year', obtaining a neighbouring living to hold in plurality, 'of which the fruit does not exceed £8 a year'. Usually conditions were attached to such dispensations: Richard Jaques in June 1572 'obtained from Edmund archbishop of Canterbury a grace to possess the church of Ashen alias Esse in the diocese of London and the rectory of Althorp in the diocese of Lincoln . . . being not more than twenty miles distant from each other, on the condition of preaching in each of them thirteen sermons, and that he shall exercise in them hospitality for two months every year'; and Richard Laing, another Lincolnshire pluralist, was ordered in 1584 'that he shall in each of them have sixteen sermons and exercise hospitality for two months'.[154] The curates and readers employed by these pluralist incumbents were frequently far from satisfactory and sometimes unlicensed. Many livings joined in this way, however, were so close to each other that they could easily be served by a single minister. Myles Whale was in 1603 the Rector of Willoughby and Vicar of Osbornby, 'both in this deanery and the distance is very small soe that he servethe both Cures himself'.[155]

Certainly the number of pluralities was very high. Out of a list of 484 Norfolk clergy published in 1592, 112 were pluralists, although with two exceptions none of them was holding more than two benefices.[156] It was frankly admitted in 1603 that, despite every attempt to reduce and regulate pluralities, a thousand clergymen held two thousand and five hundred livings between them. These pluralists usually held two livings each, which were sometimes less than a mile apart, while their combined incomes did not normally exceed £20.[157]

According to the official valuations of the *Valor Ecclesiasticus*, which had been compiled in 1535, but never revised, and remained the standard reference book for clerical incomes until the end of the seventeenth century, out of the 8,803 benefices named: 4,543 had less than £10, 2,978 less than £5, and 1,000 less than £2; 3,642 varied between £10 and £26, and 144 rose above £40. Thus nearly 90 per cent of the livings were worth less than £26. The lowest endowments were usually found in the extreme north where few benefices were worth more than £5. However, none of the official compilations of this period can be taken too seriously. For example, if we take at random the Lincolnshire deanery of Aslackhoe and compare the official values in 1524 and again in 1680 we find that they have changed very little in more than a hundred years. Out of the 21 livings in the deanery in 1524: 4 were worth between £10 and £19; 1 less than £4; 16 between £4 10s. 0d. and £10.[158] In 1680 out of the 18 livings listed: 4 were respectively £27 13s. 4d., £22, £19, and £11 10s. 0d.; 13 between £4 and £10; and 1 under £4.[159] Yet it is certain that all these incomes must have doubled if not trebled during this period.

The truth is that the Elizabethan parson's exact income is very difficult to assess at all accurately, since tithes were still often paid in kind and he normally farmed his own glebe. The sixteenth century was a time of agricultural revolution when the switch from corn to pasture or an intensive agriculture was gathering momentum. It was accompanied by the introduction of new crops, and made possible by the practice of enclosure. This led inevitably to a loss of great tithes; but an increase in small, particularly in wool and lambs. Where, in fact, tithe was paid in kind according to the old law of the biblical tenth, the parson had little to grumble at; for as the price of wheat or wool went up so too did his stipend. But, alas, in all too many cases a *modus decimandi* had been adopted earlier in the century, whereby tithes had been commuted for a money payment, or some other fixed agreement had been arrived at with the incumbent that took the place of the old dispensation. These commutations now represented a mere fraction of the original market price. The economic world between 1540 and 1600 had been turned upside down by the flood of precious metals pouring in from the Americas; and this inevitably resulted in a depreciation of money values and a sharp rise in prices. As always the clergy suffered severely from such changes. Common land was being rapidly enclosed, wastes and fens were drained and reclaimed; but as these lands had never paid tithe in the past, the parson was no better off, while he lost his rights on the old common. The Reformation had put an end to the payment of various small dues and gifts at festivals and on other occasions, which the clergy had been accustomed to take as a matter of course, but now sadly missed.

The outgoings from the parsonage were alarming. These included the payment of first fruits and tenths by all vicarages over £10 and rectories over £7; and the annual subsidies. The laity also paid subsidies; but, declared Harrison wrathfully, 'if these paie after foure shillings for land, the cleargie commonlie after six shillings of the pound, so that of a benefice of twentie pounds by the yeare, the incumbent thinketh himselfe well acquitted, if all ordinary paiments being discharged, he may reserve thirteene pounds six shillings eight pence towards his own sustentation and maintenance of his familie'.[160] Then there was a charge for armour and munitions. Archbishop Parker wrote to Bishop Grindal in 1569: 'That every one of the clergie, having benefits, spiritual promotions or pensions, the clere value whereof either by themselves, or joyned together, do amounte to the clere yerely value of xxxl or upwards, shall be bound and charged to provide have, and maynteyne armour, and other provision requisite, according to such proportion and rate, as the temporaltie are bound and charged . . . by reason of their moveable goodes'.[161] Dues were payable to the Bishop or Archbishop at their visitations, to the archdeacon in his synod, and to the Royal Visitors who 'doo visit the whole realme under the forme of an ecclesiastical inquisition, in which the clergy do usuallie paie double fees, as unto the archbishop'.[162] Finally there were the demands of hospitality. The Royal Injunctions of 1559 had instructed parsons with benefices worth more than £100 to contribute £3 6s. 8d. to help poor scholars at the university;[163] all the clergy were expected to give alms;[164] and those who held two or more livings were obliged to contribute one fortieth part of their income to poor relief where non-resident, and 'keep hospitality' in the parish they inhabited.[165] John Holme, Vicar of North Clifton, for example, was presented in 1567 because 'he is not resident upon his benefice nor dothe distribute the Xltie parte to the pore'.[166]

Lay patrons of advowsons, following Queen Elizabeth's lead with her bishoprics, frequently required simoniacal payments, favourable leases, remission of tithe or even surrenders of glebe land, before they would appoint to their benefices. So much so indeed that Parliament was compelled in 1571 to pass an Act, Eliz.13., which 'provided that no spiritual person, college, or hospital, shall let lease other than for the term of twenty-one years or three lives; the rent accustomed, or more, reserved payable yearly during the said term'.[167] The Lambeth Articles of 1561 had threatened to deprive any parson who made a simoniacal compact; and 13 Eliz. c. 20 was later further strengthened by 3 Car. I c. 5, which decreed that leases of livings were only valid while the minister was in residence. Pensions, too, could no longer be charged upon a benefice. However, all real attempts to curb the growing control of the squire over the parson were doomed to failure as long as a benefice was still regarded as a piece of property rather than as a cure of souls, the advowson of which could be legally bought and sold. No wonder Harrison complained that 'Not a few find fault with our thred-bare gowns, as if not our patrones but our wives were causes of our wo. But if it were knowne to all, that I know to have been performed of late in Essex—where a minister taking a benefice (of less than twentie pounds in the Queenes books) was inforced to paie to his patrone, twentie quarters of otes, ten quarters of wheat, and sixteene yeerelie of barleie, which he called hawkes meat; and another lett the like in farme to his patron for ten pounds by the yeere, which is well woorth fortie at the least,— the cause of our thred-bare gownes would easlie appeere; for such patrons doo scrape the wooll from our clokes'.[168] Archbishop Parker, writing to Lady Bacon in 1567, informed her: 'I sent my visitors into Norwich . . . to know the state of the country, whereof I heard, of credible and worshipful persons, that Gehazi and Judas had a wonderful haunt in the country, that Quid vultis mihi dare? had so much prevailed there among the Simonians that now to sell and to buy benefices, to fleece parsonages and vicarages, that omnia erant venalia'.[169] Consequently the clergy were often driven to desperate expedients, such as cutting down the timber on their glebes without any regard to the ultimate effects on the property as a whole. This could most profitably be done in the south and east where wood was now comparatively scarce. The relatives of a certain Essex vicar, who died in 1600, suppressed the news of his death and concealed his body for three weeks, during which time they felled one hundred and twenty acres of woodland and pulled up all the fences on the glebe lands.[170] However, by 1604 the average living had probably doubled in real

D

value and risen from the pre-Reformation norm of £6 or £7, to between £10 and £20. Curates' stipends were much smaller, generally in the region of £5 per annum.[171]

What sort of house did the Elizabethan parson occupy? Just as an incumbent's stipend was slightly better than the ordinary wage of the agricultural labourer, so his parsonage was considerably more comfortable and commodious than their cottages. The smallest of them would probably have contained a parlour, hall, kitchen and chamber; while the larger ones would have had many more rooms. Ezekiel Taylor, Rector of Thorpe-on-the-Hill, Lincolnshire, who was a married man with five children, possessed no less than sixteen in his rectory: kitchen, parlour, new study, little parlour, maid's parlour, entry, hall, kitchen-chamber, bolting-house, beer-house, milk-house, 'blynd chamber', chamber over the hall, little buttery, little chamber, and upper chamber. Even allowing for the fact that the 'entry' was simply a porch, and that the 'milk-house', 'bolting-house', and 'beer-house' were no more than out-buildings, this must have been a large house by Tudor standards; while the inclusion of a study and 'maid's chamber' showed how standards of comfort and culture were rising. The perennial problem of non-existent parsonages and tumble-down mansions were as much an Elizabethan headache as our own! George Aslabie, Vicar of Tickhill in Yorkshire, complained in 1571 of his vicarage being 'in decay because yt is suche a greate house'. And the suggestion is made that the parish should 'appoint suche house of the same vicaredge as shalbe sufficient for the lyvinge and that suche other houses thereof as ar superfluous may be pulled downe wherewith the other may be sufficiently repayred'.[172]

By the end of Elizabeth's reign the study appeared to have become an indispensable part of every country parsonage. As time went on the furnishing also improved. In pre-Reformation days the necessities of life and labour—beds and bedding, pots and pans, tools, sacks of grain, cheeses etc—filled the house; but there were usually few chairs, forms, or tables, let alone luxuries like carpets or hangings. However, by the end of the sixteenth century such items were on the increase. Furthermore we note that the framed table was displacing the trestle-table; and chairs and window-seats (sometimes furnished with cushions) were taking the place of stools and forms. Stained glass windows, carpets, tester-beds, arrases, and painted cloths were also to be seen in the richer type of parsonage. Most parsons possessed books and considerable quantities of clothes and plate. Fisher, Rector of Bassingham, owned four gowns (two furred and lined), three jackets of camlet and two of cloth, three pairs of hose, two tippets of velvet, and one of cloth. Another Lincolnshire parson, Roger Routh of Hellawe, possessed twelve platters, eleven dishes, seven saucers, two plate dishes and a double salt of pewter; besides six silver spoons. The whole of these last were valued at £3.

All country parsons were farmers and owned such things as ploughs, carts, and other farm implements; and their houses, and sometimes even their churches, were used to store their grain in. As regards live stock: most of the clergy kept oxen and cattle, pigs and poultry, and a horse or two to get about on. Many, like Hooker in Walton's apocryphal story of Drayton Beauchamp,[173] tended their little flock of sheep; while some were also keen bee-keepers. Their wives were invaluable as unpaid milk-maids and poultry keepers; and sons and daughters, as soon as they were old enough, were profitably employed on the glebe farm. William Harrison wrote: 'By reason that marriage is permitted to him that will choose that kind of life, their meat and drink is more orderlie and frugallie dressed; their furniture of household more convenient and better looked unto; and their poore oftener fed generallie than heretofore they have beene'.[174] It would almost certainly be true to say that the married Elizabethan country parson was better off than his celibate predecessor: his house was larger and more comfortably furnished; he possessed more books, clothes, and plate; his glebe was better stocked, and more hands were available for its cultivation. Despite therefore the economic and social upheavals of the times, the miserable stipends recorded in the official returns, and the voracious greed of lay patrons, the inventories of clerical estates show that the average country Elizabethan parson would leave as much as £120, as compared with a mere £28 in the reign of Henry VIII.[175]

APPENDIX TO CHAPTER II

Elizabethan churchwardens' and parish account books reveal that a great deal of work was done to keep the churches in repair. Here is a typical entry from Northill, Bedfordshire, in 1561:

'Anno domini Mcccclxi vicesimo secundo die Junii: alowance askyd by John Flynt for certen money layde owt for the reparacyon of the stepull and the cherche.

	s.	d.
Imprimis payde to the plummer	13	4
Item to Appluelyn for 4 dayes worke	4	8
Item to Nycholas Edlyng for 2 dayes worke	12	
Item to Careless for 2 hundred nayles & di	2	0
Item to Careless for stapulls for the bells	12	
Item payde for a loode sande caryage	8	
Item payd to the plummer	6	8
Item payde to William Hawkyns for a pece of tymber for the stepull to make a beame	21	ob.

Item payde to Edlyng for makyng cleane the gutters   1   ob.

Item payde to the plummer the 13 day of July in full recompense of & for hys hole bargayne for the hole cherche & stepull   20——0

Item payde to the plummer the same daye for 36 li. sauder   28——4 ob.

Item payde to Webster's wyffe for drynke for laborers at the cherche at settyng up ladders & other laburs   10

Item payde to Richard Webster for wood for the plummers   20

Item payd to Appluelyn for mendyng the wyndowys in the nether loffte   3

Item payde for twentye six peny nayles   1

Item payde for dressyng the wether cocke   2——0[176]

NOTES

[1] Fuller, *Church History*, II, pp. 522–3.

[2] *Harrison's Description of England*, I, p. 26.

[3] *Correspondence of Abp Parker* (Parker Society), p. 120

[4] *Fulke's Works*, (Parker Society), Vol. II, p. 118.

[5] *Works of Abp Whitgift* (Parker Society), Vol. I, p. 316.

[6] Lincoln Record Society, Vol. 23, pp. 140ff.

[7] *Annals of Evangelical Nonconformity*, pp. 88–99.

[8] Lincoln Record Society, Vol. 23, xviii.

[9] Lincoln Record Society, Vol. 2, *Lincoln Episcopal Records in the time of Thomas Cooper*, p. 138. See also Vol. 23, p. xix.

[10] Injunction XVI. See Frere and Kennedy, *Visitation Articles and Injunctions*, Vol. III, pp. 13–14; & 177.

[11] *The Essex Review*, Vol. XXXII, 'Visitation of the Archdeaconry of Colchester. 1588', pp. 132–7.

[12] Lincoln Record Society, Vol. 2, pp. 189 & 211. Bishop Cooper's Register discloses his diligence in insisting upon a sober and learned clergy: on 6 October 1574, Robert Andrewe, curate of Market Harborough, 'appeared and the bishop enjoined him to forbeare taverne and ale howse in all places whatsoever and to increase his knowledge in the latine tongue,' p. 113. On 29 October, 'John Leech, curate of Northeyell [Northill], co. Bedford, appeared and satisfied the bishop with his study and the bishop admitted him', p. 113.

[13] *Bullinger's Decades*, (Parker Society).

[14] Lincoln Record Society, Vol. 23, p. xx.

[15] *Remains of Abp Grindal* (Parker Society), pp. 129–30. See also *Tudor Parish Documents of the Diocese of York*, ed. J. S. Purvis, p. 98.

[16] The fact that a man had a university degree did not necessarily imply that he was learned. Some degrees were very easily obtained by the undeserving, who indeed attended the university, but did very little study.

[17] *Fifty-fifth Report of the Associated Architectural Societies*, Vol. XXIV, Part II, 'Institutions to Benefices in the Diocese of Lincoln, 1540–1570. Calendar No. 1', ed. C. W. Foster, pp. 467–525.

[18] Lincoln Record Society, Vol. 2, pp. 90–8.

[19] Lincoln Record Society, Vol. 23, p. lviii.

[20] *Norfolk and Norwich Archaeological Society*, Vol. XVIII, Part I, 'A List of the Clergy of Norfolk and their Status: 1592–3' by H. W. Saunders, pp. 78–104. But as late as the fifteen-eighties there were still only too many ignoramuses of the type of Mr Glascock, Vicar of Hockley, Essex, who was described as 'sometime a serving man; unable to preach, for he cannot render an account of his faith neither in Latin nor English, yet made minister within these three or four years': See *Annals of Evangelical Nonconformity*, p. 93.

[21] Usher, *Reconstruction of the English Church*, Vol. I, p. 207.

[22] *Tudor Parish Documents* (Visitation Book 1561–4) p. 103.

[23] *Annals of Evangelical Nonconformity*, p. 93.

[24] The Clerical Subsidy Rolls at the Public Record Office disclose that large numbers of benefices in the Lincoln diocese, owing to their extreme poverty, remained vacant throughout the reign.

[25] Edmund Lee, incumbent of Shenley, Bucks, was said to be 'a scholar studying at Oxford'. See *55th Report of the Associated Architectural Societies*, Vol. XXIV, Part II.

[26] Lincolnshire Record Society, Vol. 23, p. xxxii. Readers had, too, to subscribe to certain general injunctions before they could be admitted. See Cardwell, *Documentary Annals*, Vol. I, pp. 268–70.

[27] Lincolnshire Record Society, Vol. 2, p. xv.

[28] Lincolnshire Record Society, Vol. 2, p. 122.

[29] Lincolnshire Record Society, Vol. 2, p. xiv.

[30] *Correspondence of Abp Parker*, p. 128.

[31] *Correspondence of Abp Parker*, pp. 154 & 308.

[32] *Correspondence of Abp Parker*, p. 142; Strype, Bk. II. App. No. 1.

[33] *Correspondence of Abp Parker*, p. 142.

[34] Norfolk Record Society, Vol. 18, *Bishop Redman's Visitation, 1597*, p. 135.

[35] Norfolk Record Society, Vol. 18, p. 149.

[36] Frere, *The English Church*, p. 60, and see also Frere and Kennedy, *Visitation Articles and Injunctions*, Vol III, p. 71.

[37] Abp. Sandys, *Sermons and Miscellaneous Pieces*, (Parker Society), p. 434. See also Strype, *Annals*, Vol. I, Part I, chapter xxx.

[38] *Remains of Abp. Grindal*, pp. 165 and 168.

[39] Norfolk Record Society, Vol. 18, p. 144.

[40] Norfolk Record Society, Vol. 18, p. 159; 'crabbs' were crab apples which he crushed for cider.

[41] Norfolk Record Society, Vol. 18, p. 128.

[42] Norfolk Record Society, Vol. 18, p. 77; privately for gain.

[43] Strype, *Annals*, Vol. I, Part I, pp. 515, 265.

[44] Injunction IV. Frere and Kennedy, *Visitation Articles and Injunctions*, Vol. III, p. 10.

[45] Injunction III. Frere and Kennedy, *Visitation Articles and Injunctions*, Vol. III, p. 9.

[46] *Tudor Parish Documents* [Visitation Returns of 1567], pp. 20, 22, 134.

[47] Norfolk Record Society, Vol. 18, p. 135.

[48] Norfolk Record Society, Vol. 18, pp. 40, 45.

[49] Norfolk Record Society, Vol. 18, p. 62.

[50] Oxfordshire Record Society, Vol. 23, *The Archdeacon's Court 1584*, Vol. I, p. 94.

[51] *Tudor Parish Documents*, p. 140.

[52] Norfolk Record Society, Vol. 18, pp. 138, 121.

[53] Lincolnshire Record Society, Vol. 2, xiii.

[54] *Norfolk and Norwich Archaeological Society*, Vol. XXVIII, Part I, pp. 78–104.

[55] Harleian MSS. 595.

[56] Norfolk Record Society, Vol. 18, p. 17.

[57] Lincolnshire Record Society, Vol. 23, p. 140.

[58] Usher, *Reconstruction of the English Church*, Vol. 1, p. 242.

[59] Lincolnshire Record Society, Vol. 2, pp. 107–8.

[60] Lincolnshire Record Society, Vol. 2, p. 107. Bishop Cooper's Register, folio 31d.

[61] *Tudor Parish Documents*, p. 12.
Kennedy, *Elizabethan Episcopal Administration*, Vol. I, pp. lxxxiv–lxxxvii, gives a good account of clerical dress as derived from visitation articles and injunctions.

[62] *Tudor Parish Documents*, p. 28. Visitation of 1567.

[63] *Harrison's Description of England*, Vol. I, p. 32.

[64] Lincolnshire Record Society, Vol. 2, p. 107.

[65] Usher, *Reconstruction of the English Church*, Vol. I, p. 213.

[66] *Tudor Parish Documents*, p. 25. Visitation of 1567.

[67] *Tudor Parish Documents*, p. 28.

[68] Lincolnshire Record Society, Vol. 2, p. 136.

[69] Lincolnshire Record Society, Vol. 23, p. xxxviii.

[70] Oxfordshire Record Society, Vol. 23, Vol. I, p. 67.

[71] Norfolk Record Society, Vol. 18, p. 40.

[72] Norfolk Record Society, Vol. 18, p. 40.

[73] Norfolk Record Society, Vol. 18, pp. 78 and 57.

[74] Norfolk Record Society, Vol. 18, p. 82.

[75] Norfolk Record Society, Vol. 18, p. 144.

[76] Norfolk Record Society, Vol. 18, pp. 39 and 84.

[77] *Annals of Evangelical Nonconformity*, pp. 91–2.

[78] *Tudor Parish Documents*, p. 195.

[79] *Remains of Abp. Grindal*, p. 166.

[80] Lincolnshire Record Society, Vol. 2, p. 107.

[81] *Tudor Parish Documents*, p. 196.

[82] *Viewe of the Clargie of Essex*, 1610, p. 19.

[83] *Tudor Parish Documents*, p. 167.

[84] *Records of Oundle Parish Church*, ed. W. Richardson and S. C. Harries, p. 6.

[85] *Tudor Parish Documents*, p. 211.

[86] Lincolnshire Record Society, Vol. 2, p. 135.

[87] Quoted from W. Addison, *The English Country Parson*, p. 29.

Archbishop Grindal in 1571 instructed the unmarried clergy not to 'keep in your house any woman under the age of three-score years', unless she also happened to be a close relation such as mother, aunt, sister, niece, etc. See *Remains of Abp Grindal*, p. 130.

[88] Norfolk Record Society, Vol. 18, p. 154.

[89] S. L. Ware, *The Elizabethan Parish in its Ecclesiastical and Financial Aspect*, p. 27.

[90] Taken from Abp. Parker's Lambeth Register 1570/71. See, Lincolnshire Record Society, Vol. 2, p. 307.

[91] Lincolnshire Record Society, Vol. 23, p. xxii. Two thirds of the Lincolnshire clergy were married by 1576. See Lincolnshire Record Society, Vol. 2, p. xiii.

[92] Oxford Record Society, Vol. 10, *Oxfordshire Peculiars*, ed. S. A. Peyton, p. 286.

[93] *Tudor Parish Documents*, p. 212.

[94] Lincolnshire Record Society, Vol. 23, p. xxxviii.

[95] Norfolk Record Society, Vol. 18, p. 117.

[96] Lincolnshire Record Society, Vol. 2, p. 116.

[97] Oxfordshire Record Society, Vol. 23, Vol. 1, p. 89.

[98] Usher, *Reconstruction of the English Church*, Vol. 1, p. 257.

[99] R. H. Mason, *The History of Norfolk*, p. 393.

[100] *Tudor Parish Documents*, pp. 12–15.

[101] Oxfordshire Record Society, Vol. 23, Vol. II, pp. 200, 201, 205.

[102] Essex Record Society, Vol. 17, *English History from Essex Sources*, ed. A. C. Edwards, Vol. I, p. 6.

[103] *Tudor Parish Documents*, pp. 31, 152, 162.

[104] *Remains of Abp. Grindal*, pp. 134–40.

[105] Lincolnshire Record Society, Vol. 2, p. 139.

[106] Oxfordshire Record Society, Vol. 23, Vol. II, p. 155.

[107] *Tudor Parish Documents*, p. 56. The Vicar of Rochdale, Lancs., was possibly one of the worst offenders in this last respect since he had 'not worne the surplesse these twentie years'. Ibid.

[108] Lincolnshire Record Society, Vol. 23, pp. xxxix; xli.

[109] Norfolk Record Society, Vol. 18, pp. 19, 100, 101, 47, 53.

The surplice was an expensive garment. The one bought for Northill, Beds., in 1604 cost 28s. 4d. See Bedfordshire Record Society, Vol. 33. p. 49.

[110] Usher, *Reconstruction of the English Church*, Vol. I, p. 263.

[111] *Annals of Evangelical Nonconformity*, pp. 83, 119.

[112] Essex Record Society, Vol. 17, Vol. I, p. 8.

[113] Usher, *Reconstruction of the English Church*, Vol. I, p. 264.

[114] Trevelyan, *English Social History*, pp. 179–80.

[115] Archbishop Grindal had instructed the Parish Clerk, 'if he be able also to rede the firste lesson the epistle and the psalmes'. *Remains*, p. 142.

[116] *Harrison's Description of England*, Vol. I, p. 30.

[117] *Abp. Grindal's Remains*, p. 123. Harrison also wrote: 'whereas there was woont to be a great partition betweene the quire and the bodie of the church; now it is either very small or none at all: and to saie the truth altogither needlesse, sith the minister saith his service commonlie in the body of

the church, with his face toward the people, in a little tabernacle of wainscot provided for the purpose'. See *Harrison's Description of England*, Vol. I, p. 31.

[118] Harrison said, too, of Holy Days: 'they are all brought into seaven and twentie: and with them the superfluous number of idle waks, guilds, fraternities, church ales . . . with the heathenish rioting at bride-ales, are well diminished and laid aside'. *Harrison's Description of England*, Vol. I, p. 32.

[119] Robert Kennion, Rector of Harpley, Norfolk, 'hath not declared to his parishioners what holidayes and fasting dayes be the weeke following for the space of a yeare'; and the minister of Great Bricett was one of a large company in the puritanical diocese of Norwich, who used a basin in the font. See, Norfolk Record Society, Vol. 18, pp. 66 and 147.

[120] Enormous quantities of wine were used at these communions. At Shillington in Bedfordshire two gallons were always purchased for the Easter celebration. See Bedfordshire Record Society, Vol. 33, p. xxvii.

[121] *Abp. Grindal's Remains*, p. 131. See also, Royal Injunctions 1559. No. 13.

[122] *Tudor Parish Documents*, pp. 203. It is noteworthy that Grindal expected these repairs to be undertaken not only by rectors but 'vicars and clerks'. *Remains*, p. 131.

[123] *The Essex Review*, Vol. XV. 'Essex Churches 1540–1618', p. 43.

[124] Norfolk Record Society, Vol. 18, p. 133.

[125] 'State of the Churches in the Archdeaconries of Lincoln and Stow, August 1602', Lincolnshire Record Society, Vol. 23, p. 229.

[126] Lincolnshire Record Society, Vol. 23, p. 229.

[127] See Appendix to this chapter.

[128] *Norfolk and Norwich Archaeological Society*, Vol. XXVIII, pp. 79–82, 'An Episcopal Visitation in 1593', ed. J. F. Williams.

[129] Lincolnshire Record Society, Vol. 23, p. xlvii.

[130] Norfolk Record Society, Vol. 18, p. 10.

[131] *Harrison's Description of England*, Vol. I, p. 32.

[132] *Tudor Parish Documents*, pp. 87–9.

[133] Oxfordshire Record Society, Vol. 23, Vol. II, p. 171.

[134] Royal Injunctions of 1559, No. VI.

[135] Royal Injunctions of 1559, No. X.

[136] *Tudor Parish Documents*, pp. 183–5. See also Ware, *The Elizabethan Parish*, p. 25.

[137] Strype, *The Life and Acts of Whitgift*, p. 375. Here he refers to some churchwardens as 'poor artificers and other labouring men'.

[138] *Abp. Grindal's Remains*, p. 142.

[139] Injunction XLIV.

[140] *Abp. Grindal's Remains*, pp. 124–5.

[141] Norfolk Record Society, Vol. 18, pp. 53 and 72.

[142] *Tudor Parish Documents*, p. 52.

[143] Oxfordshire Record Society, Vol. 23, Vol. II, p. 169.

[144] *Tudor Parish Documents*, p. 92.

[145] Norfolk Record Society, Vol. 18, pp. 40 and 76.

[146] *Tudor Parish Documents*, p. 92.

[147] Norfolk Record Society, Vol. 18, pp. 136 and 88.

[148] Strype, *Annals*, Vol. III, Part I, p. 328.

[149] *Tudor Parish Documents*, pp. 85 and 92.

[150] *Tudor Parish Documents*, p. 86.

[151] Quoted from W. B. Whitaker, *Sunday in Tudor and Stuart Times*, p. 29.

[152] *Harrison's Description of England*, Vol. I, p. 20.

[153] *Harrison's Description of England*, Vol. I, p. 21.

[154] Lincolnshire Record Society, Vol. 23, p. 144.

[155] Lincolnshire Record Society, Vol. 23, p. 235.

[156] *Norfolk and Norwich Archaeological Society*, Vol. XVIII, pp. 78–104.

[157] Usher, *Reconstruction of the English Church*, Vol. I, p. 211.

[158] A. Gibbon, *Valuations in the Diocese of Lincoln in 1524*, p. 96.

[159] *A Book of Valuations of all the Ecclesiastical Preferments in England and Wales*, London, 1680, pp. 184–5.

[160] *Harrison's Description of England*, Vol. I, p. 25.

[161] Cardwell, *Documentary Annals*, Vol. I, p. 314. See also *Letters written by John Chamberlain during the reign of Queen Elizabeth*, ed. S. Williams, (Camden Society), p. 56.

[162] *Harrison's Description of England*, Vol. I, p. 26.

[163] Injunction XII.

[164] *Abp. Grindal's Remains*, p. 129.

[165] *The Elizabethan Parish*, p. 31.

[166] *Tudor Parish Documents*, p. 20.

[167] Fuller, *Church History*, Vol. II, p. 566.

[168] *Harrison's Description of England*, Vol. I, p. 34.

[169] *Correspondence of Archbishop Parker* (Parker Society), p. 311.

[170] Lambeth MSS. Carta Miscellanea, V.f.24.

[171] Here is an analysis of ninety-two benefices taken from the *Valuatio Beneficorum* of 1604 in the Lincoln diocese and included in the rural deaneries of Walshcroft, Aslackhoe, Corringham, Lawres, and Manlake.

Benefices not exceeding £5 5

,,	,,	,,	£10	22
,,	,,	,,	£15	17
,,	,,	,,	£20	18
,,	,,	,,	£25	2
,,	,,	,,	£30	13
,,	,,	,,	£40	6
,,	,,	,,	£50	2
,,	,,	,,	£60	3
,,	,,	,,	£80	3
,,	,,	,,	£120	1

Curates' Stipends		£5,	£10,	£15,	£20,	£36
	Lincoln and Stow Archdeaconry:	40,	29,	7,	5	
	Bedford ,,		3,	1,	1,	1
	Buckingham ,,	4,	16,	7,	1	
	Huntingdon ,,	1,	10,	2,	1	
	Leicester ,,	1,	6,	5,	3	

[172] *Tudor Parish Documents*, p. 199.

[173] Richard Hooker was appointed to Drayton Beauchamp in December, 1584, but never resided there. 'It appears to have been a mere stop-gap until his appointment as Master of the Temple could be definitely settled in February, 1585'. F. G. Shirley, *Richard Hooker and Contemporary Political Ideas*, pp. 37–8.

[174] *Harrison's Description of England,* Vol. I, p. 33.

[175] This account of the Elizabethan parson's home and property is based on F. W. Brooks, *The Social Position of the Parson in the Sixteenth Century,* which is reprinted from the Journal of the British Archaeological Association. Third Series. Vol. X, 1945–1947.

Mr Brooks has made an exhaustive study of several thousand inventories for probate in the Diocesan Archives at Lincoln, covering the sixteenth, seventeenth and eighteenth centuries.

[176] See Bedfordshire Record Society, Vol. 33, p. 6.

Anglican and Puritan in the Reign of James I

THE ACCESSION OF James I was hailed by all the religious parties as an occasion for rejoicing. The Roman Catholic recusants expected much from the son of Mary Stuart; and the extreme Puritans from the King of John Knox's Scotland; but the Anglicans were the true beneficiaries.

James's policy towards the Roman Catholics was marked by fits and starts. Excessive tolerance, resulting in increased recusancy, led in turn to renewed persecution and the violence of the Gunpowder Plot. Parliament then passed some savage penal laws that sought to drive them to communion by the threat of heavy fines. But, despite the growing number of convictions and the many crushing fines imposed, the majority of papists still escaped relatively lightly, since they were often able to evade payment either totally or partially. Convictions were frequently never followed up at all, and very few seem to have suffered the full penalties proscribed by law.[1] Of these the most unfortunate were those recusants whose forfeitures had been granted by James to his greedy courtiers, who then ruthlessly blackmailed their victims into penury. This practice was, however, discontinued after Charles I had succeeded to the throne; when the penal laws were also relaxed.

In 1603 a Roman Catholic priest, Roger Gwynn, had estimated that a third of the population was still secretly papist; but the diocesan returns for that year showed that out of some 9,254 parishes there were only 8,590 recusants. These numbers had certainly increased considerably by 1625.[2]

The Puritans were James's real enemies. He never forgot how the Scotch Presbyterians had 'audaciously asserted the right of subjects to control their rulers';[3] and almost in self-defence, propounded the contrary doctrine of the 'Divine Right of Kings', which he summarized in his political treatise: *True Law of Free Monarchies or the Mutual Duty betwixt a Free King and his Subjects*. This doctrine maintained that monarchy was divine, hereditary right unassailable, kings accountable to none but God, and all resistance to one's lawful prince unforgivable and indefensible. And since the Anglicans supported these views, James further adopted the aphorism: 'No Bishop, No King'.

The moderate Millenary Petition presented by a thousand ministers, while James was still on his way to London, carefully refrained from any mention of the presbytery or the holy discipline; and concentrated on such practical reforms as the crossing in baptism, the ring in marriage, the reading of the Apocrypha, and baptism by laymen. It also, *inter alia*, renewed its demands for a preaching ministry, the abolition of pluralities, the return of lay impropriations, and the curbing of excommunication by lay officials for 'trifles and twelve-penny matters'.[4] The restoration of the impropriate tithes and pro-vision of a more learned ministry certainly appealed to the English Solomon. Half-hearted attempts were made to deal with the former. James promised to restore some Crown tithe and suggested that the universities, which were large holders of it, should do the same. But nothing happened. Indeed, it was pointed out that if the universities disgorged too much they would be ruined and so unable to fulfil their obligations towards learning. However, the king did not entirely forget the poverty of many of the clergy; and when in 1621, at a time when funds were low in the royal exchequer, it was suggested to him 'that a new valuation should be made of all spiritual preferments to bring them up to or near the full value thereof' and thus increase the sums secured to the Crown both from first-fruits and tenths, James preferred the advice of his Lord Treasurer, the Earl of Middlesex: 'Let it not be said that you gained by grinding them'.[5]

As regards a learned ministry: Archbishop Whitgift instituted enquiries into the dioceses which showed that at least half the beneficed clergy were now preachers and that pluralism had been greatly reduced. There were, for example, 920 preachers out of the 1,255 parishes in the Lincoln diocese in 1603,[6] and in that of Norwich three-quarters of all the men instituted between January 1603 and January 1608 had degrees. The 140 pluralists of Lincoln in 1585 had been reduced to 90 by the beginning of the new reign; while in the Archdeaconry of Norwich there were only 55 double-beneficed men.[7]

The codification of Canon Law in 1604 and its royal authorization had destroyed the former Puritan contention that since the laws of the Church were uncertain their own practices were justified: i.e. to sub-stitute *The Book of Discipline* for the Book of Common Prayer, and Presbyterianism for the three ministerial Orders. The canons moreover had specifically commanded that the minister must use the Prayer Book, don the surplice and hood, preach once every Sunday if licensed or else read a homily, catechize the youth, and visit the sick.[8] He was forbidden to maintain a conventicle, conduct private exercises, or marry out of hours.[9] The parishioners, on the other hand, were told that 'in time of divine service and of every part thereof, all due rever-ence is to be used ... no man shall cover his head in church or chapel in the time of divine service, except he had some infirmity: in which case let him wear a night cap or coif'. The congregation must also 'reverently kneel upon their knees' for the General Confession, Litany, and Prayers; stand up for the Creed; do 'lowly reverence' at the Name of Jesus; quietly attend to the Lessons and Sermon; audibly join in the Confession, Lord's Prayer, and Creed, while 'making such other answers to the public prayers, as are appointed in the Book of Common Prayer'; and finally no-one might disturb the service in any way 'by walking or talking' or departing 'out of the church during the time of service and sermon, without some urgent or reasonable cause'.[10] Everyone over sixteen years old had to make his or her Easter communion, and they must receive it kneeling, while those who failed to put in an appearance would be presented by their minister.[11] The churches themselves had to be provided with a Book of Common Prayer, a copy of the new Canons and certain other books; with the Ten Commandments inscribed at the east end; and a table of prohibited degrees.[12]

The returns to the very searching Visitation Articles of Bishop Chaderton of Lincoln in 1604 reveal that the canonical demands on the clergy that they should wear the surplice and conform to the rites and ceremonies of the Prayer Book, and on the churchwardens that they should furnish their parish churches in accordance with their rulings, were being very widely evaded. In the Archdeaconries of Lincoln and Stowe, for example, the churchwardens of 194 parishes had not yet obtained the new Prayer Book; while out of the whole diocese some ninety-three clergymen were cited for refusing to wear the surplice. Churchwardens and their ministers were frequently in alliance over such matters. At Glentworth the wardens omitted to present their incumbent despite the fact that he had neglected to wear the surplice and to use the sign of the cross in baptism. For which offence they were compelled to appear in their parish church clad in a white sheet and bearing a document setting forth their perjury.[13] Nevertheless many of the nonconforming clergy were now open to argument. One said: 'I will not refuse to weare a surplusse, so that it be a comly or decent one'. Others were less accommodating. Of Thomas Wooll, Vicar of Boston, it was reported: 'that the surplis hath bene tendred to him and he in scorn maketh it his cushion to sitt on'.[14] Thirty Lincolnshire ministers headed by John Burgess of Waddesdon sent a petition to the King in December 1604, which was later published under the title of *The Abridgement*.[15] Herein they urged that certain ceremonies were sinful or led to superstition; and although they were prepared to subscribe to the Royal Supremacy, they could accept neither the Prayer Book nor the thirty-nine Articles.

Bancroft, the new Archbishop of Canterbury, was determined to enforce the Canons; but, in order to prevent making unnecessary martyrs, he and the other bishops began by argument. The Bishop of Peterborough, for instance, held a public disputation with his Puritan clergy in the cathedral which lasted for two whole days; and other bishops conferred with them privately. However, 'nothing would prevayle';[16] and Bancroft at length wrote to his suffragans that the time had come to deal drastically with 'obstinate ministers'. Those as yet unplaced in the Church should not be given any office until they subscribed; those already in office who were observing the rites and ceremonies of the Prayer Book but appeared reluctant to subscribe again, might be leniently dealt with; but those who refused either to conform or subscribe were to be deprived immediately. In the Lincoln diocese actually no more than eight incumbents and nine curates were finally ejected; and Bishop Chaderton displayed inexhaustible patience in dealing even with the most refractory Puritans. It is noteworthy, for example, that some who never conformed at all, but were 'godly and peaceable men' were spared. The Peterborough diocese, the most puritanical of them all, reported fifteen deprivations, for which the Bishop actually apologized to the Privy Council, and over the whole country probably not more than 49 finally lost their livings. The Puritans themselves claimed that between 270 and 300 were evicted; but Archbishop Bancroft's figures are the more accurate, although no account is taken by them of the unbeneficed clergy, who were not formally deprived, but had their licences withdrawn by the Bishop. The more militant Puritans, of course, did not take this 'persecution' lying down. They contested the legality of their conviction in the courts, harassed the new incumbents, and petitioned the King, the Privy Council, and Parliament. Catlyn of Northampton locked the door of his pulpit and put the key in his pocket; while others locked the church door. Robert Swett of Weybread in Suffolk cleverly provided his own substitutes, who refused the request of the churchwardens either to display their licences to preach or to sign the preachers' book. At Preston Capes in the Peterborough diocese the deprived vicar, Mr Smart, remained in the parish and deliberately created a disturbance in church both on Palm Sunday and Easter day, when his successor was celebrating the Holy Communion.[17]

However, eventually the mass of the moderate Puritans conformed and accepted the position, at least for the moment; and the laity followed suit, although a certain number of the latter also proved obstinate. At Fenny Drayton in 1607 it was reported that 'George Heard and George Pegge, the churchwardens, and eleven others hauve not receaved the communion at Easter last and the reason is because they refuse to take the same kneeling': and at Thurlaston Agnes Wallen was presented 'for goinge out of the parishe to bee delivered of child because it should not be baptized with the signe of the Crosse and not be churched after the booke of common prayer'. Occasionally there were cases of threats and even violence towards the conformers. Robert Burbage, Vicar of Market Harborough, was accused of calling Thomas Gowen, Vicar of Great Bowden, 'lowsie roge, cogging companion and scurvie rascall and did challenge him to the feilde and did lay waite for him for usinge the rites and ceremonies of the churche, as by proof it may appeare. And further hee saide he would incense the parishioners of Great Bowden againste their minister, whiche hee did indeed, and they expostulated of him thereof. And also did call this minister puppie'.[18] At Sydenham, Oxon, the churchwardens themselves appeared to be in league with the abusers, judging from the following letter:

'Sydnam the xvi daye of October [1606].

'I the minister of Sydnam doe present Robert Sule for his common contempte of mee his minister, boethe at home and abroade usinge at all tymes and in all places so abuseively odious and intollerable skoffinge and chestinge on mee; when he is most in company, most given to abuse mee, I never givinge him any occasion soe to doe; he never receyved the communion since easter nor yet his brother who at all this twelmonth dwellinge with him and of yeares, nor none of his howse since easter, he beinge now married, and wee havinge a communion on Sundaye last was fortenight: his brother John Sule of xvi or xvii yeares of age and will not be browghte to catachising beinge often tymes warned givinge contemptuos answers when he is called and keepinge ivell rule in the streetes at eleven or xii of the clocke at night and very commonly at ten a clocke in the nighte in lowde straynincg out most filthy bawdy songs, and especially on sondaye nightes and holly nights, to the great disturbinge of those that bee well disposed and woold reste and that allwayes neere the vicaredge and once in my close hardeby my howse. . . .

Robert Cunney minister of Sydnam.

The churchwardens have refused to confeire with mee abowte presentments, as beinge the townne miller lothe to offend any of them, and seeminge boeth of them to take Robert Sules parte nightelye'.[19]

The Puritans themselves also came in for their share of abuse. John Tabor of Margaretting was indicted in 1618 for publishing a libellous doggerel on a local Presbyterian, John Gowers:

'Gowers the Puritane sayth yt ye signe of the Crosse ys the marke of the beast,
But his understandinge ys grosse: and hes a knave att the least.
He is become an headboroughe of late,

And all his witt runs through his pate;
Yea more he is the great commaunder att Tye [Margaretting Tye]
Who will not sweare but slaunder and lye;
He carryes the bible under his arme
Howe ys yt possible his neighbour he sholde harme,
He hath not learnd suche evill out of gods booke,
But from the Davill the same hee tooke.
Let him taketh sentence from a frende,
Without true repentance, badd wilbee his end,
He by a slighte can handle a sickle,
And by candle lighte have a conventicle'.[20]

The Puritans undoubtedly still possessed a large following in the country as a whole, and especially in the midlands and East Anglia. Petitions on behalf of the silenced ministers and against the Canons poured in from all sides—the one from Essex, which was addressed to James himself, declared that 'worthye lights are in part extinguished, and we heavily threatened to be deprived of the remnant that are left'[21] —and the alliance between nonconformity and the gentry and merchants, which had been forged in Elizabeth's reign, was strengthened. These were the classes that dominated the House of Commons at the time; and henceforward it became a struggle between the Puritans, who stood for the exclusive authority of the Bible in religion and of individual liberty and constitutional government in politics, and those churchmen who venerated and enforced the traditions of the Catholic Church, whilst allying themselves with the royal doctrines of divine right and absolute government.

The archiepiscopal visitation of the Province of Canterbury in 1605 vigorously upheld the new Canon Law; and a larger number of presentments were everywhere made than was customary, for which penances were rigorously exacted. The charges certainly covered a very wide field of behaviour and included cases of incontinency, refusal to attend church or communion, sabbath-breaking, drunkenness, 'scolding', debt, desecrating the churchyard, non-payment of church rates, unlicensed teaching, non-residence and omission to catechize on the part of the clergy, non-production of accounts by the churchwardens, decayed churches, want of proper vestments and ornaments, and the improper dress of incumbents. As regards this last, Canons 74 and 75 had decreed that ministers were, *inter alia*, to wear square caps and 'in their journeys cloaks with sleeves, commonly called Priests' cloaks, without guards, welts, long buttons, or cuts'. They are not to wear 'any coif or wrought night-cap, but only plain night-caps of black silk, satin or velvet'. In their houses their apparel may not be 'cut or pinkt'; and they are forbidden to don 'any light coloured

A Purge for Pluralities, shewing the unlawful nesse of men to have two Livings.

OR

The Downe-fall of Double Benefices.

Being in the Clymactericall and fatall yeare of the proud Prelates.
But the yeare of *Iubilee* to all poore hunger-pinch'd Schoilers.

LONDON,
Printed for *F. Cowles*, *T. Bates*, and *T. Banks*. 1642.

An ever-present problem

E

stockings'.[22] The Bishop of Lincoln's Visitation Returns for 1607 contained several complaints against the clergy on this score: the churchwardens of Gainsborough reported that their minister 'is in all things conformidable, savinge they never saw him weare a cornered cap or ride in a cloke with sleeves'. The Reverend Mr Burke of Covenham St Bartholomew 'used to travel without his canonical cloak'; and Mr George Buddle, the minister of Wickenby, 'doth not wear his tippet and hood'. But perhaps the worst offender of the lot was William Wood, Rector of Somerby in Leicestershire, who was presented for 'wearinge a wrought night-cap'.[23]

The archiepiscopate of Bancroft was marked by attempts to meet the more moderate and reasonable grievances of the Puritans, particularly as regards a more learned ministry, increased benefice endowments, and the reduction and regulation of pluralities. In the first of these, indeed, there was considerable progress: the number of preachers increased, more clergy were taking university degrees, and they were being drawn on the whole from a better class in society. In 1603, out of the 920 preachers in the Lincoln diocese 226 were non-graduates; but out of 66 ordinands in 1606 35 were M.A.s and 24 B.A.s, while out of the 80 men instituted to livings in 1610, 74 possessed a university degree of one kind or another.[24]

In the field of increased endowments the archbishops were by no means so successful. They suggested that livings might be augmented through a return to the strict payment of tithes in kind or at least a reassessment of the *modus decimandi* in the light of changed economic circumstances; by the union of miserably poor benefices; and above all by the return of some of the impropriated tithe. Parliament, however, consistently turned a deaf ear to demands either for the extension of tithe to minerals or the redemption of impropriations by means of a parliamentary subsidy. Instead the Commons proposed that the value of poor livings could be increased by diminishing the revenues of bishoprics, cathedrals, and rich benefices.[25]

The friction between the clergy and the farmers increased: for, with the growth of enclosure and the consequent incentive to improve their land, the latter found the imposition of the tithe most irksome, while the former hurried into litigation in order to secure every tittle of their rights. A vicar, for example, in 1595 had instituted a suit for the payment of tithe on turkeys and tame partridges, although both were then regarded as *ferae naturae*. Another incumbent claimed on fallen apples; and a third demanded his tenth of wild cherries! The introduction of new crops like turnips and hops, saffron and tobacco led to complicated and often costly disputes; and by 1630 all of them had been adjudged to the vicar as small tithes.[26]

Coke's *Institutes* of 1628 declared: 'Tithes shall not be paid of anything that is of the substance of the earth and not annual, as coals, turf etc. nor beasts that be ferae naturae, nor of agistment of such beasts as pay tithe, nor of cattle that manure the ground, but of barren beasts the parson shall have tithe on agistment of herbage, unless they be nourished for the plough and so employed. No tithe shall be paid for after-pasture, nor for rakings, nor for sylva coedua employed for hedging and repairing of plough, and two tithes shall not be paid of one land in one year.'[27] Despite this authoritative pronouncement voices were still raised affirming that lead and gold veins of ore were subject to annual growth and therefore liable to tithe. Obstacles were sometimes put in the way of an incumbent collecting his tithe in kind; and it actually needed a legal action to establish the rector's right to drive his waggon, already loaded with sheaves from the land of one farmer, onto that of another. There was also the question of the parson's right to have his tenth reaped by the farmer. Such problems found their way into the ecclesiastical courts, whose judgments were frequently disputed and led to a head-on collision with the courts of the Common Law.

Monastic lands, now largely in the possession of the laity, paid no tithe; and it was reckoned that approximately a quarter of all tithes were in lay hands.

Economic necessity alone forbade the abolition of pluralities—even Puritans were compelled to accept them—but vigorous efforts were now made by the bishops to regulate them. Small adjoining benefices were united, and by means of a widespread system of exchange very many incumbents, who already held parishes in plurality but at considerable distances from each other, were enabled to secure two livings so close together that one man could serve both himself without the need to employ a curate.

By 1610, when Bancroft died, the position of the parochial clergy was certainly far easier and more satisfactory, apart from the matter of income, than it had been since the Reformation. In social status and learning, in housing, in discipline and spiritual fervour, there had been an all-round advance. The Church's ritual and liturgy were more strictly observed, the repair of the parish churches increased apace, and now almost every parish possessed a copy of the Prayer Book, the Canons, and Jewel's Works.

The progress in church repair was indeed slow and irregular during the early years of the seventeenth century; and it was not really until Archbishop Laud's policy of 'Thorough' got into its stride that any rapid and regular progress was made. Nevertheless there is much evidence to show that substantial repairs and improvements were carried out in various parts of the country under James I, in those places where ecclesiastical authority was at once observant and vigorous, and also strong enough to ensure that its commands were obeyed. The need for action was certainly still urgent. The Essex Act Books for the years 1607 to 1618 are a good illustration of this: St Martin's Colchester in 1607 possessed 'no book of Homilies, no decent table, no stoope for the wyne, no chest for the poore; and the church is not in reparacon in the windows, and the chancell; no stooles or seats; no cushion'. However, the churchwardens, with the consent of the parish, undertook to take down two of their bells and sell them 'for the covering of the church'. Mr Keltridge, in the same year, described his church of Bergholt as 'ruinous wanting tyling, paving and glazing to the offence of the parishioners'; while his brother rector of West Mersea suffered 'the chancell to be out of reparacon so yt it doth snow and rayne in and the dawes and other vermine come and build therein'. And so the sorry tale continued. Five years later in 1612 the state of many Essex churches was no better. Great Wakering chancel was declared to be 'so out of reparacon, that yf it be not speedily repayred it will fall into utter ruyne. . . . There is never a pulpitt; the wall of the churchyard ruinayed and fallen downe in divers places; the N. door of the church decayed and broken'; and others were even worse off. Judging from the report of the churchwardens on the condition of Rawreth church in 1617 little improvement had occurred since 1612. 'We present', they declared, 'these wants and defaults in our church. First we want a ladder to our steple. . . . By reason of a tempestuous winde some fyve weekes since some smale part of the leades were blown up, and since that we neither could nor can get a fitt workman to amend them. We present also that the chancell wanteth amendinge with shingle or tyle'.[28]

A good instance of sound and steady church repairs, re-furnishing, and re-decoration over the first half of the century is to be found at Upton-by-Southwell, Notts., where the parish account books reveal what progress was made year by year. In 1603 Upton church was in a bad way: a dilapidated porch, hard earth floor, cracked windows, and damp green walls. The chancel was bare of ornaments, but contained a simple trestle table standing longways at its centre, which was covered with buckram. Under the east window, where the altar formerly stood, there now reposed a beautiful thirteenth-century chest that housed the communion vessels, the prayer book, and surplice. From the account books we can trace its gradual restoration and re-beautification over the next thirty years:

1604. Given to Harper for porche mendeing. 9/-.
1605. Pade for the beautifyeing of the church. £2-13-4.
1608. For a yeard & three quarters of seae & buccorum for the
      cussion. 4/8.

For a silke fringe for the pulpite cloth. 1/8.

Pade for silke tasiels for the cossing for the pulpit. 3d.

1613. Spent at setting forth the wood at the forest. 5/4.

Pade for cordes for scafoldes for the church. 1/-.

Spent at Winkebourne at fetching home the wood. 2/-

Pade for ale & breade at casting the leads. 1/-.

Pade to the masons for stones & for paveing the church & the porch. £1-2-6.

Pade to Hutchvnson for the pulpit. 11/6.

And for fetching it from Kertlington. 6d.

Pade for a peese of ern which holds the pulpit to the wole. 6d.

Pade towardes oure seates making. 7/-.

Pade for the table mending & Master Wilson's desk the second time. 2/-.

Pade for the nayles for Mester Wilson's desk. 4d.

Pade to Harper for making Mester Wilson's desk twice over. 4d.

1636. Paide at Chapter for wantinge some ornaments for the church. 15/-

1638. Paide to John Hollitt for raileing of the alter table. £1-12-6.[29]

So by 1640 both the interior and exterior of the church had altered considerably for the better. There was a new porch of Sherwood oak, the church floor was solidly paved, box pews with doors had taken the place of the rough benches, and a finer pulpit and reading desk, the former with its tasselled cushion, have replaced the plainer ones; while in the chancel a framed table now stood under the east window with a panelled wall behind and a low oak rail in front. Furthermore the church walls had been freshly whitewashed; the Creed, Lord's Prayer, and the Ten Commandments painted at the east end; the windows repaired; and there was a new oak roof of slightly lower pitch. Some of these improvements reflected the Laudian reaction; but it is noteworthy that many were begun early in James's reign.

As the reign progressed and more and more livings fell into Anglican hands, the Puritans sought to restore the balance by inaugurating afternoon lectureships, which were liberally endowed by their well-to-do friends. Here in his Geneva cloak, unfettered alike by the need to wear the surplice or use the Prayer Book, the nonconforming divine preached and prayed as he pleased. 'Some', wrote Tom Fuller, 'meddled with state matters; and generally, by an improper transposition, the people's duty was preached to the king at court; the king's to the people in the country. Many shallow preachers handled the profound points of predestination; wherein, pretending to guide their flocks, they lost themselves'.[30] Consequently James I, instigated by

William Laud, issued his *Directions* to the clergy, forbidding them to preach 'deep points of Predestination, Election, Reprobation, or of the Universality, Efficacy, Resistibility or Irresistibility of God's grace', and urging them instead to catechize the children in the afternoon. All sermons must be based on the Articles or the Book of Homilies. The archbishops and bishops were furthermore warned 'to be more wary and choice in their licensing of preachers, and revoke all grants to any chancellor, official or commissary to pass licences of this kind'.[31] Immediately there was an uproar. James was accused of wishing to abolish sermons and the bishops of discriminating against Puritans; and despite all the Anglican authorities could do, many such lectureships continued. More will be heard of them in the next reign.

The Primary Visitation of Bishop Neile of Lincoln in 1614 is of interest in this respect, since it was much concerned with these lectureships. They were maintained in nine towns of the diocese and often by a considerable body of the clergy. At Hornchurch, for example, twenty preachers took part; and so strongly were they entrenched that even the loyal Anglicans advised against their suppression: since it would 'make a clamour as though the bishop was the enemy to the preaching of the Gospel'. Instead, it was suggested, they should be carefully regulated and controlled. For, 'like as factious and schismatical preaching hath broken down the walls of our Church discipline, so it is to be hoped that the godly sermons of orthodoxical and conformable preachers may build them up again'.[32] The following abuses associated with these lectureships were then enumerated: age amongst the lecturers counted more than learning; one lecturer might undertake three or four lectures besides his own parish duties; the omission of the prayer for the king before the sermon; the contempt for the doctrines of the Fathers as being only those 'of men'; the ridiculing of conformable ministers as 'dumb dogs'; the deprecation of the Prayer Book services and sacraments in comparison with the efficacy of preaching, 'as if religious worship consisted only in speaking and hearing'; and finally that such lectureships merely encouraged 'factious spirits . . . men who are so desirous to preach in other men's parishes upon the working days', but who 'very seldom or never peached upon Saints' days in their own'.[33]

However, even the episcopal commissaries were obliged to recognize the sterling qualities of many of the Puritan clergy. 'A young man', they reported to the Bishop of Mr Cotton, Vicar of Boston, 'not past some 7 or 8 years Master of Arts; but by report a man of great gravity and sanctity of life, a man of rare parts for his learning, eloquence, and well-spoken, ready upon a suddaine, and very apprehensive to conceive of any point in learning though never so abstruse, in soe much that these, his good gifts, have won him soe much credit and acceptance, not only with his parishioners at Boston but with all the ministry and men of account in those quarters, that grave and learned men, out of an admiration of those good graces of God in him, have been, and upon every occasion still are, willing to submit their judgments to his on any point of controversie as though he were some extraordinary Paraclete that could not err'.[34] Cotton, who was Vicar of Boston from 1602 to 1633, later became associated with the town of that name in America.

Neile's visitation returns also showed that many of the parochial clergy were negligent in the matter of presenting their children for confirmation. The Bishop's Registrar afterwards drew up some *Observations concerning the Clergy of the Diocese Taken in your Lordship's Last Visitation*, in which he commented: 'I cannot pceive any fordwardnesse in any of ye ministers to have ye children of yeir parishes confirmed'. He likewise provided a most interesting footnote on the problem of 'tolerations': 'I have everywhere', he wrote, 'inhibited Tolerations, yet not simplie. For then many churches should be totally unserved, but conditionally, soe as if any man in orders, bringing with him his letters of orders and a testimonie of his conversation, do sue to the ordinary for any such place, that then the pty tolerated and not in orders instantly give place: and soe we have removed some in the time of the Visitation.'[35]

Communion services were still comparatively rare events in many parish churches; and were celebrated often simply for the sake of conformity. Some incumbents, indeed, crowded several such services into the eight days from Palm Sunday to Easter Day,[36] and held few others during the rest of the year. But a regular monthly communion was gradually establishing itself in certain quarters, with men like Nicholas Ferrar at Little Gidding in Huntingdonshire, Luke Grosse of Great Gidding, and Joshua Mapletoft of Margaretting in Essex leading the way. The numbers of communicants were usually very high;[37] and apart from an occasional extreme puritan or cantankerous recusant, most incumbents could complacently report to their bishops: 'all others both men and women doe frequent the Church and doe communicate orderly'.[38]

The question of Sunday observance had become by the beginning of the seventeenth century a sore bone of contention between Anglican and Puritan. On the whole, as we have already seen, Queen Elizabeth and her bishops had accepted the view-point that once the religious duties of the day had been observed, the people were free to do as they pleased either in work or play. The Puritans bitterly opposed this practice. In 1595 Nicholas Bound had published his famous book, *The True Doctrine of the Sabbath*. This firmly equated the English Sunday with the Jewish Sabbath, and transferred to it the dictates of the Fourth Commandment, prohibiting not merely sports but any unnecessary work on the seventh day. 'It is almost incredible', wrote Tom Fuller, 'how taking this doctrine was, partly because of its own purity, and partly for the eminent piety of such persons as maintained it'.[39] The thirteenth Canon had forbidden any profanation of Sunday; but this was still popularly interpreted to mean only during the actual hours of divine service, and was supposed to have no direct reference to what happened either before or afterwards, although a royal proclamation of 1603 had expressly named certain pastimes, such as bearbaiting, bull-batiting, and play-acting, which might cause disorder, rioting, or immorality, and ordered their suppression. Apart from the Puritan, who wished to confine the activities of this day to churchgoing, Bible-study, private devotions, visitations of the sick, and the collection of alms for the poor, the ordinary magistrate up and down the country, who was concerned with enforcing law and morality amongst the common people, found the lax Sunday a burden. To the Puritan all recreation or unnecessary work on the Sabbath was a sin; but to the upholders of law and order it was frequently a crime. Football, dancing, and excessive drinking often led to quarrelling and brawling, and sometimes even to murder. People wandered from one village to another on a Sunday for their sports, and 'riotous assemblies' were not uncommonly the result. The magistrates certainly did what they could, as the records of Quarter Sessions all over the country conclusively prove; but they were handicapped by the Law's vagueness. When alehouses were open and people danced and played during service time, as happened only too often, or there was brawling, or shops offered goods for sale and traders hawked their wares at forbidden hours, then they acted firmly enough. Cuthbert Cowston of Normanby, for example, was punished in 1606 for opening his alehouse on a Sunday for drinking and dancing in service-time: 'The number of a hundred persons', it was complained, 'were assembled with pipes and drums and dancing all the time of Divine service'.[40]

An order of Exeter Assize Court in 1615 forbade wakes, churchales, and clerk-ales altogether in that part of the country because they had been responsible for several manslaughters. Wakes were those jollifications held on the Feast Sunday of a parish church, when, after the afternoon service, the congregation betook itself to the village green and there indulged in athletic sports, and of course much heavy eating and drinking. Church-ales were similar festivities organized to raise money for church repairs; clerk-ales to pay the parish clerk; and bid-ales to provide money for the poor.

Eventually the Lancashire magistrates, supported by the Judge of Assize, attempted to enforce a stricter control of Sunday observance than the laws really warranted. This raised a hubbub; and in August

1617, when James was on his way to Scotland, he was met by a Lancashire petition 'desiring greater freedom to spend part of the Sunday in sport'. That led to the famous *Declaration of Sports*, which in May 1618 was extended to the whole country. Compulsory attendance at church, the illegality of carrying offensive weapons and the prohibition of unlawful pastimes[41] were all reaffirmed by the Declaration, which then went on to demand that 'our good people be not disturbed, letted or discouraged from any lawful recreation, such as dancing, either men or women, archery for men, leaping, vaulting or any such harmless recreation, nor from having May games, Whitsun ales, and Morris dances, and the setting up of May-poles and other sports therewith used, so as the same be had in due and convenient time, without impediment or neglect of Divine Service: and that women shall have leave to carry rushes to the church for the decorating of it according to the old custom'.[42] These loosely worded sentences could be and were widely interpreted and abused: little attempt was made to distinguish between 'before' and 'after' service time; knives and other offensive weapons continued to be carried; bull-baiting and bear-baiting flourished; and very heavy drinking went on in the alehouses regardless of the hour of day. At Thirsk in Yorkshire on a certain Sunday in October 1621, 'there was one so drunk' at the inn during service time 'that he drew forth a knife and would have killed divers but that good help was made'.[43]

Meanwhile no-one attempted to hinder Sunday labour: tradesmen cried their wares in the street; carriers, waggoners, and carters rattled over the cobblestones; cattle were driven to market; and butchers slaughtered their fat beasts. But as long as James I lived he steadfastly set his face against any further legislation which would either limit or control Sunday work or pleasure.

The parishioners of Elsfield in Worcestershire complained that their puritanical vicar, Gerard Prior, had preached a sermon against the profanation of the Sabbath by dancing, in defiance of the *Declaration of Sports*. He had, in fact, prayed publicly that 'the King's heart might be turned from profaneness, vanity and popery'.[44] For such outspokenness Bishop Thornborough suspended him from his benefice; and he was not reappointed until Archbishop Abbot had thoroughly examined into his case. Prior's sermons in general, or so it was alleged, had 'tended for the most part to death and damnation';[45] and certainly the puritanical preacher of this period was over-fond of the plain scriptural sermon that dealt bluntly with the sins of the individual. Neither did he mince his words about what was likely to happen to the un-elect after they were dead. John White, Rector of Barsham in Suffolk declared: 'When we certainly know by the Scriptures and without controversie believe, no small part of mankinde, in God's decree and eternal purpose, to stand reprobate and rejected from salvation, and all the effects of election, whether in the masse of sin or otherwise (all is one to the point of this difficultie). When, I say, it is of all hands yielded that there be so many reprobates, denied the grace of election, and from all eternitie prepared or finished, as the Scripture speaketh, to destruction (for what God executes in time he wills in eternity); what shall we say to Prayer and Thanksgiving for these? or what benefit can they or we receive thereby?'[46]

Puritan services and sermons were both of long duration. At Boston the afternoon service lasted five hours; for when his two-hour sermon was over, the vicar started to catechize the youth of the town and 'this being done, he spends two hours more in ye explanation of these his own questions and answers, soe that they keep the same tenour all the yeare which they did when we were with them. Theire afternoone worship, as they used to term it, will be five howes, where, to my observation, there was as many sleepers as wakers, scarce any man but sometimes was forced to wink or nod'.[47] At a somewhat later date John How, Cromwell's chaplain, used to begin his service at 9 a.m, which he did not conclude until about 3.15 p.m. The Puritan preachers were once described as 'the starres that give light in the night; they are captaines that are foremost in service; they are the soules that shield others from danger'. They preached 'The Word of Wisdom' as opposed to 'the Wisdom of Words', and the structure of their sermons rested upon the triple division of Doctrine, Reason, and Use; or as we might say today: the Declaration, the Explanation, and the Application. The text was carefully explained and defended, and then finally driven home by emphasizing the practical advantages to be derived from pursuing this particular line of teaching. Two such lengthy sermons were expected to be preached every Sunday from notes, each pregnant with vehement gestures and an affecting diction. Quotations were from the Scriptures alone; and the preacher, looking his congregation straight in the face, demanded of them that they should 'know nothing save Jesus Christ and him Crucified'.[48] God, so the Puritan believed, spoke to man through the sermon; and hence its importance was infinitely greater than the mere offering up of prayer and praise by man himself to his Creator.

On the other hand the Anglican parson when he preached—and many preferred to catechize or read the homilies—might indulge in a wealth of classical quotation, deal largely with Church doctrine and tradition, and rely heavily upon the Fathers. As likely as not, too, he would model himself upon the 'witty' and 'metaphysical' style of Bishop Andrewes; a good example of whose preaching is to be found in a sermon he delivered one Christmas Day from the text: 'Unto us a Child is born, unto us a Son is given'. 'All along in life', he said, 'you shall see these two. At His Birth; A Cratch for the Child; a Starre for the Sonne; A company of shepheards viewing the Child; A Quire of Angels celebrating the Sonne. In His Life: Hungry Himself to shew the nature of the Child; yet feeding five thousand to show the power of the Sonne. At His death: dying on the Crosse, as the Son of Adam; at the same time disposing of Paradise as the Sonne of God'.[49]

Ornaments and ceremonies continued to creep back into the parish churches: bowing to the altar and turning to the east for the Creed, a credence table, a veil for the cup, and even water to mingle with the wine.[50] The ritual itself was again chanted, square caps and surplices were being worn by the clergy with less objection, and fasts and festivals were more regularly observed. New and fine stained glass was often replacing the plain white variety in the churches, while illuminated texts appeared on their walls. Much of all this was probably due to the example and widespread influence of Launcelot Andrewes, the saintly Bishop of Winchester; but also partly as a reaction against the dogmatism of the extreme Calvinists. The growth of the Arminian movement was, indeed, now in full swing, and many erstwhile Roman Catholics were drawn into it, providing just that flavour of popery that was ultimately to prove its ruin.[51]

In the set-up of the seventeenth-century village community the Church continued to play an all-important part. Besides the parson himself and his two churchwardens, who were elected yearly by the vestry and were unpaid, although obliged to serve by law, there were their three parish servants: the clerk, the sexton, and the beadle; all of whom received a yearly stipend from church funds, supplemented as occasion arose by fees and gifts in kind. The ninety-first Canon had decreed that the clerk should be chosen by the incumbent, who must notify his choice to the parishioners 'in time of Divine service'. The candidate had to be 'twentie yeares of age at the least', and able to read, write, and sing. He was responsible for ringing the church bell, putting out the Bible and Prayer Book, and making the necessary arrangements for christenings and communions. He wore a surplice and led the congregation in the responses and singing of the Psalms. The Elizabethan clerk, as has already been noted, could read the first Lesson and Epistle; and, on occasion, might even read prayers, although this last was often objected to. At Cropredy, Oxon, in 1620 William Reade, the clerk, was presented 'for readinge devine servis upon Sundayes and holy dayes having not his lettors of ordors'.[52] If he possessed a modicum of learning he might also act as village schoolmaster. On the other hand, unless he combined in his office the humbler duties of sexton, he was not technically expected to do the church cleaning himself. Methusaleh Sharpe, parish clerk of Bathealton in Somerset, was presented in 1623 because 'he doth not make cleane the

Churche and keepe yt in decent and cleanely manner as yt ought to be'. On being cited, however, Sharpe replied 'that the Clark ought not to make Cleene the Church'.[53] The position was certainly one of considerable trust and responsibility, which, alas, was sometimes abused. A jury at Richmond Quarter Sessions in Yorkshire during 1625 condemned 'Jas Cotes of Arde-town in Arkengarthdale, one of the churchwardens there, and an ale-house keeper, for keeping disorder in his house and playing at cards with the Parish Clerk and other disordered company on the Sabbath day during Divine Service and Evening Prayer'.[54]

The sexton was the village grave-digger, for which task he received fees. James Dobson of Houghton-le-Spring, for example, was paid 2d. for a grave in the nave and 6d. for one in the chancel of the church; but only an obolus or half-penny for each cottager buried outside in the churchyard. In addition he was entitled to 'bunns at Christmas and eggs at Easter'. He was likewise church cleaner, stoker, and verger.[55] The beadle's work was of a more exciting nature. He wore a special kind of dress, carried a whip in his hand, and drove the dogs out of the church when they became a nuisance. 'Given to John Baillie', recorded an entry in the Upton account books for 1612, 'for whipping the dogges forthe of the church, 6d'.[56] His more secular occupations included helping the village constable to arrest and punish rogues and vagabonds, impounding strange cattle, inspecting hedges and fences, and bidding the villagers to the parish meetings.[57]

The church's income for the upkeep of the fabric and payment of its officials was derived from various sources: rents from houses and lands, pew rents, church-ales, and of course from the church rate. The last was an ancient tax dating from at least the fourteenth century and imposed by custom upon real property. A meeting of churchwardens and parishioners was convened, after due notice, in the church, and here the rate was agreed upon by a majority vote. This rate was actually chargeable not upon the land itself, but the occupier, even if non-resident, and it was always the tenant who was liable, not the owner. Those who refused to pay were presented by the churchwardens to the Ordinary. The rate was for the repair of the fabric of the church only, and could not be used for such items as the sacramental bread and wine or the fencing of the churchyard, which required special assessments or devolved upon a particular section of the inhabitants, i.e. those whose land abutted upon the mounds or were the tenants of certain farms.

Non-churchgoers could still be fined a shilling for every Sunday they stopped away. The churchwardens of Cropredy, Oxon, in 1619 declared in reply to a visitation article: 'Ther is few absent themselves from ther parish church at morninge prayre wherby the xiid a piece hathe not bene demaunded'; while at Banbury in the same year it was reported: 'we have not levied 12d of every one absent from the Church because our Justices doubt of granting their warrant'.[58] For a month's continuous absence a master-man could be penalized £20 and his servant £10. Parents, too, were severely punished if they neglected to bring their children for baptism.

It was the duty of the churchwardens to attend the Archdeacon's, or more occasionally the Bishop's, Visitations. These visitations began with the arrival in the parish of the apparitor bringing the articles and mandate of citation; then at the visitation itself, which in the case of the Archdeacon's was held twice a year at some convenient centre, the clergy had to produce their letters of orders and institution documents, the curates and schoolmasters their licences, and most important of all the churchwardens were sworn in and made their presentments of such offences as immorality, absenteeism from church, misbehaviour in church, sabbath-breaking, teaching without a licence, drunkenness and swearing, or a refusal to pay church rates. The culprits were then summoned before the archdeacon's court, and unless they were able satisfactorily to clear themselves by compurgation or otherwise, were sentenced. This might consist of nothing worse than a dismissal with an admonition or a slight penance that could be promptly commuted by handing over a few pence. On the other hand for a serious fault such as unchastity the offender would have to appear in church at service time, with bare feet and legs, clad in a white sheet, and holding a white rod in his hand. He had then publicly to recite his fault, express his sincere sorrow, and ask for forgiveness. Failure either to appear in court or to perform the required penance led directly to either the greater or lesser excommunication, which meant that in the former case a man was a complete outcast from society, and in the latter could not attend divine service and was deprived of the use of the sacraments. These were the maximum penalties the Church could inflict; since by herself she had no power to fine or imprison. However, the church could and did exact heavy fees before granting absolution; and might invoke the aid of the lay magistrate in order to supplement punishments should they prove inadequate. It was, therefore, scarcely surprising that the ecclesiastical courts, Archbishop's, Bishop's, and Archdeacon's, were most unpopular. They sat without a jury, encouraged spies and informers, were more than a trifle corrupt, and exacted excessive fees. Much of a parish's annual income must have been absorbed in this way. No one lamented their abolition by the Long Parliament, when their functions were taken over by the Justices of the Peace and the Courts of Quarter Session.[59] The duties of the churchwardens themselves increased considerably as the seventeenth century went on; and can roughly be summarized as follows: the repair of the church, the care of its property, the provision of the necessary books, ornaments, vestments, and furnishings for its services, the keeping of its accounts and the presentment of offenders against its laws.[60] But they also became associated with the constable, surveyor of highways, and overseer of poor relief in many social duties outside the church, such as; the supervision of alehouses, the control of vagrancy, the observance of Sunday, the repair of bridges and highways, the relief of pauperism, and the arming and payment of men enlisted by the parish to serve in the Trained Bands. 'By canon and custome and statute', wrote Professor Claude Jenkins, 'they had duties and obligations as well as rights and the historical student at any rate will not be slow to recognize the debt of gratitude which the Church owes to those who from generation to generation have filled an office which well justified the medieval quip of being not only honourable but onerous'.[61]

What of the parson himself? The Elizabethan and early Stuart parish priest was expected to live up to an ideal. Except under necessity he was prohibited from entering a public house; he might not engage in trade or 'servile labour'; he was forbidden to touch cards or dice; and, clothed in suitable attire, was expected to expend his leisure in studying the Scriptures and improving his learning. Canon Law, as we have already seen, ordered him to preach (if licensed) or read the homilies, catechize, conduct the Prayer Book services in surplice and hood, and visit the sick. But he also played his part in the secular life of the village. No labourer could leave the parish without his signed certificate; he recorded the whippings of the sturdy rogues, and sent them back to their place of origin; he was responsible for his parishioners eating fish on the statutory fast days; and also for keeping the churchwardens up to the mark in presenting offenders. A convicted recusant had to make his public confession and submission before the incumbent at divine service; and the latter saw to it that the penance imposed by the ecclesiastical court was duly carried out.[62]

All too many of the clergy, of course, failed to live up to expectations and were condemned accordingly. We hear repeatedly of incumbents who failed to preach, to catechize or to visit the sick; who were absentees, drunkards, and were even incontinent; while they frequently neglected to repair either the chancel or the parsonage. Mr Stone, curate of Curry Rivel, Somerset, in 1623, was presented because, the churchwardens complained, 'they had no service red in due tyme since the last visitacion, neither had they prayers on the xiith of October last being Sundaie at morning and that they have noe catachizing according to the Cannon, and that the Vicaridg howse and barne is in decay and fallen downe'. Of Mr Sharpe, Rector of Bathealton, in the same visitation it was reported 'that they had noe sermons preached in the Church sithence Easter last', i.e. nearly four months ago, and he was also accused of not undertaking 'the perambulacion according to the Cannon'.[63] But more serious charges were not lacking. At Benson, Oxon, in 1625 a certain Joan Coxe confessed 'that she hath had a childe unlawfully begotten of which Mr John Shurlock the Curat of Benson is the father'; and Mr Garth, Vicar of Charlton, 'about Midsommer last . . . and this examinant did play togeather against William Witham and Thomas Preist . . . att football att which tyme the said Mr Garth was overtaken wth drinck that hee did sometymes reele, and att that tyme one Mumford a cooper was wrastling there with another and afterwards lying along upon the ground on his back, the said Mr Garth uppon a wager then offered to be layd did attempt to take him up. Where uppon the said Cooper catched hold of him that the sayd Mr Garth fell downe backward and thereby the sleeve of his Jerkin or gowne was torne'.[64]

A favourite pastime among the less desirable elements in a parish was to abuse their minister. Richard Jones, curate of Towersey, for instance, complained in 1608 that John Thornton 'hathe misuseth me the Curat of Towersy beinge a ministere of the word of god and a bachelere of arts by callinge me jacksauce and welsheroge, and by chalengeinge me to ye fields: and by reportinge to his neighbours that he kept every day in the weeke servants and slaves bettere men than I'.[65] On the other hand, as always, little is heard of the well-deserving majority of spiritually-minded, hardworking parsons. The tribute paid by the churchwardens of Cropredy, Oxon, to their Vicar in 1619 shines all the brighter then in the darkness of this silence: 'Our vycar hath preached many yers as 40 and more and we think he hath lycence and authoryte so to do. We thinke and beleve our vycar cam by his lyvinge without eny symonichall practyce, the same then beinge in quene elyzabethes gyfte. We have had and have every sabbath day a sermon at morninge prayers. The parents and governors send ther children and servants to be catechised one the sabbath dayes in lent when he catachisethe. Our minister bestoweth his greatest tyme in redinge the scriptures and no offender in the other parts of that artycle. Our minister ys knowen to be a modest man in all things and maker of peace not cawsinge dissension. Our minister at all tymes weareth but such apparell as ys befytting his calling neyther ys he frequenter of ale house or taverne. Our minister is marryed and kepth servants fyttinge ther bodelye labor and not any otherwise. Our minister at all tymes useth the surplus in his tyme of devyne servyce and we beleve he hathe subscribed according to that artycle. Our minister usethe no other forme of common prayer then is in the booke of common prayer prescribed and useth the ryttes and ceremonies in servyce and administration of the sacraments. Our minister admytteth to the commyon no such offendors as our mentioned in the artycles neyther addmyteth any straungers. Our minister at all tymes for the most parte Redeth our devyne servyce and . . . the sacrament oftener then twyce in the year. Our minister in his owne person or by his deputation visyteth the sycke with prayers accordinge to the boke of comon prayer. The vycaradge house chauncell and church is kept in good and suffycient repayre neyther hath eny things bene defaced or pulled downe. . . . We beleve our minister hath at all tymes performed such deatyes as the article enquyreth'.[66]

The parish church itself, as in medieval times, was still the meeting place of the parish where its business was discussed and transacted. Here the village schoolmaster often taught his pupils; while in the vestry the parish armour and powder barrels were deposited, and above in the belfrey the country parsons might store their wool and grain. Vestry meetings, the monthly meetings of the overseers of the poor, J.P.s' meetings, and the coroner's inquests on dead bodies were held there regularly; besides, on occasion, the Archdeacon's court. From the pulpit the minister read aloud the visitation articles, gave warning of the yearly perambulation of the parish boundaries, and published briefs, testimonials and enclosure Acts. In 1609 the parish church of Arthuret in Cumberland was actually rebuilt by means of a national brief issued on 24 September 1606 and published in this way. But judging from a circular letter sent out to the bishops by Bancroft, the collections were not at first very strenuously enforced. 'His majesty', wrote the Archbishop, 'is not well pleased with the negligence generally of almost all the bishops in England touching the collections prescribed heretofore by his majesty for the building of the church and chapels of Arthuret in Cumberland; and therefore I pray you in any wise call your officers before you, and take a strict account of them; first, how many collections have been made, and where the money remaineth; for I am persuaded in many dioceses, much doth rest in the collectors' hands. Besides, there be sundry dioceses wherein there has been no collection at all, and in some not past one or two. Let me receive your lordship's particular letter to be showed to his Majesty, how his pleasure and directions touching this collection have been accomplished in your particular diocese'. Unfortunately in this case much of the money raised was later stolen, and eventually the church was finished through the energetic efforts of its rector, Dr Todd, who contributed some £60 out of his own pocket and procured £50 more from his friends. Bancroft's letter certainly disclosed that seventeenth-century churchwardens were no more in favour than their twentieth-century successors of allowing money to go out of the parish!

The rogationtide perambulations, sanctioned by the Royal Injunctions of 1559, appear to have been widely observed in the early part of the century; and were further encouraged by Archbishop Laud, who instructed the clergy 'to go in perambulation of the circuit of the parish'.[67] This involved a procession once a year round the parish boundaries, the recitation of prayers and psalms at stated intervals along the route; the beating and otherwise maltreating of small boys in order to impress indelibly upon their minds the precise extent of the area wherein the parish law ran, and finally of course the consumption of much food and drink. The Upton account books duly record this last:

1604.   For breade and ale in Rogation week. 1/8.
1615.   Paide for breade and drinke in Procession weeke. 5/-
1616.   For breade and drinke at the perambulation about the feildes. 6d.[68]

Despite strong puritanical criticism the church bells were still in great demand and rang out to celebrate all village and national occasions. They cost a lot in repairs, recastings, and wages for the ringers. From Shillington parish in Bedfordshire for example, we have the following outlay for their bells during the years 1603 and 1604:

'Laied foorth by the churchwardens about the bells . . .   £—s—d
Paide to the bellfounder   10—0—0
Paied for the writing of bonds   2—0
Paied to the bellfounder's men   12
Paied for William Ensam his charges to Leicester
    when the bells went to be cast   9—10
Paied at the same time for John Miles and Leach charges   13—4
Paied to Cheese for hanging the bells   4—0—12
Paied for timber to Mr Vites   15—0
Paied moor for timber   7—0
Paied to Thomas Pryor for boord for to make the bell
    wheels   6—0
Paied for nailes for the bels   4—0
Paied moore for nailes   8
Paied to William Goodale for iorn work for the bells   53—4
Paied for the carriage of the bells to Leicester   6—0—0
Paied to the bellfounder at the second payment   10—0—0
Paied for bell roopes   15—8
Paied to John Burley for a dinner for the labourers &
    for bread & beare for them at the taking downe of
    the bells & the hanging them up   9—9
Paied more for bred and bear   6
Paied for oyle for the bels   12
Paied for mending the upper bell loft   2—6
Paied to Cheese   5—0

F

By the time they had met all their bills the churchwardens of Shillington had expended some £48 8s. 7d. in these two years on the church bells.[69]

NOTES

[1] Magee, *English Recusants*, pp. 205–8.

[2] These astonishing numbers many have been due to a kindly 'blindness' on the part of incumbents and their churchwardens. In the Act Book of the Archdeacon of Lincoln in 1603 the Aveland deanery recorded that in its 20 parishes there were 3,619 communicants, but only one recusant. The Calcewaith deanery with 37 parishes and 4,484 communicants likewise only had one recusant! The majority of Lincolnshire deaneries had none at all. See Lincolnshire Record Society, Vol. 23, p. 443. In Norfolk the numbers were larger. Out of 238 parishes 41 recusants were returned, but 21 of these came from the three Wiggenhall churches. See *Norfolk and Norwich Archaeological Society*, Vol. X, Part I, pp. 1–49.

Towards the close of the reign the Act Book of the Archdeacon of Taunton revealed that 54 persons had failed to communicate in their parish churches, and these came from only 20 parishes. But the reason for their abstention is not always recorded. See Somerset Record Society, Vol. 43, p. 22. The Oxford diocese in 1620 also showed a growing number of non-communicants. At Benson, for example, 3 were presented. See Oxfordshire Record Society, Vol. 10, p. 27.

[3] G. P. Gooch, *Political Thought from Bacon to Halifax*, p. 9.

[4] Frere, *The English Church*, pp. 292–3. See also Neal, *History of the Puritans*, Vol. II, p. 5.

[5] Fuller, *Church History*, pp. 323–4.

[6] Lincolnshire Record Society, Vol. 23, p. lvi.

[7] Lincolnshire Record Society, Vol. 23, p. lxiv; *Norfolk and Norwich Archaeological Society*, Vol. X, Part I, pp. 10–49. It should be noted however that most of these livings were very close together, often less then half-a-mile apart; and their endowments were very small, not more than a few pounds each. It was most exceptional to hold 3 livings. The only case quoted here is that of Acle cum Wickmere cum East Dereham, whose combined income amounted £70 3s. 1d.

[8] Canons 14, 58, 45 and 46, 59, 67.

[9] Canons 72, 73, 62.

For the 'Constitution and Canons Ecclesiastical' of 1604, see E. Cardwell, *Synodalia*, Vol. I, pp. 245–329.

[10] Canons 18, 111.

[11] Canons 112, 27, 114.

[12] Canons 82, 52, 87, 70, 80, 99.

[13] See Lincolnshire Record Society, Vol. 23, p. lxvii.

In connection with this Lincolnshire Visitation of 1604 it is of interest to note that John Garbrore, curate of Stane, was excused the visitation fees because 'his stipend is but 20s a year, and therefore in meare pitty he is dismissed'; and that the churchwardens of Ludborough refused to answer the visitation articles, 'being so many and so hard', until they were threatened with excommunication. Ibid. p. lxvii.

[14] Alexander Cooke, Vicar of Louth, declared 'that he will rather loose his living then weare the surplice'. Several others said the same thing. See, Lincolnshire Record Society, Vol. 23, p. lxvii. And not only in the Lincoln diocese: at Towersey, Oxon., in 1608 'Mr Jonns our curate' was presented 'for not wearinge his Surples uppon the sabot day at Evninge prayer at the christninge of a child. And also uppon Esterday, and divers other Sabothe dayes'. Oxfordshire Record Society, Vol. 10, p. 193. At Monksilver in Somerset, as late as 1623, the Rector, William Wilmoth, was presented because 'Hee did bury a dead man not wearinge his Surplisse and doth not weare yt oftentimes in reading morning and evening prayer'. Somerset Record Society, Vol. 43, p. 79. In the Archdeaconry of Essex Act Books for 1605 and 1607 the Vicars of Childerditch and Little Leighs were charged with refusing to wear the surplice, to use the sign of the cross in baptism, 'to read the Book of Common Prayer established in the last parliament', and 'also for administering the sacrament to those that do not receive the same kneeling'. Essex Record Society, Vol. 17, Vol. I, p. 8.

[15] Neal, *History of the Puritans*, Vol. II, pp. 48–53.

[16] Lincolnshire Record Society, Vol. 23, p. lxxv.

[17] Usher, *Reconstruction of the English Church*, Vol. I, p. 423. Some of the worst of the extremists could not be touched at all since they were only lecturers or private chaplains.

[18] Lincolnshire Record Society, Vol. 23, p. lxxix–lxxx.

[19] Oxfordshire Record Society, Vol. 10, pp. 161–2.

[20] Essex Record Society, Vol. 17, Vol. I, p. 10.

[21] *Annals of Evangelical Nonconformity*, p. 132.

[22] Bancroft wrote to his bishops in 1610: 'Never was their pride in that respect so great as it is now'. This type of ostentation applied particularly to double-beneficed men, 'which', the Archbishop went on, 'is one principal motive why there is such exclamation against double-beneficed men. . . . By such their bravery in apparel they do procure no manner of credit unto themselves, but . . . great envy and heart burning against their calling and estates'. See Cardwell, *Documentary Annals*, Vol. II, pp. 154, 162; see also, for Canons 74 and 75, Cardwell, *Synodalia*, Vol. I, pp. 288–90.

[23] Lincolnshire Record Society, Vol. 23, pp. lxxviii, lxxix, lxxx.

[24] Lincolnshire Record Society, Vol. 23, p. lvii.

[25] Fuller, *Church History*, Vol. III, p. 224.

[26] J. A. Venn, *The Foundations of Agricultural Economics*, pp. 153–6.

[27] Institutes, II, p. 652.

[28] See, *Essex Review*, Vol. XV, Jan. 1906, 'Essex Churches . . . in the XVI and XVII centuries', pp. 45–9.

[29] F. H. West, *Rude Forefathers*, pp. 10–14.

[30] Fuller, *Church History*, Vol. III, p. 356; W. Haller, *Liberty and Reformation in the Puritan Revolution*, p. 11.

[31] Fuller, *Church History*, p. 357. See, also, Cardwell, *Documentary Annals*, Vol. II, pp. 149–51; Neal, *History of the Puritans*, Vol. II, pp. 116–17.

[32] *38th Report of the Associated Architectural Societies*, Vol. XVI, Part I, 'The Primary Visitation of the Diocese of Lincoln by Bishop Neile. A.D. 1614', ed. Rev. Precentor Venables, p. 38.

[33] *38th Report of Associated Architectural Societies*, Vol. XVI, Part I, pp. 39, 40.

[34] *38th Report of Associated Architectural Societies*, Vol. XVI, Part I, p. 40.

[35] *38th Report of Associated Architectural Societies*, Vol. XVI, Part I, p. 43.

[36] A reason for this may have been the comparatively small space in the chancel for the communicants to kneel on round the Table; necessitating at a festival like Easter a number of services in order to cater for the very large congregations involved.

[37] The following ten rural deaneries with their communicants are taken at random out of the Archdeaconry of Lincoln in the year 1603.

Deanery	No. of Parishes	No. of Communicants
Bolingbroke	22	3522
Grantham	23	3685
Holland N.	19	8066
Holland S.	13	5082
Horncastle	22	3197
Lafford	30	4763
Loveden	14	3000
Ness	13	2593
Walshcroft	25	3263
Yarborough	34	6712

[38] Lincolnshire Record Society, Vol. 23, pp. 337–40.

[39] Fuller, *Church History*, Vol. III, p. 159.

[40] Whitaker, *Sunday in Tudor and Stuart Times*, p. 74.

[41] These included bowling 'for the meaner sort of people' by a statute of Henry VIII.

[42] Neal, *History of the Puritans*, Vol. II, p. 105.

[43] Whitaker, *Sunday in Tudor and Stuart Times*.

[44] See *The Victoria County History of Worcestershire*, Vol. II, pp. 57, 58 and 61.

[45] Frere, *The English Church*, pp. 381–2.

[46] W. F. Mitchell, *English Pulpit Oratory from Andrewes to Tillotson*, p. 199.

[47] *38th Report of Associated Architectural Societies*, Vol. XVI, Part I, p. 41.

[48] Quoted from W. Haller, *The Rise of Puritanism*, p. 143.

[49] Mitchell, *English Pulpit Oratory*, p. 152.

[50] This was certainly unusual at the beginning of the century, judging from the following complaint made about the minister of Gosberton in 1602: 'he did minister the communion in the said parish church of Gosberton about Lammas last, and wanteing wine at the latter end of the communion he mingled water with wine and did deliver the same to the communicants, for that otherwise he should have sent away some of the communicants without wine'. See *Lincoln Episcopal Visitations*, ed. E. Peacock, p.19.

[51] 'On the doctrine of the sacraments', wrote J. B. Marsden, 'this new party began to speak a language long unknown in England. The Lord's supper they affirmed, was not only a sacrament, but a sacrifice. They carefully insisted that the communion table should be called an altar; and having obtained this point . . . we have the wood, said they, and the altar but where is the lamb for the burnt offering. Thus they inferred the doctrine of the real presence', *The History of the Early Puritans*, p. 365.

[52] Oxfordshire Record Society, Vol. 10, p. 253.

[53] Somerset Record Society, Vol. 43, pp. 55–6.

[54] Whitaker, *Sunday in Tudor and Stuart Times*, p. 102.

[55] In many country villages the offices of parish clerk, vestry clerk and sexton were all held by one man. See Eleanor Trotter, *Seventeenth Century Life in the Country Parish*, pp. 6–8.

[56] West, *Rude Forefathers*, p. 15.

[57] He was therefore also town crier.

[58] Oxfordshire Record Society, Vol. 10, pp. 214, 251.

[59] The visitation itself concluded with the issuing of injunctions.

[60] This duty must have rendered them very unpopular at times, and explains why undoubtedly in many parishes the wardens turned a blind eye to minor peccadilloes, and with their tongues in their cheeks wrote in their report: 'All well'.

[61] Somerset Record Society, Vol. 43, p. 14. The Act Book of the Archdeacon of Taunton in 1623 certainly showed that the churchwardens were performing their duties conscientiously, since in that volume there were only presentments from thirteen parishes that directly affected them.

[62] See A. Tindal Hart and E. F. Carpenter, *The Nineteenth Century Country Parson*, 1954, pp. xvii–xviii.

[63] Somerset Record Society, Vol. 43, pp. 67, 64, 54, 55. Mr Sharpe also left his chancel unpaved.

[64] Oxfordshire Record Society, Vol. 10, pp. xviii, 28.

[65] Oxfordshire Record Society, Vol. 10, p. 194.

[66] Oxfordshire Record Society, Vol. 10, pp. 249–50.

[67] W. A. Bewes, *Church Briefs*, p. 99.

[68] *Works of William Laud*, Vol. V, Part II, p. 427.

[69] Bedfordshire Record Society, Vol. 33, p. 108.

The Policy of 'Thorough'

THE LAUDIAN REACTION, that began early in Charles I's reign while Laud himself was still only Bishop of St David's, had a definite three-fold purpose: the destruction of Calvinism, the restoration of Catholic Order, and the thorough disciplining of clergy and laity alike. It based its power upon the unfettered exercise of the royal prerogative and supremacy, and enforced its will through the well-oiled machinery of the Courts of High Commission and the Star Chamber.

When John Cosin was Archdeacon of the East Riding of Yorkshire in 1625, he received a memorandum from a certain Mr R. Claphamson, a notary-public at York, concerning the slackness of the parochial clergy. 'Well may your Worship terme these tymes of neglect', he wrote, 'for even in the Clergy I fynd a great defect in the performance of reall duties; and I am not alone in this: others suffer as well, and cannot amend it, and if a man use lawfull meanes to compell them to do what they ought, then do they exclame and rayle as if they had in-justice done: these be the tymes that a man may well say, O tempora! O mores'.[1] Two years later Cosin issued his own Visitation Articles, which indirectly confirm this indictment. Does any clergyman, he asked, 'give himself over to base and servile labours' or 'vain and idle pastimes', such as 'drinking at the alehouse, or ryot at the taverne; in resorting to common bowling allies . . . in playing at dice, cards . . . in hawking and hunting like a gallant; in sporting and dancing like a wanton person'. Could he be said 'to be a swearer, a blasphemer of God or his saints; a fighter, a brawler,[2] a fornicator, an usurer, a sower of discord?'[3] Was his dress 'decent and comly'; did he misbehave himself 'like a gentleman' or buy and sell 'like a merchant'? Had any clerk come 'to his holy order by any corrupt means' or acquired his benefice unconstitutionally? Was he resident and diligent in his duties, and careful to preserve the property of his living?

As these Articles went on it quickly became apparent that the Archdeacon was even more concerned with ceremonial and doctrinal questions than with clerical morals; for evidently the old puritanical omissions and commissions were as rife as ever. These included the refusal of many parsons to kneel at the reception of the sacrament or for public prayers; the 'new devise' they had adopted for baptizing their children 'in a bason or some other vessell brought from private houses'; their failure to adhere to the Table of Lessons or always to wear 'and never omit the wearing of the surplice'; the omission of the sign of the cross in baptism; the use of 'outlandish' catechisms instead of the standard version in the Prayer Book; the marriage in private houses and without a ring; the neglect of the Rogationtide perambulations; the preaching of sermons without a licence; and the persistent habit of many Calvinistically-minded lecturers 'to absent themselves from the Congregation, to stay at home or to walk abroad, or to retire into the vestrie, till all or greater part of the Service be done'. But the most searching enquiries were reserved for the subject matter of the sermon, where the nonconformist was accused of soaring 'too high' and meddling 'with unrevealed mysteries', of 'rude and undecent reviling of persons', of broaching 'new and strange doctrines' or 'old and condemned heresies'; and worst of all of seeking to undermine the Prayer Book, the Episcopate, and the 'Canons and Constitutions of the Church'. The main purpose of any sermon, the Archdeacon declared, ought to be 'to exhort the people unto obedience, peace and unitie, teaching them a godly, righteous and a sober life'.[4]

In this same year of 1627 Cosin published *A Collection of Private Devotions or the Hours of Prayer*, which fairly represented the Laudian ideals. Herein the individual churchman was directed to join in saying the daily services, resisting the Seven Deadly Sins, practising the Seven Corporate Works of Mercy, and carefully preparing himself through private confession for the receiving of the Eucharist.[5] Such a work, which quickly became a best-seller among the Arminian clergy, was of course utterly condemned by Puritans like Burton and Prynne, the latter of whom attacked it in his book *A Brief Survey and Censure of Cozens his Cozening Devotions*, strongly objecting to the canonical hours, prayers for the dead, and the frontispiece. This last contained 'the Name of Jesus, figured in three Capital Letters (I.H.S.) with the Cross upon them, incircled with the Sun, supported by two Angels, with two devout Women praying toward it'.[6]

Archbishop Abbot of Canterbury, who appeared to favour the Puritans, was sequestered from his metropolitical jurisdiction and confined to his house at Ford in Kent, while under his Commission the Bishops of London, Durham, Rochester, Oxford, and Bath and Wells (William Laud) exercised his authority from October 1627 until late in 1628 when the Archbishop was restored to power. During this period, egged on by Laud, they did much to encourage the high churchmen in their 'popish practices', particularly the removal of the communion table to the east end, where it was 'set up in the place where the altar stood, and there commonly covered as thereto belongeth'. Here the second service was usually read and reference began to be made in certain quarters to 'the Sacrament of the Altar' and 'the Sacrifice of the Altar'.[7] All the bishops, however, were not in favour of these proceedings; and in particular John Williams of Lincoln,

who favoured a policy of moderation and compromise. At Grantham
the Laudian Vicar, Tyler, tried to move the table and was obstructed
by his puritanical congregation. In a rage, and relying on the backing
of the Commission, Tyler informed them that he intended to set up a
stone altar at the east end. A complaint was made to Williams, who,
according to Heylin, 'takes hold of the opportunity to discourage the
work'[8] by writing to Tyler and urging him to adopt the Elizabethan
ruling. He further reproved the Vicar for 'needless controversies' and
suggested, 'You shall find no such ceremony equal to Christian
Charity'. This incident led to a pamphlet warfare in which Heylin's
A Coal from the Altar received a crushing rejoinder from Williams
under the title of *The Holy Table, Name and Thing*.[9] But a notable
victory was won by the Laudians at St Nicholas Abingdon, where a
Chancery Commission decreed 'that the Table given by Mr Blucknall
should not by the multitude of People coming to Service, or otherwise
by sitting or writing upon it, nor by any other unreverent usage be
prophaned, spoyled or hurt; We do order and decree that the said
Table shall continually stand at the upper end of the Chancell, upon
which a Carpet (by him given) should be laid, where it shall continually stand close to the upper Skreen . . . and there to be covered with
the Carpet aforesaid, and in no place else'.[10]

In 1628 a royal proclamation utterly forbade the teaching of Calvinism from Anglican pulpits; and the following year Laud was
instrumental in drawing up certain instructions that were issued by the
King to the bishops.[11] These commanded their lordships to reside in
their dioceses, take particular pains with their ordination candidates,
and to deal sternly with the puritanical lecturers. They were also
ordered to give an account year by year to the King of their steward-
ship. John Selden, who compared the lecturers with the friars, declared
that just as the latter had helped to divide Christendom at the Reformation, so the former would eventually disrupt the Church of
England, since they secured for themselves 'not only the affection,
but the bounty that should be bestowed on the minister'.[12] Laud urged
that wherever possible catechizing should be substituted for the afternoon sermon; but in any case each lecturer must be compelled to read
the Prayer Book service in his surplice before commencing his dis-
course. This at least would put a stop to the growing practice, whereby
an orthodox incumbent read Evening Prayer in an almost empty
church, which then immediately filled up to hear the Puritan preacher
in his Geneva cloak. Furthermore no Town Corporation or any other
body or individual might now appoint a clergyman to a lectureship
unless he also held a cure of souls; thus ensuring the maximum of
episcopal control over the preachers. Laud would, of course, have
liked to abolish these lectureships altogether; but unfortunately owing

to the usual chronic financial difficulties, the spiritual needs of the towns could only be fully met by sermons of this type that were subsidized by Puritan business men. Many of these lecturers were undoubtedly very popular with both clergy and laity, judging from the streams of petitions from all over the country which poured into the episcopal postbags. A good example of this kind of thing was the one sent to Laud himself, who was now Bishop of London, on behalf of Thomas Hooker, the lecturer at Chelmsford, which was signed by large numbers of Essex beneficed clergy, and ran: 'We all esteeme and knowe the said Mr Thomas Hooker to be, for doctryne, orthodox, and life and conversation honest, and for his disposition peaceable, no wayes turbulent or factious, and so not doubting but he will contynue that good course, commending him and his lawfull suite to your lordship's honourable favour'[13]. No notice was taken of this petition, and Hooker was eventually compelled to flee to Holland.[14] In 1633 the bishops were again warned that no man was to be ordained except to a title and also that the number of private chaplains were to be drastically reduced by restricting them to those people only who possessed the privilege by law.[15] In such ways the prestige and authority of the episcopate were further enhanced and advanced.

Part of the Laudian plan for controlling and shaping the future of Anglicanism was to reduce, and eventually abolish altogether, lay patronage and lay impropriations. This meant in the latter case buying them out; and to his intense chagrin the Bishop found that in such a project he had been forestalled to some extent by a group of wealthy London nonconformists, who had clubbed together to purchase impropriated tithes, and proposed to use the income for maintaining extreme Calvinists. These 'feoffees for impropriations', as they were called, had 'acquired by purchase or gift impropriations, lands and tenements, advowsons to rectories and vicarages, and the nomination and maintenance in whole or in part of vicars, curates, preachers, lecturers and schoolmasters'. They made no pretence of restoring these impropriations to their original ecclesiastical owners; but used the revenues from them to maintain 'godly' ministers, who were exclusively selected and controlled by themselves. In particular they favoured 'removable' men over whom the bishops had little or no power. This type of preacher was trained through the Calvinistic St Antholin lectureships in London and then dispersed throughout England to fill the large number of ecclesiastical offices now at the disposal of the feoffees. By that means they hoped eventually to mould the Anglican Church more to their way of thinking.[16] 'It is incredible', wrote Fuller, 'what large sums were advanced in a short time towards so laudable an employment'. But Bishop Laud feared that they might shortly become 'prime patrons, for number and greatness of benefices' and so promote

Laud dining off the ears of Puritan divines (1637)

'a secret growth of nonconformity'.[17] This was not to be tolerated for a moment, and the whole weight of the royal authority was brought into play in order to crush it. Peter Heylin, who was a fellow of Magdalen College, Oxford, was put up to preach the Act sermon against the feoffees in Great St Mary's Church before the University on 11 July 1630. He took as his text Matthew XIII 25 and described them as those enemies that sowed tares among the wheat. 'What', he asked, 'are those intrusted in the managing of this great business? Are they not the most of them the most active and the best affected men in the whole cause, and *Magna Partium momenta*, Chief Patrons of the Faction? And what are those whom they prefer? Are they not most of them such as must be serviceable to their dangerous innovations? And will they not in time have more preferments to bestow, and therefore more dependencies than all the Prelates in the Kingdom?'[18] The Laudians awoke to their danger, and two years later a Bill was introduced into the equity side of the Court of Exchequer accusing the feoffees of behaving like a corporation, but without letters patent, and so holding property without the sanction of the Crown. Judgment was delivered against the feoffees, who were ordered to hand over their advowsons and funds to the King, and to dissolve their organization.[19]

Nevertheless Laud himself had not the same means of acquiring the huge sums needed substantially to reduce impropriations, which remained the real flaw in his policy of 'thorough'.

At Charles I's personal request it became Laud's practice, as soon as he was made Primate, to render an account of his province, year by year, to the King. These reports began in January 1633/4 and continued until 1639, revealing the conditions of the church, diocese by diocese. It is significant that as time went on the iron hand undoubtedly began to show results, with more and more outward conformity and a noticeable weakening of the opposition. By 1638, for example, the lecturers were giving very little trouble. The extreme Puritans had gone, and the rest conformed to the rules; while the 'Combination-Lecturers', who were appointed by the bishops, actually read the second service at the communion table clad in their surplices and hoods. The following year the great majority of dioceses could certify complacently 'that everything is well'.

This was far from the case in 1634 when there was trouble with the nonconformists in practically every county. In Essex Nathaniel Ward, Rector of Stondon Massey, had to be excommunicated and deprived 'for refusing to subscribe to the articles established by the canon of the Church'; and John Beedle, Rector of Barnston, was admonished 'for omitting some parts of divine service and refusing conformity'. In Northamptonshire a certain Mr Elmes of Peterborough kept, contrary to law, 'a schoolmaster in his house and useth him as a chaplain to preach a lecture upon Sundays in the afternoon in the church of Warmington'. The Bishop of Coventry and Lichfield had to suppress 'the running lecture so called, because the lecturer went from village to village, and at the end of the week proclaimed where they would have him next, that his disciples might follow. They say this lecture was ordained to illuminate the dark corners of that diocese'; while there were many people in Bedfordshire who used to wander away from their own parishes in order to follow 'preachers affected by themselves'. The Bishop of Salisbury found 'the greatest part of Wiltshire overgrown with the humours of those men that do not conform'; and his brother of Norwich, a notoriously puritanical diocese, had to contend with wandering preachers and 'unsound doctrine' on every side. Zealous Laudian bishops like Pierce of Bath and Wells, and Wren of Norwich (later of Ely) vigorously enforced the Archbishop's policy, particularly after the test case of St Gregory's Church near St Paul's had been decided in favour of the Archbishop's ruling that in the matter of the placing of the communion table parish churches should follow the example of their cathedral and the judgment of the Ordinary.[20] They put down the puritanical lectureships, insisted upon the railing in of the Holy Table at the east end of the church, kneeling at the rails in order to receive the sacrament, bowing towards the altar and at the name of Jesus, and the publication and enforcement of the *Book of Sports*. Lincoln, where Bishop Williams boldly opposed the Primate, especially in the matter of the placing of the communion table, was the chief stumbling block in Laud's path, until Williams had been committed to the Tower in 1637 and the Archbishop could triumphantly report to the King that this gigantic diocese was 'now in my charge'.[21]

Prynne picked out five bishops from the episcopate who seemed to him excessively zealous Laudians. These included, besides Pierce and Wren, Augustine Lindsell, Bishop of Peterborough (later of Hereford), Richard Montague, Bishop of Chichester (later of Norwich,) and Robert Skinner, Bishop of Bristol (later of Oxford and Worcester); and were in his opinion 'the chiefe promoters' of Laud's 'innovations'.[22] The fiercest of them all was probably William Pierce, who bragged 'that he had not left one lecturer in all his Diocess, of what sort soever, whether he lectured for his Stipend, or by a voluntary combination of some Ministers amongst themselves'; and further declared that his arguments about the altar had 'prevailed so far, that of 469 Parishes which were in that Diocess, 140 had conformed to his Order in it . . . in this present year 1635'.[23] He was not, however, to have it all his own way, for in the large and populous parish of Beckington in Somerset he met with considerable opposition. Here it was true the high church incumbent, Alexander Huish, was perfectly willing to conform, but the two churchwardens and the majority of the parishioners were not. The communion table 'had for 70 years stood in the midst of the chancel, enclosed with a very decent wainscot border and a door, with seats for the communicants to receive in round about it'.[24] Bishop Pierce was determined to have it moved to the east end; and when the churchwardens, Wheeler and Fry, refused to comply with his order they were excommunicated. Their appeal, first to the Court of Arches and later to the King, was disregarded; and eventually, proving contumacious, they were imprisoned in the county jail under a writ of *capias excommunicatum*. Here their health broke down and they were obliged to make submission. The prescribed penance consisted of publicly confessing their fault in their own parish church, in the great church of Bath, and finally in Frome church. Shortly afterwards Wheeler died of tuberculosis, which he had contracted in prison; and neither ever 'enjoyed themselves' again.

The churchwardens' case, which was a strong one, ran as follows:

'We the churchwardens of Beckington doe give these reasons for our refusal to remove the Communion table from the place it nowe standeth and hath stood since the reformacon:
1. We have noe iniunction from his Royall Matie.
2. Noe statute confirmed by act of parliamt.
3. Noe Canon at all for alteringe the table.
4. Noe article to which we are sworne.
5. We expecte noe change of Religion blessed be God.
6. We are to continewe the peace of the Church.

7. If we should be hereafter questioned in a parliament we knowe not howe to answere it.'

The Bishop countered these arguments with his own:

'1. That it was ordered by the Queen's Injunctions that the Communion Table should stand where the Altar did.

2. That there should be some difference between the placing of the Lord's Table in the Church and the placing of a Man's Table in his House.

3. That it was not fit the People should sit above God's Table, or be above the Priest when he Consecrateth.

4. That when the Communion Table standeth thus, the Chancel would be the fairer, and so there would be more room for the Communicants.

5. That the Table standing thus, the face of the Minister would be better seen, and his voice more audibly and distinctly heard, than if it stood upon a Level in the midst of the Chancel.

6. That it was expedient that the Daughters should be like their Mother, and that the Parochial Churches should conform themselves in that particular to their own Cathedrals.

7. That should it be permitted to stand as before it did, Churchwardens would keep their Accounts on it, Parishioners would dispatch the Parish business at it, Schoolmasters will teach their Boys to Write upon it, the Boys will lay their Hats, Sachels and Books upon it, Many will sit and lean irreverently against it in Sermontime, the Dogs would piss upon it and defile it, and Glasiers would knock it full of Nail-holes'.[25]

Legally the Bishop was not on such strong ground as the churchwardens. The Elizabethan Injunction of 1559, which ordered that the Table should be set 'in the place where the altar stood', had qualified this command with the words, 'saving when the communion of the Sacrament is to be distributed'; a passage deliberately ignored by the Laudians. Neither could the churchwardens be gainsaid when they declared that to date (1635) there was no parliamentary statute or ecclesiastical canon specifically ordering the permanent removal of the table to the east end of the church. The Bishop's arguments, apart from the first, were based in fact entirely upon the expediency and decency of the thing itself.

Running through the Archbishop's yearly reports to the King are some heart-rending glimpses of the extreme poverty of some of the parochial clergy. In 1634, for example, Laud admitted that in all the dioceses of his province 'I find one great complaint, and very fit to be redressed, it is the general grievance of the poor vicars, that their stipends are scarce able to feed and clothe them'. The Bishop of

Lincoln had likewise reported in 1637: 'there are a great number of very poor miserable vicarages and curateships in many parts of this large diocese, and which are almost past all cure and hope of help, unless by your majesty's grace and favour some may be had'.[26] Many of the petitions concerning the Kentish clergy that came before Sir Edward Dering's sub-committee of Religion in 1640 contained much the same story. The nigger in the woodpile was frequently the impropriator. The minister of Shoreham and Otford, for instance, received the princely salary of £20 and a free house, whilst the impropriators, the Dean and Chapter of Westminster, drew £160 from Shoreham and two hundred marks from Otford each year.[27] The Vicar of Bradborne, another rich impropriate rectory, had £30 per annum and a ruinous vicarage. 'This present incumbent', wrote his petitioners, 'hath the ruines of much old housing left unto him by his predecessor, which he could never yet be able sufficiently to repayre; he hath alsoe a wife and five children to sustayne upon this small meanes'. And it was said of Waltham: 'our parsonage by lease held from the See of Canterbury is att the least of an hundred and twenty pounds annuall value; our vicarage poore, and not worth above thirtie and five pounds yearely, or thereabouts; our moderne Vicar Mr David Neishe, a man of exemplar life and conversation; and a most diligent preacher, for whom wee humbly begg that there might bee some competent addition of necessarye maintenance; and not knowing how this may be affected (as wee most heartily desire), wee humbly implore the aide and assistance of this most honourable and highe Court of Parliament'.[28] The down-trodden curate was also very much in evidence: John Streating had been curate of Ivychurch for twenty-six years when his parishioners dispatched the following letter to Westminster: 'Wee holdinge it an unreasonable and unconscionable thinge, that the livinge of Ivychurche, being worth, as it is farmed out, above two hundred pounds a yeare, the poore Curate should have but thirtie pounds a yeare, he takinge all the paines; and the doctor [Dr Jackson] under whom he serves, seldome cominge and preachinge amongst us; no, not havinge bin once amongst us for the space of these fower or five yeares'.[29] Francis Marsh, perpetual curate of Guston next Dover, was in even worse plight, since, it was complained, in the course of the last three years he had received £9 for the first two and £13 for the last;[30] and his was by no means an exceptional case either in Kent or elsewhere.[31] Laud had indeed attempted to augment poor vicarages by seeking to compel impropriators to increase their small incomes; but the successes achieved, as for example in the huge diocese of Lincoln, were very meagre.

The condition of many parish churches, chapels of ease, and churchyards, despite the improvements effected under James I, was still truly appalling. *The Peterborough Church Survey Books* for the first half of the seventeenth century fully confirm and illustrate this neglect, which indeed was to be very largely remedied after the famous Metropolitical Visitation of 1633 to 1636. These surveys recorded serious flaws in the actual fabric of nave and chancel alike in church after church; multiple defects in communion tables, pulpits, chests, fonts, bells, and church-yards; while large numbers of parishes lacked proper church furnishings or vestments such as communion plate, 'carpets' for the holy table, and an adequate surplice. Tumble-down seating and insufficient Bibles and Prayer Books were also complained of. Polebrook church in 1605/6 was described as follows:

'The pulpit standeth too low; the carpet for the Holy Table is very old; the bible is insufficient, wanting leaves; there is a seat next behind the Minister's seat not fit to be there for that it is inconvenient; the Surplice is insufficient; the Seats in the church are not paved nor built in the bottom, but straw strewn in them, very unseemly. The third bell is cracked. They have not a pewter pot'.[32] In 1631 their condition was little better. A typical entry is that concerning Cranford St John:

'A window in the chancell wants glassing and two windows on the southside are stopped. The chancell and church wants plaistering and pointing in divers places. The uppermost seate of the middle space is very undecent being patched up with rough bordes unbecoming the place. They want a poore man's box. The north Ile joyning to the chancell wanteth whiting and the pavement is broken and uneven. The communion cloth and carpet are insufficient. The Booke of Common Prayer is old and unsufficient. The Bible is not of the last edition but an old one which hath divers leaves loose and it is unfit for use. They want two tomes of Homilies and Erasmus' Paraphrases and the booke of Canons and the booke called *God and the King*. They want a flagon for the communion wine. The cover of the Font is broken and insufficient'.[33]

Peterborough was not the only diocese to suffer from decayed churches; for it was equally true of all the rest. At the Archdeacon of Essex's Visitation of 1633 it was reported of All Saints Church in Colchester:

'Their church walls want pargeting on the outsides towards the North. The lead of the steeple wants repairing; their bell wheels are broken and want repairing and their second bell wants a rope; their church wants paving; divers of the seats in their church want boarding in the bottoms; their church wants glazing; the partition between the church and the belfry wants repairing; they want a new Book of Common Prayer; they want the books of homilies, Bishop Jewel's works and the book of Canons; they want a napkin and a plate for the communion; there is two posts set up in the churchyard for drying of yarn which are forthwith to be pulled down; their church porch wants planchering; their chancel wants glazing'.[34]

At a time when the sermon was growing in importance the Peterborough diocesan surveyor apparently took particular care to mention any tumble-down or inconvenient pulpits. At Woodford near Kettering there was an outstandingly bad instance: 'in the church the pulpit standeth too lowe and is shattered in divers parts thereof. The pulpit staires are very undecent, fitter for a hynds' lodging than for the house of God'; while he reported of Irchester church: 'The minister's reading pew standeth unconveniently to go from thence into the pulpitt and so he is faine to turne himselfe upon the top of an ill-favoured and dangerous ladder and as it were creepe between the pulpitt and seate before he can go up into the pulpitt'.[35] The churchyard was a source of considerable anxiety. It was only too often inadequately fenced, churned up by cattle and pigs, the scene of rowdy carnival, or simply neglected. The unsatisfactory parish of Woodford possessed a churchyard which 'seemeth to have no mounds of its own on the southside'; and on the east 'the mound seemeth to be placed on other men's ground and there is a ditch between the true churchyard and other men's mounds; and they are but ill mounds and as ill maintained.[36] Similar complaints were common elsewhere. At Cropredy in Oxfordshire, for example, the churchyard had become disfigured 'by gorge in of hoggs and swayne'.[37]

The question of Sunday sports and labour came to a head early in the sixteen-thirties. Puritanical parliaments at the beginning of Charles I's reign had insisted upon legislation directed against both; and zealous puritanical Justices of the Peace strove vigorously to suppress them. When, however, in 1632 Lord Chief Justice Richardson and Baron Denham, who were on the western circuit, ordered at the Somerset Assizes that 'Revels, Church Ales, Clerk Ales and all other public Ales be henceforth utterly suppressed' because of the many and notorious disorders they had been responsible for—a judgment the clergy were told to read from their pulpits—Laud himself decided to intervene. He asked the Bishop of Bath and Wells to investigate the matter; whereupon the partisan Pierce immediately replied that he had consulted seventy-two of 'the better sort of clergy', i.e. hand-picked by himself, who all swore that the wakes, ales, and other church jollifications were perfectly respectable and orderly. 'The true cause of the outcry against them', the Bishop declared, 'was sabbatarianism . . . if people should not have their honest and lawful recreations upon Sundays after evening prayers, they would gather into tipling-houses and there on their ale benches talk matters of Church and State, or else into conventicles . . . By church-ales many poor parishes have cast their bells, repaired their towers, beautified their churches, and raised stock for the poor.'[38]

Richardson was summoned to London and compelled to recant, after being more than half-choked by a pair of lawn sleeves. In tears he informed the Somerset magistrates that although he and Denham sincerely believed that they had only done their duty, yet 'it had been misrepresented to his majesty', and 'I do as much as in me lies, reverse it, declaring the same to be null and void, and that all persons may use their recreations at such meetings as before'.[39] Twenty-five of the magistrates petitioned the King in vain on Richardson's behalf; and on 18 October 1633, Charles re-issued his father's *Declaration of Sports*, to which he added the following command: 'The rather because of late in some counties of our Kingdom, we find that under the pretence of taking away abuses, there has a been general forbidding, not only of ordinary meetings, but of the Feasts of Dedication of the Churches, commonly called Wakes. Now our express will and pleasure is, that these Feasts with others shall be observed. . . . And that publication of this our command be made by order from the Bishops through all the Parish Churches of their several Dioceses respectively'.[40]

The Puritan clergy either evaded or ignored the order. The more timid among them got over the difficulty either by leaving this un-pleasant task to their curates or complied themselves but read the Fourth Commandment immediately afterwards; the more resolute refused point-blank to obey and 'were suspended ab officio et beneficio, some deprived, and more molested in the High Commission; it being questionable, whether their suffering procured more pity to them, or more hatred to the causers thereof'.[41] The bishops as a whole ruthlessly enforced the order, 'laying the publication of this Declaration on the backs of the Ministers'; but, of course, the intensity of the persecution varied in the different dioceses. The Bishops of Norwich and Bath and Wells were two of the worst offenders in this respect; while on the other hand John Davenant of Salisbury frankly refused to report delinquents. 'I will never', he said, 'turn an accuser of my brethren; there be enough in the World to take that office'.[42] Archbishop Abbot had been of the same way of thinking; but he died that year and Laud was enthroned in his room. The battle with the Puritans was to be fully joined. One of the nonconformists indeed commented: 'It was suspicious that now night did approach, because the shadows were so much longer than the body, and ceremonies more in force than the power of godliness'.[43]

The famous Metropolitical Visitation, which covered the years 1633 to 1636, was especially designed to enforce such a uniformity and promote a vigorous and effective discipline of clergy and laity alike. It was conducted by Laud's Vicar-general, Sir Nathaniel Brent, who was also accompanied by the Archbishop's chaplain, Peter Heylin. The actual visitation articles had little new in them; 'but', remarked Heylin,

G

'he [Laud] had given [private] directions to his Vicar General'.[44] These instructed him to see that in all churches the communion table was placed 'where formerly the Altar stood' and securely railed in to prevent any desecration.[45] The Ten Commandments were also to be set up at the east end, together 'with other sentences of Holy Scripture'; the clergy must 'deliver the bread and wine to every communicant severally and kneeling' at the altar rails; and 'as for the duties of the people . . . it was expected at their hands that due and lowly reverence should be made at their first entrance into the Church'.[46] Furthermore Brent was ordered 'to enquire after such impropriations whose cure is not well served', to look into cases of churches ruined by enclosures and schools held in chancels, 'to take order yt the surplis and other decent ceremonyes of the Church be duly used', to restore fonts to their proper place in the church, and 'whereever you fynd the Chancell severed from ye Church or any other waye prophaned, to see it remedyed'.[47]

Brent's Visitation was certainly a very thorough affair; and he insisted throughout upon the need for proper vestments, the full Prayer Book services, the substitution where possible of catechizing in place of the afternoon lecture, the proper repair and re-beautification of the churches, the upkeep of parsonages and the strong fencing of the churchyard 'to keep out swine and other noisome creatures'. In a great many parishes, especially in the eastern counties, he came up against the opposition, active or passive, of the Puritan clergy and their supporters among the laity; but he would brook no interference. In the diocese of Lincoln he began by suspending the Bishop and his six archdeacons from the exercise of their jurisdiction so long as the visitation lasted; at St Mary le Tower in Ipswich he excommunicated the churchwardens because they refused to move the communion table, whose subsequent appeal to the Dean of Arches and in the Star Chamber received no 'remedy from either';[48] and at Boston, a hot-bed of Puritanism, the Vicar and churchwardens were made jointly responsible with the Mayor and Recorder for carrying out his orders. These last included the levelling of the pavement in both the nave and chancel, the rebuilding of the seats, repairs to the exterior of the fabric 'especially the roof and glass windows of the same', the white-washing of the interior and adorning of the walls 'with devout and holy sentences of Scripture . . . divers of which sentences shall tend to the exhortation of the people to obedience to the king's most excellent majesty, his heirs and successors'.[49] The bells were to have new frames and to be rehung; and the churchyard was no longer to be 'profaned by any unclean thing, and shall also be maintained with a strong and sufficient fence to keep out swine and other noisome creatures from digging and rooting up the same'.[50]

Brent's Visitation swept on like a whirlwind from one diocese to another until the whole of the Canterbury province had been covered; but in each case he left the 'follow up' to the diocesan authorities. 'Having given the Charge', wrote Heylin, 'and allowed time to the churchwardens to return a certificate of their doings in pursuance of it, the further execution of it was left to the bishops in their several dioceses';[51] in accordance of course with their zeal or otherwise for the Laudian regime. Some, like Matthew Wren and later Richard Montague of Norwich, were particularly insistent upon enforcing all the Laudian innovations. 'The communion table', Wren declared in 1636, must 'always stand close under the east wall of the chancel, the ends thereof north and south, unless the ordinary give particular direction otherwise, and that the rail be made before it . . . reaching across the north wall, near one yard in height, so thick with pillars, that dogs may not get in'.[52] He also demanded that the daily services should be said in all churches and chapels 'with the tolling of the bell before he [the minister] begins'.[53] 'Doe your parishioners', asked Montague in 1638, 'at their entrance within the Church doores use that comely and decent deportment which is fitting for God's house . . . do they uncover their heads, sit bare all service time, kneele downe in their seates, bowing towards the Chancell and Communion Table, and use those severall postures which fit the several acts and parts of Divine Service?' Did they moreoever 'bend or bow at the glorious sacred and sweet name of Jesus?'[54] At a Synod of his clergy held in Ipswich on 8 October 1639, the same Bishop laid down rules for communicating. All would-be communicants, those over sixteen years, were to enter the chancel, whose door would then be shut in order to prevent the non-communicating 'Boyes, Girles or gazers' from looking on 'as to a Play', and there remain until their dismissal. Here they were formed into ranks, with 'the best of the parish' actually kneeling at the altar rails and the others behind them in order of precedence, while the priest and his assistant (if any) passed to and fro with the sacramental bread and wine.[55]

On the other hand, when the Bishop of Lincoln demurred about compelling communicants to come up to the altar rails, and demanded specific guidance, Laud replied evasively: 'I think for this particular, the people will be best won by the decency of the thing itself; and that I suppose may be compassed in a short time'.[56] Not all bishops, too, were prepared to enforce the command to bow towards the altar. As late, for example, as February 1640 when Ralph Josselin was ordained priest by the Bishop of Peterborough, he could boldly record in his diary: 'I was ordayned minister at Peterburg by ye Bp and 6 ministers: I would not bowe towards the Altar as others did and some followed my example'.[57]

The deluge of Laudian articles that followed in the wake of Brent'

Visitation sought, in fact, to clamp down as rigid a discipline upon the laity as upon the clergy. Churchwardens, sidesmen, parish clerks, sextons, and the parishioners in general all came under their lash. The parish clerk, for instance, was warned not 'to meddle with anything above his office: as churching of women, burying the dead, or such like'; every confirmed person must receive the sacrament at least three times a year and bring their children to be baptized in church at the font; and the churchwardens were ordered to present any unorthodox parsons. 'Doth your minister, curate, or lecturer', they were questioned, 'in his or their sermons deliver such doctrine as tends to obedience and the edifying of their auditory in faith and religion, without intermeddling with matters of state, not fit to be handled in the pulpit, but to be discussed by the wisdom of his majesty and his counsel? And if you find any fault herein you shall present them'.[58] Failure to do so would and did have very serious consequences for the churchwardens themselves.

As a result of this thorough cleansing of the Augean stables the church courts had to deal with a host of presentments. Those that came before the Court of Instance for Leicestershire in 1634, over which Sir John Lambe presided as judge, give a very good example of the kind of thing Nathaniel Brent was trying to suppress or amend. Mr Turnell, Vicar of Horninghold, was accused of 'not building the vicaridge house in such manner as it anciently stood but building it in manner of a cottage not being so wide as it was'; William Staveley of Bowden Magna was presented 'for that one chimney of the parsonage house is blowne downe with the wind and some of the windows want glaseing'; and William Johnson of the same parish 'for railing in the Church porch against the constable and churchwardens and townsmen and threatening the constable that he would have him by the eares'. Mr Thomas Coltman of Newton would not 'receave the communion att the hands of our Minister because he will not give it him standing but kneeling'; while on the other hand Richard Plummer of Evington refused 'to stand up in the time of divine service att the readeing of Glorie be to the Father,' and on being admonished by his vicar, replied: 'he would not observe every order brought in by every fantasticall fellowe'. At Easton Magna a visiting parson had preached 'in his cloake and without a surplisse'; and Mr Lamb, Vicar of Somerby, 'hath not worne the surplis for the space of two years last past but at the time of administration of ye communion'. There were certainly Puritan clergy in plenty who would neither wear the surplice nor use the sign of the cross in baptism; and one of them, James Wood, Vicar of Lockington, was described as 'a great Puritan, all run after him. He was a Taylor or Shoemaker yt could not read his Induction'. Nevertheless none of the clergy, excepting John How the curate of Loughborough, were actually persecuted for their opinions. How was imprisoned because he had publicly prayed that Prince Charles might not be brought up a papist, of which danger he alleged, 'there is a great cause to fear'.

The number of dilapidated churches in Leicestershire appeared to be legion: at Appelby, 'the Church is uncovered and out of repaire'; at Stanton-under-Bardon, 'the chancel is out of repaire'; at Muston, 'the chancel wants repaire in lead and timber'; and 'the Chappell of St Nicholas in Mountsorrel being ruinated and decaied and the chapel yard holden by Francis and the font that was a horse-trough is now made a font again in the nether Chappel in the parish of Barrow'. And so the sorry tale of ruin and neglect went on. The Laudian clergy frequently suffered abuse, if nothing worse, from their puritanical parishioners. At Anstey John Middleton was presented 'for his great and grosse abusinge our painfull orderly and peaceable minister in incivile and scandalous speeches to the disparagement of his ministry'. That was in 1634; but two years later in the same parish the boot was very much on the other foot, when the Reverend Richard Pole was accused of 'striking John Corbett one of the churchwardens with a naked sword many blowes'. At St Mary's Leicester they had not conformed to the Archbishop's Injunction concerning the holy table, and hence the Court decreed: 'that the communion table shall be placed att the upper end of the South Ile uppon the highest ascent there the ends thereof standing North and South and close unto the wall under the great window and the Minister shall administer the communion there and not remove the table from there unto any other pte of the Church'.

There were many cases before the Court of glebe that had been enclosed by the laity and of tithes lost. At Foston, for example, it was said: 'all inclosed by Sir William Fant quaere of ye glebe; a good parsonage but I doubt ye parson hath tithe. Sir Edmund Carter, Bachelor of Arts, instituted and inducted: hath £50 paid him by Sir Wm Fant but no tithe or glebe'. The same story was told of Knaptoft: 'all inclosed by Sir W. Turpin', including apparently the glebe and parsonage itself; while at Shearsby the Rector, Mr More, 'hireth', or so it was reported, 'a house and dwelleth and hath a lease of grownde to stopp his mouth quaere of the glebe'.

The clergy themselves were often far from satisfactory: the curate of Market Harborough had to be dismissed for attending conventicles; the parson of Allerton, Mr Biddle, was described as 'a bold saucey fellow'; and Mr Richardson, Vicar of Garthorpe, 'quarrelled and fought in ye churchyard.' Worse still, the Rector of Shawell, 'beate downe all ye painted glass in ye windowes' and omitted portions of the Prayer Book services.[59]

This policy of 'thorough' was of course especially aimed at the puritanical clergy, both licensed and unlicensed. Professor Norman Sykes has recently pointed out that there is much evidence to show that 'ministers of the foreign reformed churches, presbyterally ordained, were admitted without episcopal reordination to benefice with cure of souls in the Church of England during the three-quarters of a century dividing the accession of Elizabeth I from the Civil War'; and a classical case was that of Dr Peter de Laune, who was instituted by Bishop White of Norwich to the rectory of Redenhall on 2 November 1629. In the Consignation Book of Matthew Wren, de Laune was later described in 1636 as 'ordinatus presbyter per Doctores et Professores Collegii de Leyden, 26 Junii 1599'.[60] Probably Caesar Calindrinus, who was instituted to the rectory of Stapleford Abbotts in Essex on 20 June 1620, was yet another beneficed clergyman in presbyterian orders, who had never received episcopal reordination. No doubt there were others. But it was not this type of man the Archbishop was worrying about so much as the unlicensed Calvinist preacher; and those who 'not being in orders do execute priestly and ministerial office'.[61] Churchwardens were closely questioned: 'Whether do ye see the names of all preachers which are strangers and preach in your parish churches, to be noted in a book for that purpose, and whether every preacher do subscribe his name, and of whom he had his licence'.[62] Such men when caught were severely dealt with. A certain Mr Latropp, for example, was haled before the High Commission, where he confessed that he had never received Anglican orders, declaring defiantly: 'I am a Minister of the Gospell of Christ and the Lord hath qualified me'.[63] And in 1637 Laud made use of the Star Chamber to pass a decree imposing a censorship upon the press, 'to regulate the trade of printing and prevent all abuses of that excellent art, to the disturbance of the Church'.[64]

The weapon, in fact, that he mainly employed for smashing his enemies and enforcing his policies lay in these twin Courts of the Star Chamber and High Commission. If then one takes two periods at random, 1631–2 and 1634–5, during the eleven years of Charles I's personal rule, it is possible to gauge the type of ecclesiastical offender who appeared before these courts and how the Archbishop and his colleagues dealt with them. First, there were those people who caused disturbances in church either in opposition to Laudian divines or in pursuance of their own private vendettas. The incumbent of Sudbury in Suffolk brought a Bill into the Star Chamber during 1631 against certain of his parishioners 'for divers riotts and misdemeanours', in the course of which 'they indeavoured to dispossess the plaintiff because he would not suffer them to receive the Sacrament sitting'; and also indicted them for refusing to kneele at the Sacrament and for throwing 'The holy Sacrament most contemptuously under their feet'.[65] Such insults to God and his own servants Laud had punished by savage penalties both in fines and imprisonments; and even the gentry had to toe the line. When Messrs Young and Broughton quarrelled and fought in Eccleston chapel, Lancs., during a Sunday morning service in May 1631 over which of them should occupy a disputed pew, they too were haled before the Star Chamber, fined a hundred pounds each, and bidden to keep the peace in the future.[66]

Secondly, of course, there were those puritanical ministers who refused to conform: a particularly notorious case was that of Alexander Leighton, which, although it lies outside our selected periods, will be dealt with here in order to illustrate, what is often forgotten, that if Laud became a martyr he had first been a tyrant and a brute. Leighton had written a book entitled: *Sion's Plea against Prelacie* in which he had called the Queen 'the daughter of Heth, a Cannanite and an idolatress'. For this he was seized under a warrant from the High Commission, carried to Newgate, clapped into irons and thrust into a 'loathsome dog-hole, full of rates and mice', with a leaky roof. Here he remained for some fifteen weeks without proper bedding or heating and more than half-starved, until 'his hair and skin came off'. In the meanwhile his house was ransacked, his wife misused, and his children frightened to death. His case was tried before the Star Chamber on 4 June 1630, where, without allowing him to say a single word in his own defence, he was sentenced to be degraded, twice whipped and pilloried, to have both ears cut off and both sides of his nose slit, to be branded in the face with the letters S.S. (sower of sedition), fined £10,000, and imprisoned for life in the Fleet. As this cruel judgment was pronounced Laud pulled off his cap, held up his hands in joy, and 'gave thanks to God who had given him the victory over his enemies'. The sentence was fully carried out and Leighton lay in the Fleet for eleven years until eventually freed by the Long Parliament, when, we are told, 'he could neither walk, see, nor hear'.[67]

Samuel Pretty of St Michael's Pater Noster Royal, London, was degraded and imprisoned because he said: 'Justification and Salvation differ not and that this is the doctrine of the Church of England';[68] John Vicars, who was described as 'vicar of Stamford', was likewise deprived of his living, excommunicated, and degraded for saying in a sermon 'that he that doth not when he may heare two sermons every Sabbath day committeth a greate sinne, and is in the way to fall into the sinne against the holy ghost, and if they were not where two sermons a day were, they were to remove unto another place where they might enjoy a fiery ministry, and that they that neglected this preaching twice a day to their people would never see the greatnesse of their sinne till they fryed in hell for the same'; and referred to those who disagreed with him as 'hell hounds', adding that destruction was their portion.[69]

Dᵣ Laighton, for writing a booke, called Sions
Plea, was first by a warrant from the high-Com:
mission-Court, clapt up in Newgate for the space
of 15 weekes, where hee suffered great miserie
and Sicknes, almost to death, afterward lost
one of his Eares on the pillorie, had one of
his nosthrils slitt clean thorough, was whipt
with a whip of 3 Coardes knotted, had about
36 lashes therwith, was fined 10000. ℔
and kept prisoner in the ffleet 12 yeares,
where hee was most cruelly used a long ti
me, being lodged, day & night amongst the
most desperately wiked villaines, of yᵉ who
le prison.

Vicars was undoubtedly a fanatic. He called all the church ceremonies 'a stinking heap of atheistical and Roman rubbish', and demanded that the nation should 'throw away the rubbish with the Lord's enemies. Vex the Midianites, abolish the Amalekites; let popery find no favour'.[70]

Dr Hooke, Rector of Nettleham, Lincolnshire, was however probably even more reprehensible since, on resigning his archdeaconry, he took it upon himself to abuse his ecclesiastical superiors, calling 'my Lordes the Bishops' by such odious names as 'caperpillars and cancarwormes'.[71] John Bastwick of Colchester was equally outspoken, referring to the prelates as 'Grolls', and remarking scornfully 'that the reverend bishops lived like beasts and drones and that there was more profaneness in their houses than in any temporal lords'.[72]

George Burdett, a lecturer at Yarmouth, was summoned before the High Commission in February 1634/5 on the charge of preaching that the merits of Christ's suffering were limited to a certain number of souls only, 'all others being utterly excluded' and further affirming 'there could be no resemblance or delineation of any of the persons of the Holy Trinity'. A boy, he said, having seen such a picture of God the Father, and later being asked who God was, answered: 'An old fool in heaven with a white beard'. For these sentiments he was deprived of his lectureship, suspended from ministerial functions, ordered to make a public confession of 'his scandalous, blasphemous, erroneous, heretical, and schismatical opinions', and compelled to pay all the costs of the suit.[73]

The manner in which Laud himself used to brow-beat such men, refusing to listen to their arguments and always voting for the maximum penalties, is well brought out in the case of John Etsall, who had boldly defended other already condemned ministers and their unanimous opinion 'God seeth noe sinne in his elect'. After Laud had ranted away for some time attacking Etsall's so-called blasphemies and suggesting that he ought to be sent to Bedlam for having uttered them, the latter mildly interjected: 'I pray speak in love'. He promptly received the furious reply: 'I may censure you to deprivation in love for your base heretical opinions. It is not wont that men should choppe in and talk soe when the Court is speakinge; these are blasphemies . . .I doe deprive him and degrade him, and cost of suit. I goe higher, because he hath contradicted the sentence of this Court against others heeretofore'.[74] Laud's normal attitude towards the clergy was, indeed, so arrogant and autocratic as to be almost papal; and justified Prynne's contention that he had 'trayterously assumed to himselfe a pappall and tyrannicall power both in Ecclesiasticall and Temporall matters'.[75] Dr William Slater, when he appeared before the High Commission, was advised to be more careful in his habit. 'That band', he was told, 'is not fitt for a minister, nor those ruffles up to your elbowes almost'.

Slater humbly pointed out that he was in riding clothes, to which Laud retorted: 'If he sawe him in the like hereafter he would looke out some canon or other to take hauld of him.'[76] Another parson who was arguing a suit about tithes, 'was reprehended for cominge into the Court with his great ruff, ban strings and cloake lyned with velvett'. 'That', Laud declared 'is a great sinne, and will bring down the judgment of God upon the land . . . Minister's cloakes are lyned with vellut or plush, that they may be taken for Noblemen's secretaries, or else for merchants' factors of the best sorte'.[77]

The Puritan laity did not escape. Laymen of Hardwick, Oxon., were accused of 'christening of a catt'[78] and very severely punished; while at Kettering, Northamptonshire, the parishioners were indicted for refusing to kneel or ring the church bells; and also for objecting to Sunday sports, the surplice, and the use of the cross in baptism and the ring in marriage. They were reported to have said that 'all children were within the covenant of God, and were saved though not baptized'; and that 'to bow at the name of Jesus was to bow to five letters . . . it was as lawful to bow at the name of Judas or Satan or the Devil'.[79] The laity for their part frequently had to complain of much overbearing conduct on the side of their ministers. Francis Abbot, Vicar of Poslingford in Suffolk, infuriated his parishioners by his strong words and even stronger actions. From the pulpit one Sunday morning he pointed to Mistress S——, 'wife of one of the chiefest parishioners', and shouted: 'When your husbands are gone abroad you send for your comrades, and then you play the wantons . . . and you are not ashamed to come into the house of God with your whorish face'. On another Sunday morning he stopped in the middle of the service, 'and coming out of his reading desk violently pulled three men off a form at the bottom of the church and carried the form into the chancel'.[80] Anthony Lapthorne, Rector of Tretire in Herefordshire, was if anything even more outspoken, since he announced that those of his flock who had not benefited by his teaching 'were possessed of devils'. He likewise attacked the neighbouring Arminian clergy, referring to them as 'the Great Rabbis, the Great Clergy-monsters, Idol Shepherds, Dumb-dogs and Soul-murtherers, and that their sermons were strawberry sermons and dawbing sermons'.[81]

Many cases that appeared before the High Commission dealt with moral offences or conduct unbecoming a clergyman. Joseph Harrison, Vicar of Sustead in Norfolk, was accused of frequenting alehouses and associating with 'beggars, tinckers, bedlam men and all sorts of people'. It was further alleged that he was often 'soe distempered with drinke that he could not reade divine service'; and among other sins had baptized illegitimate children privately, conducted clandestine marriages, and abused the Bishop of Lichfield. Worse still he was 'a professor of the Art Magick and in particular charmeing of piggs'. Every charge, excluding the last, was proved up to the hilt and he was heavily punished, being deprived, degraded, imprisoned, and excommunicated, fined £50, and compelled to pay all the costs of the suit.[82] Cases of immorality (especially with maidservants), swearing, dishonesty, simony, and similar offences abound in the records of this Court; and it is of interest to note that, as in persecutions under the Commonwealth,[83] there was always a tendency to try to bolster up attacks on so-called heretical opinions by including charges of a purely moral nature. These latter were often far from proven, yet were frequently punished most cruelly and unjustly by both these arbitrary and prerogative courts.

Laud's policy of 'Thorough' came to a head with the celebrated Canons of 1640, by which he sought to secure a solid legal basis for his innovations and at the same time clamp down his ecclesiastical system once and for all upon clergy and laity alike.[84] Herein it was categorically laid down that all resistance to one's lawful prince 'upon any pretence whatsoever', was not only treasonable, but literally damnable; and any clergyman who refused to take the highly controversial *et caetera* oath, contained in Canon 6, could first be suspended *ab officio* and then, if he remained obstinate, be finally deprived. The bishops were ordered to administer this oath before ordination, and licensing a cleric to preach or serve a cure.[85] By Canon 7 the placing of the holy table 'where the altar stood', the railing of it in, and the practices of kneeling there for communion and bowing to the altar when entering or leaving the church, were all confirmed.[86] Other Canons dealt with clerical behaviour, chancellors' patents, episcopal censures, absolutions for excommunications, penances etc. Twice a year each incumbent had to instruct his people 'that the rites and ceremonies in the Church of England were lawful and commendable; and that the people ought not only to conform themselves to those rites and ceremonies: but cheerfully to submit themselves unto the government of the Church as it was then established under his Majesty'.[87] The Archbishop rushed these Canons through Convocation in his usual high-handed manner; but they were never accepted by Parliament; and Prynne was perfectly right when he asserted that Laud had 'caused a booke of Canons to be composed and published without any lawfull warrant and authoritie in that behalfe'.[88]

A contemporary ballad of 1635 entitled *The New Churchman* sums up not unfairly what the great majority of Englishmen thought about the Laudian regime and the Laudian clergyman.

> A ceremonious, light-timbred scholler,
> With a little dam-mee[89] peeping over his coller;
> With a Cardinal's cap, broad as a carte wheele,
> With a long coate and cassocke down to his heele.

With long haire and a short grace,
Which, being sharpe set, he snaps up apace,
And after dinner, such a little touch——
His belly is so full he cannot say much.

His gavity rides up and downe
In a long coate or a shorte gown;
And swears, by the halfe-football on his pate,
That no man is predestinate.

His Divinity is trust up with five points,
He drops, ducks, bowes, as made all of joints;
But when his Romane nose stands full East,
He feares neither God nor beast.

He hopes to be saved by prevision
Of good workes, but will do none;
He will be no Protestant, but a Christian,
And comes out Catholike the next edition.

Some halfe-dozen benefices gone downe his gullet,
Yet he gapes as though his belly were not full yet;
And sure his Curate must be turned away,
If he chance to preach twice a day.

On fasting nights, he hath a collation;
And on Sundayes a great preparation
Of cardes, dice and high joviality
And all to confute the formality.[90]

Laud wrote in his diary on Saturday 17 August, 1633: 'I had a serious offer made me again to be a Cardinal. . . . But my answer again was, that somewhat dwelt within me, which would not suffer that, till Rome were other than it is'.[91] Protestant England would certainly never have believed him. Prynne declared: 'Hee hath traiterously and wickedly endeavoured to reconcile the Church of England with the Church of Rome';[92] and a libel pinned on the south gate of St Paul's Cathedral on 23 August 1637, announced that 'the Devil had left that house to him for the saying of Mass'.[93] Another fastened to the north gate two days later affirmed 'That the Government of the Church of England is a candle in the snuff, going out in a stench'.[94]

NOTES

[1] *Correspondence of John Cosin* (Surtees Society), Vol. I, p. 82.
[2] Fighting parsons alas still abounded. The Rector of Towersey, Oxon., Richard Jones, was presented in May 1609 as 'both a quarreler, a fighter and

a drunkard in publicke places upon Common fame'. See Oxfordshire
Record Society, Vol. 10, p. 195.

[3] Mrs Thomas Eyres of Nettlebed, Oxon., was presented in 1626 because
she had 'abused our Minister Mr Sheppard in her speeches which she spake
of him that he was a divell and not a Minister, and that when he should die,
he was such a troublesome man none should be troubled to bury him for the
devill would fetch him away'. Oxfordshire Record Society, Vol. 10, p. 49.

[4] *Correspondence of John Cosin*, Vol. I, pp. 107–23.

[5] 'After the Kalendar it began with a Specification of the Apostles Creed
in Twelve Articles, the Lords Prayer in Seven Petitions, the Ten Commandments, with the Duties enjoined, and the Sins prohibited by them; the
Precepts of charity, the Precepts of the Church, the Seven Sacraments, the
Three Theological Virtues, the Three kinds of Good Works, the Seven
Gifts of the Holy Ghost, the Twelve Fruits of the Holy Ghost, the Spiritual
and Corporate Works of Mercy, the Eight Beatitudes, Seven Deadly Sins,
and their contrary Vertues.' P. Heylin, *Cyprianus Anglicus*, p. 173. It also
contained forms of prayer for the canonical hours, prayers for sickness,
death, and preparatory to receiving communion, the Litany and seven
penitential psalms.

[6] Heylin, *Cyprianus Anglicus*, p. 173.

[7] Heylin, *Cyprianus Anglicus*, p. 22.

[8] Heylin, *Cyprianus Anglicus*, p. 171.

[9] B. Drew Roberts, *Mitre and Musket*, pp. 136–8.

[10] Heylin, *Cyprianus Anglicus*, p. 171.

[11] *The Works of William Laud*, Vol. V, Part II, pp. 307, 308.

[12] John Selden, *Table Talk*, p. 75.

[13] *Annals of Evangelical Nonconformity*, p. 153.

[14] B. Brook, *The Lives of the Puritans*, Vol. III, pp. 65–6.

[15] Cardwell, *Documentary Annals*, Vol. II, pp. 177–84. Many wealthy
puritan laymen employed private chaplains who were then largely independent of the bishops.

[16] See Isabel Calder, *The Activities of the Puritan Faction of the Church of
England: 1625–1633*, p. xv.

[17] Fuller, *Church History*, Vol. III, pp. 407 and 417.

[18] Heylin, *Cyprianus Anglicus*, p. 211.

[19] Neal, *History of the Puritans*, Vol. II, p. 201. See also, Calder, *Activities
of the Puritan Faction*, p. xv. It should be noted that all the revenues were to
be restored to perpetual incumbents. Haller, *Liberty and Reformation in the
Puritan Revolution*, pp. 11–13 sums up the situation succinctly.

[20] This case was decided before the King in Council in November, 1633.
See, Heylin, *Cyprianus Anglicus*, p. 257.

[21] For these Reports see *Works of William Laud*, Vol. V, Part II, pp.
318–70. Sir John Lamb and Dr Robert Sibthorp had once pressed Williams
to take action against some Puritans in Leicestershire, describing them as
men who, although they would not 'swear, whore nor be drunk, yet . . . lie,
cozen and deceive'. Williams refused, remarking unguardedly: 'the Puritans
are the King's best subjects, and . . . will carry all at last'. See Neal, *History of
the Puritans*, Vol. II, p. 153; and Roberts, *Mitre and Musket*, p. 115.

[22] William Prynne, *Canterburies Doome*, pp. 93–4.

[23] Heylin, *Cyprianus Anglicus*, pp. 289 and 312.

[24] Somerset Record Society, Vol. 43, p. 185.

[25] Somerset Record Society, Vol. 43, pp. 183–6. See also Prynne, *Canterburies Doome*, pp. 90–100.

[26] *Works of William Laud*, Vol. V, Part II, pp. 327 and 349.

[27] *Proceedings principally in the County of Kent*, (Camden Society), p. 126.

[28] *Proceedings, . . . County of Kent*, pp. 150, 239.

[29] *Proceedings, . . . County of Kent*, p. 153.

[30] *Proceedings, . . . County of Kent*, p. 178.

[31] *Proceedings, . . . County of Kent*, pp. 154, 179.

[32] Peterborough Diocesan Records (Lamport Hall MSS). *Church Survey Books*, Vol. I.

[33] Peterborough Diocesan Records, Vol. IV.

[34] Essex Record Society, Vol. 17, Vol. I, p. 72.

[35] Peterborough Diocesan Records, Vol. IV.

[36] Peterborough Diocesan Records, Vol. IV.

[37] Oxfordshire Record Society, Vol. 10, p. 245.

[38] See Prynne, *Canterburies Doome*, p. 151; H. R. Trevor-Roper, *Archbishop Laud*, p. 157.

[39] Neal, *History of the Puritans*, Vol. II, pp. 212–15; Heylin, *Cyprianus Anglicus*, pp. 255–7.

[40] Whitaker, *Sunday in Tudor and Stuart Times*, p. 126; Cardwell, *Documentary Annals*, Vol. II, p. 193.

[41] Fuller, *Church History*, p. 424.

[42] Heylin, *Cyprianus Anglicus*, p. 295.

[43] Fuller, *Church History*, p. 428.

[44] Heylin, *Cyprianus Anglicus*, p. 285.

[45] The Archbishop had heard terrible stories of dogs that had run off with the sacramental bread, and communion wine that had been 'brought unto the Table in many places in Pint-pots and Bottles, and so distributed to the people'. Heylin, *Cyprianus Anglicus*, p. 285.

[46] Heylin, *Cyprianus Anglicus*, p. 17. See also, *Works of William Laud*, Vol. V, Part II, pp. 422–3 and 427.

[47] *65th Report of the Associated Architectural Societies*, Vol. XXIX, Part II, 'Leicestershire: The Metropolitical Visitation of Archbishop Laud', p. 485.

[48] Heylin, *Cyprianus Anglicus*, p. 314.

[49] *Works of William Laud*, Vol. V, Part II, pp. 499–500.

[50] *Works of William Laud*, p. 500.

[51] Heylin, *Cyprianus Anglicus*, p. 287.

[52] Cardwell, *Documentary Annals*, Vol. II, p. 252.

[53] Prynne, *Canterburies Doome*, p. 97.

[54] Prynne, *Canterburies Doome*, pp. 94–6.

[55] Prynne, *Canterburies Doome*, p. 100. See also Heylin, *Cyprianus Anglicus*, p. 366.

[56] *Works of William Laud*, Vol. V, Part II, p. 343.

[57] *Diary of the Revd. Ralph Josselin*, ed. E. Hockliffe (Camden Society), p. 8.

[58] *Works of William Laud*, Vol. V, Part II, pp. 427; 428–33.
[59] See *65th Report of the Associated Architectural Societies*, Vol. XXIX, Part II, pp. 487–519.
[60] N. Sykes, *Old Priest and New Presbyter*, pp. 87–93.
[61] *Works of William Laud*, Vol. V, Part II, p. 433.
[62] *Works of William Laud*, Vol. V, Part II, p. 433.
[63] *Reports of Cases in the Courts of Star Chamber and High Commission* (Camden Society), ed. S. R. Gardiner, p. 281
[64] Heylin, *Cyprianus Anglicus*, pp. 362–3.
[65] *Reports of Cases in the Courts of Star Chamber*, p. 72.
[66] *Reports of Cases in the Courts of Star Chamber*, pp. 139–44.
[67] Brook, *Lives of the Puritans*, Vol. II, pp. 476–85; Neal, *History of the Puritans*, Vol. II, pp. 188–90; Heylin, *Cyprianus Anglicus*, p. 198.
[68] *Reports of Cases in the Courts of Star Chamber*, p. 182.
[69] *Reports of Cases in the Courts of Star Chamber*, pp. 200–1.
[70] Brook, *Lives of the Puritans*, Vol. III, p. 143.
[71] *Reports of Cases in the Courts of Star Chamber*, p. 249.
[72] *Calendar of State Papers Domestic: Charles I*, 1634–35, p. 547.
[73] *State Papers Domestic*, 1634–35, pp. 537–9.
[74] *Reports of Cases in the Courts of Star Chamber*, pp. 316–21.
[75] Prynne, *Canterburies Doome*, p. 26.
[76] *Reports of Cases in the Courts of Star Chamber*, p. 186.
[77] *Reports of Cases in the Courts of Star Chamber*, p. 303.
[78] *Reports of Cases in the Courts of Star Chamber*, p. 275.
[79] *State Papers Domestic*, 1634–35, pp. 410–11.
[80] *State Papers Domestic*, 1634–35, pp. 319–20; he was suspended and imprisoned.
[81] *State Papers Domestic*, 1634–35, p. 263; he was deprived and degraded.
[82] *Reports of Cases in the Courts of Star Chamber*, p. 271.
[83] See Chapter V.
[84] Up till now many Laudian practices had no real authority behind them; bowing to the altar for example: 'for this neither rule nor rubric could be shown'. See Marsden, *History of the Early Puritans*, p. 371.
[85] He had to swear to accept 'the discipline and government in the Church of England, as containing all things necessary to salvation; and that I will not ever give my consent to alter the government of the church by archbishops, bishops, deans and archdeacons et caetera, and as by right it ought to stand'. *Annals of Evangelical Nonconformity*, pp. 86–7.
[86] Heylin, *Cyprianus Anglicus*, pp. 435–6.
[87] Heylin, *Cyprianus Anglicus*, p. 437.
[88] Prynne, *Canterburies Doome*, p. 26.
[89] A soldier's oath: God damn me.
[90] *Diary of John Rous*, ed. M. A. E. Green (Camden Society), pp. 78–9.
[91] *Works of William Laud*, Vol. III. p. 219.
[92] Prynne, *Canterburies Doome*, p. 27.
[93] Heylin, *Cyprianus Anglicus*, p. 359.
[94] *Works of William Laud*, Vol. III, p. 229.

The Sufferings of the Clergy

WITH THE TRIUMPH OF the Long Parliament over Strafford and Laud, the outbreak of Civil War, the abolition of the episcopate, and the eventual establishment first of the Commonwealth and then the Protectorate, the high church and loyalist clergy certainly suffered very severely indeed; although out of about 8,600 incumbents only some 2,425 were actually evicted. It has been estimated that at the height of the Laudian regime in 1640 there were no more than 4,000 genuine high church clergy, about 1,000 fanatical Puritans, and the rest middle-of-the-road men who had not identified themselves with either party.[1] On the other hand it has to be admitted that the mass of the laity were much more protestant than their clergy, had little sympathy with Laudian ideals, and greatly dreaded a re-introduction of popery. As soon as people realized in fact that the tide had turned and the King and Archbishop were no longer all-powerful, a flood of petitions, headed by one from London signed by more than 15,000 persons and seconded by those 'of many whole Counties and Populous Cities',[2] notably from Kent, Essex, and Lincolnshire, began to pour into the House of Commons demanding redress against the so-called 'popish practices' of the more Catholic clergy and asking for the restitution of those Puritan ministers whom Laud and his satellites had deprived. The Lincoln petition, for example, complained of 'the increase of Popery, the renewing of idle and frivolous ceremonies, and the canons . . . and some severe law might be enacted against the profanation of the Lords day';[3] while that from Norfolk wanted certain nonconformist clergy restored to office. The Reverend Paul Amarent of Wolterton, for instance, had been suspended after a visitation of Bishop Wren's in 1636 because he had referred to Sunday as the Sabbath and refused to bow 'att the name of Jesus'; so too had Henry Wilkinson, a lecturer, 'for a sermon against lukewarmness'; and an ordination candidate, Henry Langly, when he presented himself to the Bishop of Oxford, had been rejected on the plea that his answers to the following questions were unsatisfactory: 'Whether the Booke of Sportes be allowable; whether bowing towards the altar be superstitious; whether the Church have power to determine matters of fayth'. 'These questions', the bishop's chaplain declared, 'were as a shibboleth to determine who were fitt for orders, and who unfitt'.[4]

So numerous indeed were these petitions from clergy and laity alike that Parliament was obliged to set up a Grand Committee of Religion

A
REMONSTRANCE
AGAINST THE
NON·RESIDENTS
of great Brittaine :
OR
Non-Residency condemned by Scrip-
ture, by strength of Arguments, by Fathers,
Councels, Canon-Law, by the Iudgement of
Reverend and Learned Divines.

THE CARELESSE NON=RESIDENT.

I would I had

LONDON,
Printed by *T. Badger*, for *Rich. Royston*, dwelling in
Ivy-lane, 1642.

The careless non-resident

H

to deal with them, which very quickly appointed sub-committees such as the Committee for Deprived Clergymen and the Committee for Scandalous Clergymen; and these bodies, according to Heylin, 'finding . . . that Informations came not up so fast as had been expected, despatched instructions into all parts of the Kingdom for an enquiry to be made into the Lives and Actions of the Clergy in their several Parishes'.[5] Later the most important religious committees were those for Plundered Ministers, Compounding, and the Trustees for Maintenance of Ministers. When Oliver Cromwell ejected the Rump Parliament in 1653 all these committees ceased to function except the last, and he appointed his own commissioners in their place. Such were the tribunals that took over much of the administration of ecclesiastical affairs from the bishops: they deprived those incumbents whom they pronounced malignant, scandalous, or inefficient; examined the fitness of ministers to hold livings; appointed to vacant benefices; administered church property; augmented the stipends of the underpaid; and enforced the suppression of the Prayer Book. They were not concerned, however, with distinctly spiritual matters. On 12 June 1643 the Westminster Assembly of Divines was called into being: 'to confer and treat amongst themselves, of such matters and things touching and concerning the Liturgy, Discipline and Government of the Church of England'; and, as a result of their deliberations, *An Ordinance for the Form of Church Government* was promulgated in August 1648 which declared: 'That all Parishes and places whatsoever within the Kingdom of England and Dominion of Wales . . . be brought under the Government of Congregational, Classical, Provincial and National Assemblies . . . Divine duties to be performed according to the Directory and not otherwise'.[6] The Church system thus introduced represented, of course, a triumph for Presbyterianism, with the congregational eldership ruling the parish as the unit of society, while the National Assembly directed the religious life of the nation as a whole. Ordinations and institutions were carried out by the classical presbyteries, who examined all candidates, assuring themselves that they had taken the Solemn League and Covenant, possessed both 'the Grace of God' and a 'call' to the ministry, and wielded the necessary power 'to defend the orthodox doctrine'. Before entering upon his ministry each aspirant had to preach before the classis and his intended flock on three successive days; then, if no exception was taken against him, he would be ordained in the church he was to serve.[7] Nevertheless, the presbytery began to decay almost as soon as it got into its stride, owing partly to the opposition of an Erastian Parliament and Independent Army, and partly to the passive hostility of the mass of the laity. Presbyterianism and Independency could and did exist side by side; but the final triumph of the Army dealt a deathblow to the former's discipline, without which it was not able to maintain its supremacy. As a result, from 1653 onwards, there grew up in its place what became known as the Voluntary Associations, which largely took over the functions of the classis.

On the whole it would be true to say that the clerical sequestrations and evictions removed most of the extreme high church men and actively royalist Anglicans, but left the Calvinists, vicars of Bray, and in fact all those who either supported Parliament against the King or remained quiescent. It is, however, noteworthy that a number of men were deprived for purely moral offences quite irrespective of their party allegiance. Episcopal ordination went on in secret. Bishop Skinner of Oxford claimed to have conferred priests' orders on between 4,000 and 5,000 candidates, while others were ordained by Brownrig of Exeter or one of the Irish bishops; and many of these men found ways and means of getting past the parliamentary committees into benefices. All this made the return to episcopacy easy; and was the principal reason why, when the period of testing came after the Restoration, so few ministers refused to conform. It must not be forgotten either of course that, as in the case of many other temporarily successful revolutions, there were very large numbers of 'collaborators', and rightly so; for the work of the Church as a whole had to be carried on and far-seeing men, recognizing that the present regime was most insecure, quietly waited on better days. Meanwhile by their very existence they put a brake on puritanical zeal and hampered all radical attempts at change.

These attempts were certainly determined and widespread. First, every effort was made to abolish so-called ceremonies and innovations, nd to destroy sculptured figures and other marks of 'superstition' in parish churches. As early as 8 September 1641, the House of Commons had ordered the churchwardens to remove the communion table from the east end to the body of the church, destroy the rails, and level the chancel. All 'crucifixes, scandalous pictures of one or more Persons of the Trinity', together with images of the Virgin Mary and 'tapers, candlesticks, and basons' on the altar were to be swept away; while bowing at the Name of Jesus or towards the east end must be 'forborne'.[8] Two years later a further Ordinance demanded 'the utter demolishing, removing, and taking away of all Monuments of Superstition'; and this was reinforced in May 1644 by another which included 'Copes, Surplisses, superstitious vestments, roods or roodlons, or Holy-water Fonts'.[9] *The Journal of William Dowsing* describes how he and his fellow commissioners blazed a trail of ruin across Cambridgeshire and Suffolk during the years 1643 to 1644 in accordance with such instructions. A typical entry in the diary is that of 6 January 1643/4, when the visitors reached the parish church of Clare: 'We brake down 1000 Pictures superstitious; I brake, down 200; 3 of God the Father and 3 of Christ, and the Holy Lamb, and 3 of the Holy Ghost like a Dove with Wings; and the 12 Apostles were carved in Wood, on the top of the Roof, which we gave order to take down; and 20 Cherubims to be taken down; and the Sun and Moon in the East Window, by the King's Arms, to be taken down'.[10] He visited one hundred and fifty places in Suffolk in less than fifty days and everywhere the work of destruction went merrily on, despite occasional obstruction. At Ufford on 31 August Dowsing recorded: 'And we were kept out of the Church above 2 hours, and neither Churchwardens, William Brown nor Roger Small, that were enjoined these things above three months afore, had done them in May and I sent one of them to see it done, and they would not let him have the key. And now, neither the Churchwardens, nor William Brown, nor Constable James Tokelove, and William Gardner, the Sexton, would not let us have the key in 2 hours time'. Nevertheless even Dowsing could appreciate real beauty when he saw it; for in this self-same church of Ufford, after remarking 'we brake down the Organ cases and gave them to the Poor', he reported: 'There is a glorious Cover over the Font, like a Pope's Tripple Crown, and a Pelican on the Top, picking its Breast, all gilt over with Gold', and it was spared.[11]

Richard Baxter, the puritanical Vicar of Kidderminster, left the destruction of crosses and images in his church to the churchwardens, who experienced great difficulty in carrying out their task. 'A crew of the riotous party of the town (poor journeymen and servants)', Baxter wrote, 'took the alarm, and run together with weapons to defend the crucifix and the church images'; later they sought to kill the Vicar himself as the supposed author of this demolition.[12] There is a strong tradition that the parishioners of Blatherwycke in Northamptonshire barricaded themselves into their church and stood a siege rather than allow the images to be broken. Certainly the opposition to such vandalism must have been widespread, if unorganized, and reflected the stubborn conservatism of the countryman in religious matters.

The fabric of the churches themselves and the tombs of the laity were always scrupulously respected; but communion tables were ruthlessly removed from the east end, the rails taken down, and steps levelled. In March 1646/7 an Ordinance was made to provide for the repair of churches. The churchwardens were instructed 'to make rates or assessments of every inhabitant dwelling in the parish' and to use the money for the maintenance of church and churchyard, besides supplying books for the services and bread and wine for the sacrament. Little, however, was done. It is interesting to note in passing that despite the political and religious upheavals of the time the course of parochial administration apparently flowed on much as ever before. The churchwardens were annually elected, assessed the rates at Easter, and carefully kept their accounts, which unlike the church registers present a continuous and unbroken record.[13]

Secondly, the puritanical afternoon lectureships that had been either abolished, curtailed, or reformed under the Laudian regime, were now restored in all their pristine glory, and the incumbent obliged to grant the preacher the use of his pulpit. 'The preaching of God's word', declared the Commons, must be permitted 'in the several Churches and Chappels of this Kingdom, and the Ministers and Preachers be encouraged thereunto'.[14] This frequently led to clashes between lecturers and the parish clergy, as for example at Pinner in Middlesex, where in 1643 the House of Commons was informed that the curate, to elude the order, preached himself every Sunday afternoon until 6 p.m, and so kept the Puritan out.[15] William Spalden, who was appointed lecturer at Saffron Walden, Essex, was expected 'to preach a weekly lecture on such day of the week as the parishioners shall agree upon, and also on every Lord's day in the afternoon'; while it was ordered 'the vicar and all other persons should permit him to preach there without interruption'.[16] The object of such lectures was, of course, political as well as religious, since they provided an antidote to the preaching of the royalists.

Thirdly, the Prayer Book was superseded by the *Directory of Public Worship* in January, 1644/5.[17] 'Long and sad experience', declared the Preface to this Ordinance, 'hath made it manifest; That the Leiturgie used in the Church of England ... hath proved an offence not only to many of the Godly at home; but also to the Reformed Churches abroad', partly because the Book itself contained 'many unprofitable and burdensome Ceremonies', and partly due to the 'prelates and their faction' who 'have laboured to raise the Estimation of it to such an height, as if there were no other Worship or way of Worship of God amongst us, but onely the Service-Book; to the great hindrance of the Preaching of the Word, and ... to the Justling of it out, as unnecessary; or (at best) as far inferiour to the Reading of Common-Prayer, which was made no better then an Idol by many Ignorant and Superstitious People, who pleasing themselves in their presence at that Service, and their Lip-labour in bearing a part in it, have thereby hardened themselves in their ignorance and carelessness of saving knowledge and true piety'. Herein lay the core of puritanical hatred against the Book of Common Prayer. Every effort was now made to see that this suppression was absolute: 'If any persons', it was laid down, 'whatsoever shall at any time or times hereafter use, or cause the aforesaid book of Common Prayer to be used in any Church, Chappell, or publique place of worship, or in any private place or family ... every such person so offending therein shall for the first offence forfeit and pay the sum of five pounds of lawful English money, for the second offence the sum of ten pounds, and for the third offence shall suffer one whole year's imprisonment without bail or mainprize'.[18] Nevertheless the Prayer Book continued to be used extensively in private, and occasionally boldly in public. Robert Sanderson, later Bishop of Lincoln, while at Boothby Pagnell, Lincolnshire, openly conducted public worship from its pages until it was torn out of his hands by a troop of soldiers.[19]

Fourthly, each congregational eldership now had the power to enquire into the spiritual well-being of its members, to admonish the backward, to suspend and even excommunicate the 'unworthy'. The elders could actually suspend the minister himself from communion, prior to his trial before the classis, on such charges as unbecoming conduct, unsound doctrine, or simony. Admission to the Sacrament was indeed a jealously guarded privilege and would be refused not only to the doctrinally unsound, but to the 'scandalous', 'idolatrous', and 'sabbath-breakers' as well.[20]

Fifthly, although, once the fighting had subsided, the rights of private patrons to appoint to livings in their gift was not interfered with, unless they were recognized delinquents or Roman Catholics, in practice the local sequestration committees often had the last word, after consulting the parishes concerned; while the parishioners themselves frequently 'usurped' the right to appoint directly in the case of episcopal or Crown livings. The Committee for Plundered Ministers had the power of nomination to certain sequestered benefices, the Trustees for Maintenance to those livings that formed part of the trust they were administering, i.e Dean and Chapter patronage and some episcopal rectories, and the Commissioners of the Great Seal to part of the royal patronage. Cromwell took over most of the last when the Protectorate was formed. Patronage was, in fact, as widely diversified as ever; but its boundaries were no longer so cut and dried, producing a fluid situation that enabled some royalists to creep back into parsonages.

Once the nomination had been made, the selected candidate was expected to be examined first by the local classis and then by the Westminster Assembly of Divines as to his fitness to serve the cure. But as the presbyterian system began to decay such scrutinies could often be avoided altogether; and provided the Solemn League and Covenant was accepted, a nominee might often, at any rate in the case of private patronage, enter upon his ministry without further trial. In March 1653/4 Cromwell appointed the Triers, who took over from the Assembly of Divines, and from then onwards each applicant was considered as 'a person for the grace of God in him, his holy and un-blameable conversation, as also for his knowledge and utterance, and fit to preach the Gospel'.[21] They were certainly a very conscientious and broad-minded body of men who admitted Presbyterians, Baptists,

Independents, and sometimes even Anglicans to livings, provided they were satisfied of their suitability in other respects.

Finally, at the outbreak of the Civil War ecclesiastical property was seized wherever possible and applied 'to the use, and for the maintaining of the army and forces raised by the Parliament'.[22] Later, in 1646 and 1649, Acts were passed authorizing the sale of episcopal and cathedral lands, with the avowed purpose of perpetuating the overthrow of the Anglican hierarchy.[23] Neither tithes nor first fruits and tenths were abolished, much as some of the Puritans would have liked to do so. The Commonwealth was too poor to afford such luxuries; and indeed was compelled to augment clergy stipends from other sources, notably by the sale of sequestered royalist estates and capitular lands. The Trustees for Maintenance sought to bring up the average income to £100; but in order to do so they, and later Cromwell, were compelled to unite certain parishes—another bugbear of the nonconformist,[24] who in the first flush of his triumph had abolished pluralities altogether.

> 'Bigamy of steeples is a hanging matter;
> Each must have one and curates will grow fatter.'

We now come to the sad story of the evictions themselves, which began late in 1642 and continued during the following years, the reasons put forward to justify them, and the consequences that sprang directly out of them.

As regards the accusations brought against the clergy to justify their removal, we must be careful to distinguish between the purely political, doctrinal, and malicious, and those moral offences to which alas the clergy of the period were undoubtedly only too prone. The tendency unfortunately amongst royalist apologists is to regard all the evicted as martyrs irrespective of their offences; and when an historian of sense and sensibility like Tom Fuller frankly admitted that many of the clergy were no better than they should be, he called down upon his head a load of brickbats. Speaking in 1643 he had declared: 'their offences were so foul, it is a shame to report them'; for which remark he was belaboured by Laud's ex-chaplain, Peter Heylin. 'It concerns our author', the latter wrote, 'to be sure of this, that all things be well at home, both in his own person and in his family before he throws so much foul dirt in the face of his brethren'.[25] Fuller, who was never a Laudian but always a stout King's man, retorted that he must needs 'acknowledge what indeed could not be concealed, and what indeed must be confessed, viz., that some of the ejected clergy were guilty of foul offences; to whom, and to whom alone, the name of Baal and "unsavoury salt" '; and added: 'Nor was it a wonder if, amongst ten thousand and more, some were guilty of scandalous enormities'. Yet he readily enough agreed that some had been charged with idolatry 'whose positions were sound', and others simply 'for their affections to the king's cause'; and so, he concluded, although 'many scandalous ministers' were 'deservedly punished', 'the veins of the English church were also emptied of much good blood'.[26]

The kind of charge in fact that was likely to be brought against the high church clergy had already been foreshadowed in the petitions which came before the parliamentary sub-committee of Religion set up in 1640 under the chairmanship of Sir Edward Dering. These included moving the holy table to the east end, railing it in, and compelling all communicants to kneel there in order to receive the sacrament; demanding that every worshipper should bow to the altar and at the name of Jesus, and to stand up and turn to the east for the Creed and the Gloria Patri; advocating auricular confession; permitting lay baptism in an emergency; and deprecating excessive preaching or the doctrines of election and predestination. Dr Meric Casaubon of Minster in Kent, for example, together with his curate, was accused of being 'zealously observant of all innovations, as bowing and cringeing to the Communion table . . . because the Sacrament was there administrede'. He had also apparently railed in the table at his own charge 'and sett it close to the wall, at the east end of the Chancel, altarwise . . . and hath cutt and defaced the Chancell in many things . . . and threatened your humble suppliants, that, if they would not come upp to the rayle to receive the Communion they should answere it before the Lord Archbishop at the Highe Commission; for feare whereof the greatest part of your peticioners to the great griefe of their consciences did goe up to the rayle to receive'.[27] Dr Vane of Crayford had preached 'that it was necessary for every man to confesse his sinnes to the Preist', spoken against predestination, and declared 'that those children which dyed before they were baptized could not be saved, and therefore in case of necessity, laymen or midwyfes might baptize, the minister or preist being absent'. At communion, while consecrating the bread and wine, he had dared to lift them up and bow three times.[28] It was reported of Edward Boughen of Woodchurch that he perambulated round his parish at Easter 'in his surplesse and hood, reading prayers and psalmes at divers crosse wayes, and digging crosses in the earth at divers places of the bounds of the same'. He likewise said 'that Bishops are the head of the Church next under God and Christ'.[29] Jeffrey Amherst, Rector of Horsmonden, indulged, or so his detractors asserted, in every kind of 'popish practice'. Over his altar were the words: 'Wee have an Altar whereof they have no right to eate which serve the Tabernacle'; and he referred scornfully to those of his parishioners who would not come up to the rails to receive as 'itching Puritans'.[30] And so the sorry tale was told of parson after parson in the fair land of Kent. William Gervis, Vicar of Sturry, actually dared to possess 'a large Crucifix painted, in a frame, hanginge in his parlour'.[31]

Some puritanically-minded congregations, without awaiting parliamentary action, took the law boldly into their own hands: William Skynner and Jeremy Reeve went into the parish church of Latton, Essex, one Sunday morning after the service and pulled down the communion rails 'with their hands only' and cast them over the churchyard wall onto the highway 'because they gave offence' to their consciences;[32] John Pool of Halstead, Essex, went into the church on Sunday morning, 28 October 1640, during the service, took the clerk, William Till, by the throat and 'compelled him to go into the vestry, and give up the surplice and the hood', which were immediately torn to pieces. Meanwhile another man, Robert Howard, 'rushed up to the desk where Mr Carter, the curate, was reading the baptismal service at the font, struck the prayer book out of his hand and, with several others, kicked it about, saying "it was a popish book" ';[33] and at Rolvenden the Vicar, Thomas Higginson, had the mortification of standing impotently by and seeing his churchwardens 'takeinge out the Communion Table from the aulter rayle' and 'causeinge it to be sett in the most convenient place in the chancell, where it formerly stood'.[34]

Another and most unjust complaint made against the Laudian clergy was that many of them were pluralists; but this only too often was an economic necessity. Edward Nichols, incumbent of Northbourne cum Sholden in Kent, when he heard that he might be deprived of the latter living, wrote to Sir Edward Dering in the most pitiable and heart-rending terms. 'If I loose Sholden', he concluded, 'perii, I am undone, and my wife and children'.[35] Eventually, as has already been seen, the Roundheads themselves were obliged to unite small benefices.

When Civil War broke out numbers of the clergy fled from their livings to royalist strongholds like Oxford, Ashby-de-la-Zouch, Newark-on-Trent, Belvoir Castle, or Exeter. Some of these served as army chaplains, like Jeremy Taylor and Tom Fuller; and a few, such as the celebrated Michael Hudson, Rector of King's Cliffe and the original of Dr Rochecliffe in Walter Scott's novel *Woodstock*, actually bore arms. The clergy as a whole certainly showed enormous courage on the King's behalf: Thomas Jones of Offwell in Devon received a doctorate from Oxford in recognition of the fact that he was the reputed cause of Waller's defeat at Devizes;[36] Thomas Newcomen of Holy Trinity, Colchester, assisted Sir John Lucas in raising forces for the King, a proceeding that led to a riot at Colchester in August 1642; and later was accused of escorting a convoy of horses and ammunition to the cavaliers of Nottingham;[37] and the pugnacious and irrepressible Dr Matthew Griffith, Rector of Bladon, Oxfordshire, helped to defend Basing House, where his daughter lost her life. Beaumont of

Pontefract was tried and executed by the Roundheads for the part he played in the capture of that castle. 'That part of the army before Pomfrett', wrote Ralph Josselin on 25 February 1649, 'hanged a Minister, a Cavalier; they condemned him for holding intelligence with the enemy in the Castle, and that he had a hand in betraying the same'.[38] Beaumont was not the only Anglican parson to be hanged for serving the royal cause. Thomas Cooper, Rector of Edgefield and schoolmaster at Holt in Norfolk, was strung up in front of his own school door towards the end of 1650 'for being concern'd in a Rising in favour of his Majesty'.[39]

Others, who did not engage actively in the fighting themselves, provided arms or armed recruits, blackguarded Parliament from their pulpits, and exhorted their congregations to stand up for King and Country. Dr John Gorsuck of Walkern, Herts, was sequestered and plundered 'for sending a good horse to serve his Majesty, and a bad one to serve Parliament';[40] James Potter of Binfield, Berks., asserted that 'the meeke desire peace . . . but these bloodie men [i.e. the Round-heads] would yield to no propositions';[41] John Baker, Rector of Bartlow in Cambridgeshire, hoped 'to see King Pym hanged for taking bribes'; and Lionel Playters, Rector of Uggeshall, Suffolk, confidently expected to sell his crop of hemp at a good price, 'for', he said, 'if theis tymes hold many would need hanging', and added that he had 'tenne stone of hempe and he would bestow it freely to hang up the Roundheads'. Salt would be dear, too, for 'the Roundheads must be salted'.[42] John Aymes, curate of Loose in Kent, declared that it was 'a Roundedheaded Parliament and that their heads should be all shortly chopt off', and wished 'that the King might grind them in pieces like a Potter's vessell'.[43] But if Parliament disliked that kind of thing, it had little more sympathy with the type of sermon that proclaimed: 'souls went to three places, some to heaven, some to hell, and some to a middle place from which they might be resolved by prayer';[44] or the utterances of Emmanuel Utley, Vicar of Chigwell, Essex, who said: 'he loved the Pope with all his heart'.[45]

In defeat the clergy remained defiant. When the aged Vicar of Tarrington in Herefordshire was rudely asked by one of Colonel Massey's soldiers whom he was for, he boldly answered that 'he was for God and the King; for which the barbarous Rebell shot him through the head with his Pistoll.'[46] Henry Hancocks, Vicar of Furneaux Pelham, Hertfordshire, in order to stop his parishioners pulling down the communion rails, 'walked the churchyard at night sword in hand, and said he would rather lose his life than let the rails be pulled up; and that if the bishops ordered him to wear a kettle on his head he would do it';[47] and Dr Roberts, Rector of Hambledon, Buckinghamshire, declared 'it unlawful upon any pretence to raise Armes against the

King'.[48] A number of the Wiltshire clergy joined the Clubmen; while others supported underground movements of different kinds to restore the monarchy, for which, when caught, they suffered death or imprisonment. Nicholas Andrewes, Rector of St Nicholas' Guildford, was, for example, 'hurried from Jayl to Jayl, sometime Imprisoned on Shipboard and Died under this barbarous Treatment';[49] and David Lloyd in his *Memoirs* names a large number of clergy who were imprisoned. John Squire, Vicar of St Leonard's Shoreditch, was perhaps one of the most unfortunate, being incarcerated in succession at Gresham College, Newgate, and the King's Bench, while his wife and children were turned out into the street to starve.[50] The Bishops' London houses, like Lambeth Palace and Ely House, were requisitioned for this purpose in order to help accommodate the ever growing number of prisoners. Here the inmates were comparatively well treated provided they were prepared to pay the exorbitant demands of jailers like the 'vengeful Alexander Leighton. Imprisonment on board ships in the Thames, that was reserved for the worst offenders, was on the contrary a real hell on earth.

The various sequestration committees had, it must be admitted, a certain amount of justification in evicting such persistent malignants; as also in the case of gross moral offenders of whom there were only too many among the clergy. The charge of widespread sexual offences, like those levelled against the monks and nuns a century earlier, can probably be largely discounted. The reception accorded to an accusation brought against Stephen Nettles of Lexden in Essex, which was described as 'an extreme of immorality which is scarcely credible', indicated that the committee members themselves were dubious of the truthfulness of some such witnesses for the prosecution.[51] A particularly ludicrous instance was the case of Ambrose Westrop, Vicar of Great Totham in the same county. Ambrose was a suitor for the hand of a certain Ellen Pratt; and, according to the charge made against him by his enemies, 'did write upon a piece of paper these words: "Bonny Nell, I love thee well", and did pin it upon his cloake and wore it up and down a market towne, which woman refusing him, he did for five or six weeks afterwards utter little or nothing else, in the pulpit, but invectives against woman'.[52]

In such matters as drink, swearing, and fighting, however, the indictments, generally speaking, were more accurate. It may be recalled in this connection that in his regular annual reports to the King on the state of the dioceses in his province, Archbishop Laud had constantly deplored the excessive drunkenness of the Lincolnshire clergy. On the other hand it should also be remembered that local sequestration committees, when they found that parishioners, either from fear or affection or perhaps merely caution, were reluctant to speak against their incumbent, encouraged informers of an undesirable type; and rarely permitted a fair or impartial trial. The accused man was never present at the taking of depositions, although he might on payment receive a copy of the charges against him, and was given fourteen days in which to prepare his defence. In practice, indeed, a defence was seldom offered—Thomas Gibson of Horncastle was the only clergyman to do so in the whole of Lincolnshire[53]—and most ministers were condemned *in absentia*.

The Essex committee for dealing with scandalous ministers had been set up by the Earl of Manchester in February 1643/4, and that for Lincolnshire in 1644.[54] 'Your power is great', he wrote to them, 'and so is your trust. If a general reformation follows not within your county, assuredly the blame will be laid upon you, and you must expect to be called to an account for it both here and hereafter'.[55] In each case, besides having the power to eject an incumbent, they could sequester his temporal as well as his spiritual estate, for which he had to compound by fine after subscribing to the Solemn League and Covenant,[56] and in conjunction with the parishioners themselves appoint his successor, who had then to be despatched to the Assembly of Divines at Westminster 'with an account of his character for their trial and examination'.[57] They were also instructed 'to enquire the true value of every living brought in question, and to certify it to me; also the private estate of the accused, that I may know what allowance to make, on sequestration, for his wife and children'.[58] A fifth of the value of the benefice was usually granted. Incidentally the Earl also told the churchwardens of a sequestrated parish to collect the tithes and 'keep them in safe custody till they should receive farther order from himself'.[59] Curiously enough a number of parsons were actually accused, as part of their indictment, of ill-treating their wives. Jeremiah Ravens, Rector of Great Blakenham, Suffolk, was perhaps the worst culprit in this respect, since he 'hunge his wife upp by the heels and tyed her to the bedposts and whipped her'.[60] Possibly he had in mind the old country saw: 'A wife, a dog, and a walnut tree, the more you beat them the better they be'.

Drunkenness and the encouragement of it was widespread. Samuel Collins, Rector of Fen Ditton and Milton, Cambridgeshire, used so hospitably to entertain his congregation after morning service that they 'spewed most shamefully' whilst attending church in the afternoon.[61] It was said of William Underwood, minister of Harby, Lincolnshire, 'Mr Underwood is very scandalous in his life and converssacon by his continual frequenting of Ailhouses and that sometimes of the Sabboth dayes and keepinge Companie theire with men of Illfame, viz. Coblers and Pedlars and such as spend that they gett in drinkinge and Tiplinge in Ailhouses and thereby has made himselfe a skorne and derision to others in havinge the backside of his clothes besmered over with creame by those that keepe him Company'.[62] Thomas Pickard, Rector of St Mary's, Stamford, seems to have combined all three vices of drinking, swearing, and fighting, judging from the following deposition: 'he is a frequenter of Innes and Ailehouses and hath heard that hee is oftentimes distempered with drinke and quarrellsome and apt to abuse honest men and women with his tongue'. And when at a supper party a certain Mrs Susan Bullock gently reproved him for his foul language, 'the said Pickard furiously fell upon her with ill languadge giveinge her 2 or 3 blowes about the head and face and pullinge downe the cloth and all the meate from the table upon the ground'.[63]

Fighting parsons seem to have abounded. Bernard Flesher, Rector of Saddington, Leicestershire, was described as 'a notorious fighter with man woman and child in church feild and towne'.[64] Another was John Terry, curate of Smarden in Kent, who used to become so drunk 'that he hath bene found lyinge in the streete and dirt, not able to helpe himselfe ... Mr Terry is a ffighter and that nott only in his owne house but a breaker of the King's peace in strikinge others, both men and women; and that even att the churche door'.[65] Perhaps John Kidde, curate of Egerton in the same county, had more justification for his conduct when, on a communicant refusing to kneel at the rails, he 'pulled him by the haire of his head and thrust him out of the Church'.[66]

Some of the charges brought against the clergy certainly throw an interesting light on their variegated activities. Too many incumbents, for example, appear to have been farmers first and parsons second. Daniel Falconer, Rector of Aldham, Essex, bestowed, or so it was said, 'much of his tyme about worldly imployments as dressing corne, pitching cart, and that sometymes on Satterday Nine a clock at night when it were better he were in his study'.[67] Other agricultural workers were: William Proctor of Stradishall, Suffolk, who was 'seen hedging on a Sunday',[68] and Peter Waterman, Rector of Wootton Rivers, Wiltshire, who performed 'sevill offices not befitting a minister of the gospell, as goeing to plough, filling the dungpotts, serving of Hoggs and the like, and doth suffer his wife to sell matheglin in his house'.[69] A variety of secular employments were often adopted by the clergy of necessity in order to make both ends meet. William Lange, Vicar of Bradworthy in Devon, was something of a publican since he 'kept a tavern at the vicarage for 4 years past'.[70] Other complaints made by the Puritans about the Anglican clergy were that with royal encouragement they had favoured Sunday sports,[71] played cards and other games themselves of a Sunday, and were gluttons as well as drunkards. Of Thomas Holt, Vicar of All Saints' Stamford, it was reported: 'the saboth day hath beine much prophaned by ringinge of Bells in Mr Holt's Church both before and after noone, and by playinge at Stooleball in the streete neere his owne door';[72] while Lionel Playters of Uggleshall disgusted his abstemious neighbours by eating custard publicly 'After a scandalous manner', and then added to his offence by putting sack to it and eating it 'with great greediness'.[73] Some clerics were accused of being avaricious as well as greedy, extorting tithes unjustly from their poorer parishioners. It was said, for example, of Mr Lidham, Vicar of Leysdown, 'Hee exacteth tythes for working horses. . . . Hee extorteth Tithe ffish of poore men, which have taken them a mile thence, upon the sea sands with netts and hooks';[74] whilst Dr Parke, Rector of Tenterden, at his Easter Communion in 1640, 'did disgracefully put backe some poore servants of the said parishe from the receiving of the holy Sacrament, beeing there ready with the rest of the congregation to receive the same, meerlie because they would not pay him twelve pence a peece for their offerings, although they hadd beefore tendred him their accustomed offerings'.[75]

Some of the stories told were so fantastic that they would have been laughable if their consequences had not been so serious. The Vicar of Somerby, Leicestershire, 'did ride on hunting in his perambulation after a hare, in his surplice, and leapt over a gate and so teare his surplice, that the parish was forced to provide a new surplice for him to read prayers in, and to keepe the old one for him to hunt in'.[76] John Lowes, Vicar of Brandeston, Suffolk, was arraigned for witchcraft and executed at Bury St Edmunds in August 1645. He was compelled to confess to having bewitched a ship near Harwich that went down with all hands, and to admit 'he had done many other most hanous, wicked and accursed acts by the help of Six Impes which he had that frequented him daily'. It was further alleged that he had made a covenant with the Devil and subsequently had been marked by his Satanic Majesty with teats on the crown of his head and under his tongue.[77]

The actual evictions themselves were often carried out with the greatest brutality: pregnant women were thrust forth into the street; bedridden Mrs Ephraim Udal was turned out of doors and left to starve;[78] soldiers with drawn swords twice within a month pulled the eighty-year-old wife of the Rector of Thornton-in-the-Moors, Cheshire, out of her bed and lugged her off to a nearby garrison;[79] and the aged and sick John Prince, Rector of Little Shefford, Berkshire, was carried from his bed to the tithe barn where he died.[80] 'One Major Raimes his Neighbour', wrote the son of the Rev. Dr Thomas Reeve of Aldborough and Colby in Norfolk, 'having raised a troope of Horse for Parliament, got a warrant from the Committee of Sequestration to take away the saide Dr Reeve's cattle and bring him Prisoner to Norwich Jayle, which he executed with all the Riggor he coold, searching the Bed where the wife of the saide Dr Reeve had lain in but 3 days, for the said Dr Reeve; and when the women rebuked him for his Barbaritie, telling him he acted more like a Beast than a Man, he drue his Sword and stabbed through the Bed in severall places pretending to stab the said Dr Reeve as hid in the Bed; after that caused all his Troopers to pull the Bridles off their horses and whip them round the garden to tread all under foote; after that he Brake open the Barn dore and turn'd the whole Troope to the Stacks of Corn to fill their Bellyes. . . . Some few days after he broke open the dores with a plough sheere . . . and turned my Mother and six children into the street, and brought carts and carried away my father's Librairy and Household goods'. [81]

Church and parsonage were sometimes set on fire after the latter had been systematically plundered and the parson, like Humphrey Betty of Little Petherick, Cornwall, driven out into the world 'all naked';[82] or Dr Philip King, who was 'sequestered from his Rectory at Botolph Billingsgate', and then compelled 'to fly to save his life, and when he had nothing to lose but his life'.[83] Many of the clergy and their wives put up a sturdy and gallant defence: John Edshaw, Rector of Chailey in Sussex, fought off the Roundheads first with his cane and then with a hedging bill thrown him by a neighbour;[84] and Mrs George Beardsall of Arkesden in Essex refused to admit the intruding minister, Mr Bull, into her vicarage, declaring 'she would die before quitting it'. Eventually she was carried out by force kicking and screaming.[85] But she was more fortunate than her sister parson's wife, Mrs Thomas Smith of Richards Castle in Herefordshire, who on adopting similar tactics was so brutally assaulted that she never recovered from her injuries.[86] The Vicar of Wellingborough was compelled to ride on the back of a wild bear;[87] and at Cole Orton, Leicestershire, the Rector was beaten up, receiving 'above 100 blowes of a skeane on his back armes and shoulders till all was black as a shooe'.[88] A particularly atrocious story comes from Buckinghamshire: Anthony Tyringham, who held the family living of Tyringham, was out riding one day near Stony Stratford with two of his nephews when they were accosted by a party of Roundhead dragoons, robbed of their valuables and despatched under escort to a nearby garrison. Suddenly the small party halted and Canon Tyringham was ordered to remove his cassock. As he did not obey this order fast enough he was struck over the head with a sword and his fingers slashed. The cry was then raised that the prisoners were escaping and the main body of soldiers, who were not far off, summoned to the rescue. Immediately on arrival and without awaiting any explanation the commanding officer, Captain Pollard, struck Tyringham across the elbow and almost severed his arm. The nephews were not allowed to render any first aid, the prisoners were urged forward, and after some four hours riding they came to Whitchurch, where Tyringham collapsed from pain and loss of blood. He was revived, plundered of his boots, jerkin, and hat; and then compelled to ride yet another mile

on a cold dark night to Aylesbury. The next day his arm was ampu-
tated. The Canon apparently bore his sufferings with great courage and
told the rebels he hoped to live to see them all hanged. Actually he died
a year before the Restoration.[89]

Some extremely vivid stories have come down to us of how the
clergy reacted to their expulsion or attempted arrest. We see Robert
Clarke of Andover striving to escape through the 'bolt-hole' he had so
thoughtfully constructed into his next-door-neighbour's house, only
to suffer a broken thigh in the process;[90] Christopher Prior of Elve-
tham, also in Hampshire, leaping over a high wall and rupturing himself;[91] and Thomas Pestell of Packington, Leicestershire, sitting quietly
with his wife and family in the vicarage pew, listening to the intruding
Mr Pegg declare that God had justly spewed him out of his mouth,
before going on to announce his own text: 'I AM hath sent me unto
you'.[92] Subtler tactics were occasionally more successful. When
soldiers came to arrest Guy Carleton, Vicar of Bucklebury, Berkshire,
they mistook him for a servant since 'he wore a grey coat and had
his boots on';[93] and so he escaped. In order to make his living as unattractive as possible John Challice of Teigngrace in Devon let his
parsonage fall into ruins. Then when in spite of this he heard that the
sequestrators were approaching, he gathered as many of his neighbours' children together as possible, passed them all off as his own,
and thereby engendered in the hearts of his visitors 'a qualm of com-
passion' about turning so large a number of youngsters out to starve.
The ruse apparently succeeded since Challice was not evicted.[94]

Before, however, we begin to shed too many tears about the sufferings of the evicted clergy, let us first see how they put into practice the
Christian principle of turning the other cheek. Sequestered parsons
were normally expected to withdraw from their livings after eviction;
but quite a number of these royalist clerics, who had been so brutally
hounded from their parsonages, merely retired into the village where,
loyally supported in many cases by the bulk of their erstwhile parishioners, they proceed to harry the intruding ministers unmercifully.
They forbade their people to pay him any tithes, organized rowdy
scenes in church, and even pursued him into the vicarage itself.
Nathaniel Gill, Rector of Burgh-next-Aylsham, Norfolk, who had been
sequestered in 1644, continued boldly to officiate in his church aided
and abetted by the churchwardens, until in 1651 he was obliged to
retire to Bungay carrying the registers with him.[95] At Soham in Cambridgeshire the whole parish rose against the intruder, threw his
possessions out of the vicarage, and manhandled his servants.[96] W.
Anderson, the parliamentary nominee at Coppenhall in Cheshire, had
his horses legs cut off and the rectory set on fire by hostile villagers.[97]
In 1647—a year when many of the clergy attempted, with the reputed

encouragement of Sir Thomas Fairfax himself, to recover their livings—Samuel Cotton, the ex-Rector of North Kilworth, Leicestershire, helped by some disbanded cavaliers, attacked the parsonage where his successor T. Jenkins was peaceably residing, kicked his wife then with child, threw out some of his goods and kept the rest, disarmed those opposing him, and for a time held the house and church by force against all comers.[98] A final example that may be quoted from the mass of evidence available, is that of the wretched Puritan minister at Redcombe in Gloucestershire: the ex-Rector's sons used to throw stones at the pulpit when he was preaching, forced him to leave the church by threats, followed him to the parsonage accompanied by a savage mob, penned him and his wife into an attic, and made such a noise outside day and night that they died from exhaustion.[99]

How did the ejected clergy earn a livelihood? Some lived on the charity of their old parishioners, who illegally paid them their tithes. The inhabitants of Dickleburgh in Norfolk followed the party of soldiers who had plundered and arrested their Rector, Christopher Barnard, and effected his rescue; and when they heard that 'the Villains had designed to Plunder his House a second Time', men, women and children turned out in force, broke into the tithe barn at night, threshed some of the wheat and carted the rest away for the benefit of their sequestered parson.[100] Eleanor, wife of Amias Hext, Rector of Babcary in Somerset, was accused before the local parliamentary committee of keeping the glebe and collecting the tithes with the help of malignant friends, long after they had seen sequestered.[101] Another parson's wife, Mrs Thomas Glover of West Kirby, Cheshire, boldly 'intruded into the rectory house and seized the tithes'.[102] Possibly, however, the last was within her rights, since an ejected clergyman's wife, on petition, was allowed one-fifth of the value of her husband's benefice for the support of herself and her family; but such claims were sometimes successfully opposed or eluded by the intruding nonconformist ministers. The parson himself was also legally entitled to any corn that was standing on the glebe or lying in the barn at the time of his eviction.

A few sequestered clergy went abroad: to Paris to join the royal court, across the Atlantic, or even, like Isaac Basire, to missionary work in the Near East; but the majority stayed at home and sought a living where it could be found. Chaplaincies or tutorships in the homes of the royalist gentry offered a refuge to some of them, until this kind of thing was forbidden by an Ordinance of 1655; while lectureships, medical practice, and even manual labour were undertaken by many others. Occasionally in a vacant parish, where the sequestrators were not too particular, they could find their way back temporarily at least into the pulpit; or during the last five or six years of the interregnum squeeze

I

past the Triers into a living. Certainly conditions, generally speaking, were easier for the Anglican clergy after the establishment of the Protectorate. In February 1655 a proclamation declared that 'all persons in this Commonwealth fearing God, though of differing judgments' were to be protected 'in the sober and quiet exercise and profession of religion and the sincere worship of God'.[103] Unfortunately the Penruddock Rising caused a set-back. The Major Generals were instructed to tighten up the execution of the law for ejecting scandalous ministers;[104] by a series of orders in September 1655 the evicted clergy were no longer allowed to act as chaplains, schoolmasters, or lecturers; and they were to be turned out of any living into which they had been able to penetrate. Fortunately from the Anglican's point of view these regulations were not seriously enforced in practice unless the clerics concerned were making themselves a nuisance. Furthermore in June 1657 every sequestered minister was himself assured of a fifth of the income of his old benefice, provided his present income did not exceed £30 per annum and his temporal estate was less than £500. Should the intruder refuse to pay, Cromwell's commissioners had the power to sequester 'the said allowance' for the use of the ex-incumbent.[105] But, as Fuller pointed out, 'If the sequestrated minister hath any temporal means of his own, or since his sequestration hath acquired any place wherein he officiateth (though short of a comfortable subsistence), they deny payment of a fifth part unto him'. Moreover nothing at all would be paid to anyone who in any way disputed the intruder's 'peaceable possession'.[106]

In January 1640/41 Sir Simonds D'Ewes had expressed in forceful language the need for a reformed ministry: 'It would be the greatest glory of his majesty's reign', he declared, 'if we could change the greater part of the clergy from brazen, leaden—yea, and blockish—persons, to a golden and a primitive condition, that their authority might be warranted by their godly example';[107] but in 1656 Richard Baxter, who was certainly no Cromwellian, considered that this aim had been achieved: 'For all the faults that are now among us', he declared, 'I do not believe that ever England had so noble and faithful a ministry since it was a nation, as it hath at this time. . . . Sure I am, the change is so great within these twelve years, that it is one of the greatest joys that ever I had in the world to behold it'.[108]

On the whole it would be true to say that the bulk of the sufferers remained faithful to their profession. A few became Roman Catholics or adopted the tenets of the Calvinists; but only one, Francis Corker of Bradford, turned informer for a living. Scholars, helped by generous if impoverished royalist noblemen like Viscount Scudamore, produced some excellent work. Jeremy Taylor, under the protection of the Vaughans at Golden Grove, wrote copiously and well; Dr Henry

Hammond, Rector of Penshurst in Kent, published his *Paraphrase and Annotations upon the New Testament* in 1653, and John Pearson (later Bishop of Chester) his *Exposition of the Creed* in 1659. Tom Fuller and Peter Heylin and others also made splendid use of their enforced leisure for study. It was said, for example, of Dr Brian Walton, the learned incumbent of St Martin's Orgar in London, 'being assaulted, sequestered, and plundered, he had been killed, had he not fled to Oxford, where he laid the ground for the most Heroick design of the Polyglot Bible'.[109] Neither, in this period of oppression and obscurity, did poets like Robert Herrick forget to sing.

Some tiny snapshots have come down to us of a number of these parsons in exile: Robert Clarke of Andover was 'allways threadbare, often barefoot',[110] Mr Tabor, of St Margaret's Lothbury in London, died 'in Hertfordshire in want';[111] Thomas Haywood of Badby, Northamptonshire, went up and down the country on foot begging, from one royalist to another;[112] William Lane of Ringmore in Devon quarried stone at Hope's Nose near Torbay until ironically enough his tools were plundered by the crew of a French privateer commissioned by Charles II;[113] John Turner of Treneglos in Cornwall took to farming and left behind him a remarkable testimony to his skill, namely 'two Stone Fences one on either side of a Public Road ... which he built with his own hands ... the neatest and strongest in all the country';[114] and Henry Wright of Ashperton in Herefordshire opened an alehouse at Broadheath where he entertained members of the resistance movement.[115] Perhaps the most contented of them all was Robert Sibthorp, the Laudian ex-Rector of Brackley, Northampton-shire, who had escaped from the Roundheads 'in his Clark's habit that had been certainly murthered in his own'; but in his poverty-stricken exile used to remark: 'I have as much as I desire, if I have as much as I want; and I have as much as the most, if I have as much as I desire'.[116]

Another sad case was that of Thomas Campbell, the Rector of Swafield, Norfolk. An eyewitness thus recounts the tragic circum-stances: 'Thomas Campbell . . . being sequestered by ye Earle of Manchester was forced from his Rectory of Swafield to retyre to a neighbour village called Bradfield, to live in a poor cottage, where visiting him in very cold ffrost and deep snow, about ye yeare 1643, I found him at his study, reading Gerrhard's Harmony. Hee was with his wife and fower children: without fyre or fyring. I beeing dry and weary with a long walke, ask'd him for a draught of beere. Hee carryed mee to his window and showed mee a water-course, and told mee if I were drie thereof might satisfy myself; for hee had no other liquor to drink for some months past. I then asking for a morcell to eate, his reply was hee had neyther bread, or cheese, or fish, or fflesh in his howse; and he had wanted all these and fyring also, for many weeks. I wondering how hee could subsist, hee led me to an old chirn, and opening it I saw two or three very great dumplins. He sayd they were barley dumplins: and I perceived they were coarse and brown, and as cold, and hard, as vehement frost could make them: and he told me that hee lived only on such provision, and water from ye little runn of water for many weeks. I seeing his wants, told him I wondered at it, and feared that if I should fall into such circumstances and wants, I should sink under them. Hee replyed with a surprising cheerfulnesse, that I was a foole, I wanted experience for if ever God called me to suffering, hee would enable me to beare it, with courage and contentment'.[117]

Oliver Cromwell expired on 3 September 1658, regretted by few individuals outside the Army; and even that Roundhead divine, Ralph Josselin, recorded in his diary: 'Cromwell died, people not much minding it'. On 3 June 1660, he wrote: 'Ye King returned in safety, and with hopes of being a blessing to the nacon'; and added the following day, 'Rid to lay claime to the King's pardon before ye Mayor of Colchester'.[118] Josselin, of course, was not the only Vicar of Bray. 'I prayed for the king this afternoon by periphrasis', declared the Manchester Presbyterian curate, Henry Newcome, on 6 May 1660. 'On Satuday after, May 12th, they resolved to proclaim the king in Manchester, and we went first into the church, and sung a Psalm, and after I went up into the pulpit, and prayed about half an hour, wherein the Lord did affect all the people, the change was so great'.[119]

A few stories have been preserved of how the ordinary country parson came into his own again. Nathaniel Gill entered in the church register he had so grimly hung on to throughout the interregnum: 'May ye 29 [1660] King Charles ye Second arrived in London, being then 30 years ould compleat'; and a little further on recorded his own restoration: 'Neth. Gill (after 17 yeares sequestration by traitors, rebels, Anabaptists and Presbyterians) was restored to his Rectory of Burrough and preached on Christmasse day 1660'.[120] Perhaps, however, the most interesting example of all is that of Robert Clarke: on hearing the glad tiding of the King's Restoration, he returned secretly one Saturday night to his old parish of Andover. 'He lay in the house of a friend till Sunday morning', we are told, and then 'he went to the Church at full congregation and going in at the west door and going through the body of the Church he drew the eyes of all upon himself and comes up into the reader's pew and puts the intruder aside, and told him: "Sir, the King is come to his own and will reign alone, and I am come to my own too and will officiate without an assistant". And so taking a book out of his pocket went on with the Liturgy, and an excellent Sermon of forgiving injuries, to the satisfaction of most of his audience'.[121] On this pleasant note of Christian charity let us bring the tale of 'The Sufferings of the Clergy' to an end.

NOTES

[1] G. B. Tatham, *The Puritans In Power*, p. 53.

[2] Heylin, *Cyprianus Anglicus*, p. 469.

[3] W. A. Shaw, *A History of the English Church during the Civil Wars and under the Commonwealth*, Vol. I, p. 8.

[4] *Proceedings, . . . County of Kent*, pp. 81, 84, 87.

[5] Heylin, *Cyprianus Anglicus*, p. 472.

[6] *Acts and Ordinances of the Interregnum*, ed. C. H. Firth and R. S. Rait, Vol. I, pp. 180–4; 1188.

[7] Shaw, *History of the English Church*, Vol. I, pp. 334–5.

[8] Heylin, *Cyprianus Anglicus*, p. 468.

[9] *Acts and Ordinances of the Interregnum*, Vol. I, pp. 265–6; 425–6.

[10] *The Journal of William Dowsing*, ed. E. H. Evelyn White, p. 16.

[11] *Journal of William Dowsing*, p. 29: 'divers Pictures in the Windows', continued Dowsing, 'we could not reach, neither would they help us raise the ladders'.

[12] *The Autobiography of Richard Baxter*, ed. J. M. Lloyd Thomas, p. 38.

[13] Shaw, *History of the English Church*, Vol. II, pp. 253–4.

[14] Heylin, *Cyprianus Anglicus*, p. 486.

[15] *Journals of the House of Commons*, Vol. II, p. 723.

[16] *Annals of Evangelical Nonconformity*, p. 205. A Committee for Preaching Ministers had been set up by the House of Commons, which recommended lecturers to particular parishes. See Shaw, *History of the English Church*, Vol. II, p. 182.

[17] Shaw, *History of the English Church*, Vol. I, pp. 337–57.

[18] *Acts and Ordinances of the Interregnum*, Vol. I, pp. 582–607.

[19] Tatham, *Puritans in Power*, p. 227.

[20] *Acts and Ordinances of the Interregnum*, Vol. I, pp. 789–91.

[21] *Annals of Evangelical Nonconformity*, p. 317.

[22] *Acts and Ordinances of the Interregnum*, Vol. I, pp. 106 and 109.

[23] *Acts and Ordinances of the Interregnum*, Vol. I, pp. 878 et seq. Vol. II, pp. 81 et seq.

[24] Enquiries into the value of all livings were carried out by the Trustees in 1649–50 and again from 1655–8, and as a result a number of Ordinances were passed for the uniting of parishes. These affirmed that where necessary livings were to be 'consolidated and united for the better maintenance of an able and godly Minister'. See *Acts and Ordinances of the Interregnum*, Vol. I, pp. 1000–6.

[25] *Appeal to Injured Innocence*; quoted in Fuller, *Church History*, pp. 627–8.

[26] Fuller, *Church History*, Vol. III, pp. 516–18.

[27] *Proceedings, . . . County of Kent*, pp. 104–5.

[28] *Proceedings, . . . County of Kent*, p. 119

[29] *Proceedings, . . . County of Kent*, . . . pp. 122–3.

[30] *Proceedings, . . . County of Kent*, pp. 182–3.

[31] *Proceedings, . . . County of Kent*, p. 186.

[32] Essex Record Society, Vol. 17, Vol. I, p. 77.

[33] *Annals of Evangelical Nonconformity*, p. 188.

[34] *Proceedings, . . . County of Kent*, p. 238.

[35] *Proceedings, . . . County of Kent*, pp. 110–11.

[36] A. G. Matthews, *Walker Revised*, p. 116.

[37] *Annals of Evangelical Nonconformity*, pp. 203 and 228.

[38] *Diary of the Rev. Ralph Josselin*, p. 63. D. Lloyd wrote in his *Memoirs*, p. 563, 'murdered by a Council of War, who took, sentenced, and executed him in two hours . . . his nearest relation was forced to have a hand in his execution, contrary to the Civil Law among Heathens'.

[39] C. M. Hood, *Sequestered Loyalists and Bartholomew Sufferers*, p. 45.

[40] D. Lloyd, *Memoirs of the Lives, Actions, Sufferings, and Deaths of those that suffered for the Protestant Religion in our late Intestine Wars*, p. 531.

[41] Matthews, *Walker Revised*, p. 71.

[42] Matthews, *Walker Revised*, pp. 78 and 341.

[43] Mathews, *Walker Revised*, p. 210.

[44] Edward Sheppard of Great Maplestead. See *Annals of Evangelical Nonconformity*, p. 241.

[45] *Annals of Evangelical Nonconformity*, pp. 220–3.

[46] Matthews, *Walker Revised*, p. 194.

[47] Matthews, *Walker Revised*, p. 199.

[48] Lloyd, *Memoirs*, p. 530.

[49] Matthews, *Walker Revised*, p. 349.

[50] Lloyd, *Memoirs*, p. 508.

[51] *Annals of Evangelical Nonconformity*, p. 226.

[52] *Annals of Evangelical Nonconformity*, p. 252.

[53] *Lincoln Architectural and Archaeological Society Reports*, Vol. II, Part I, 'The Royalist Clergy of Lincolnshire', ed. J. W. F. Hill, p. 63.

[54] Manchester was empowered by warrant in March 1644 to establish commissioners for this purpose in the seven associated counties. See *Annals of Evangelical Nonconformity*, pp. 210–11; *Lincoln Architectural and Archaeological Society Reports*, Vol. II, Part I, N.S., pp. 42–3.

[55] Neal, *History of the Puritans*, Vol. III, p. 110.

[56] It should be noted that clergy who fled to enemy strongholds which subsequently surrendered, were often exempted from taking the Covenant and their fines reduced from a third to a tenth. See, Matthews, *Walker Revised*, xxiv.

[57] Neal, *History of the Puritans*, Vol. III, p. 110.

[58] *Annals of Evangelical Nonconformity*, p. 210.

[59] The churchwardens also had the unpleasant task of helping to eject the convicted incumbent from his parsonage. See Neal, *History of the Puritans*, Vol. III, p. 110.

[60] Matthews, *Walker Revised*, p. 342.

[61] Matthews, *Walker Revised*, p. 78.

[62] *Lincoln Architectural and Archaeological Society Reports*, Vol. II, Part I, N. S., p. 65.

[63] *Lincoln Architectural and Archaeological Society Reports*, Vol. II, Part I, N.S., p. 101. He was likewise accused of drawing a knife on one witness in a shop at Stamford.

64 Matthews, *Walker Revised*, p. 235.

65 *Proceedings, . . . County of Kent*, p. 116.

66 Matthews, *Walker Revised*, p. 220. He called such parishioners 'unreverent Puppies'.

67 Matthews, *Walker Revised*, p. 151.

68 Matthews, *Walker Revised*, p. 341.

69 Matthews, *Walker Revised*, p. 381.

70 Matthews, *Walker Revised*, p. 118.

71 The Puritans themselves when in power made a number of Ordinances for the better observance of the Sabbath. See *Acts and Ordinances of the Interregnum*, Vol. I, pp. 420–3; and Vol. II, p. 383 et seq.

72 *Lincoln Architectural and Archaeological Society Reports*, Vol. II, Part I, N.S., p. 80.

73 Matthews, *Walker Revised*, p. 341.

74 *Proceedings, . . . County of Kent*, p. 159.

75 *Proceedings, . . . County of Kent*, p. 231.

76 Matthews, *Walker Revised*, p. 232.

77 Matthews, *Walker Revised*, p. 339.

78 Lloyd, *Memoirs*, p. 507.

79 Matthews, *Walker Revised*, p. 89.

80 Matthews, *Walker Revised*, p. 71.

81 R. W. Ketton Cremer, *A Norfolk Gallery*, p. 108. See also Hood, *Sequestered Loyalists*, pp. 42–3.

82 Matthews, *Walker Revised*, p. 95.

83 Lloyd, *Memoirs*, p. 507.

84 Matthews, *Walker Revised*, p. 335.

85 Matthews, *Walker Revised*, p. 146.

86 Matthews, *Walker Revised*, p. 196.

87 Matthews, *Walker Revised*, p. 281.

88 Matthews, *Walker Revised*, p. 242.

89 See W. R. Newton, *The Church in Worcestershire, 1617–1645*, (unpublished).

90 Matthews, *Walker Revised*, p. 181.

91 Matthews, *Walker Revised*, p. 189.

92 Matthews, *Walker Revised*, p. 242.

93 Matthews, *Walker Revised*, p. 68.

94 Matthews, *Walker Revised*, p. 110.

95 Ketton Cremer, *Norfolk Gallery*, pp. 114–15.

96 Matthews, *Walker Revised*, p. 81.

97 Matthews, *Walker Revised*, p. 92.

98 Matthews, *Walker Revised*, p. 234.

99 Matthews, *Walker Revised*, p. 172.

100 Hood, *Sequestered Loyalists*, p. 39. See also Ketton Cremer, *Norfolk Gallery*, p. 106.

101 Matthews, *Walker Revised*, p. 314.

102 Matthews, *Walker Revised*, p. 90.

103 Tatham, *Puritans in Power*, p. 235.

104 Even the puritanical Ralph Josselin was moved to write of the Major

Generals; 'neither do I joy to see ministers put under ye lay power'; *Diary*, p. 115.

[105] *Acts and Ordinances of the Interregnum*, Vol. II, p. 1267.

[106] Fuller, *Church History*, Vol. III, pp. 554–5.

[107] Quoted by Shaw, *History of the English Church*, Vol. I, p. 22.

[108] *Annals of Evangelical Nonconformity*, pp. 318–19.

[109] Lloyd, *Memoirs*, p. 513.

[110] Matthews, *Walker Revised*, p. 181.

[111] Lloyd, *Memoirs*, p. 513.

[112] Matthews, *Walker Revised*, p. 279.

[113] Matthews, *Walker Revised*, p. 117.

[114] Matthews, *Walker Revised*, p. 101.

[115] Matthews, *Walker Revised*, p. 196.

[116] Lloyd, *Memoirs*, p. 278.

[117] Hood, *Sequestered Loyalists*, pp. 43–4.

[118] *Diary of the Rev. Ralph Josselin*, pp. 125, 134.

[119] *The Autobiography of Henry Newcome*, ed. R. Parkinson, (Chetham Society), Vol. I, p. 120. Later Newcome added: 'We had a public day of thanksgiving appointed by authority, on which day I preached on 2.Sam. XIX.14, the sermon which I was afterwards persuaded to publish'.

[120] Ketton Cremer, *Norfolk Gallery*, p. 115.

[121] Matthews, *Walker Revised*, p. 189.

Saints and Sinners

IN CONTRADISTINCTION TO the foregoing chapters, which were primarily concerned with the general picture and an historical sequence, an attempt will now be made to provide some tiny biographies, or rather snapshots, of individual parsons during this period. Some of them, of course, are household names; but others are little-known men who have had to be dug out of the obscurity that has long surrounded them.

Perhaps the most formidable personality noted by Fuller among the parochial clergy in Queen Elizabeth's reign was that of Bernard Gilpin, who was popularly known as the 'Apostle of the North'. Puritanically minded, he was charged with heresy under Queen Mary, whose timely death saved him from the stake; but when offered the see of Carlisle in 1559 he declined it,[1] preferring to remain the Rector of the gigantic parish of Houghton-le-Spring in Co. Durham that covered some fourteen villages. 'In his own house', wrote Fuller, 'he boarded and kept full four and twenty scholars. The greater number of boarders were poor men's sons, upon whom he bestowed meat, drink and cloth, and education in learning. He was wont to entertain his parishioners and strangers at his table, not only at Christmas time, as the custom is; but, because he had a large and wide parish, a great multitude of people, he kept a table for them every Sunday from Michaelmas to Easter. He had the gentleman, the husbandman, and the poorer sort, set every degree by themselves, and as it was ordered in ranks. . . . He bestowed, in building, ordering, and establishing of his school, and in providing yearly stipends for a schoolmaster and an usher, the full sum of five hundred pounds; out of which school he supplied the Church of England with a great store of learned men. He was careful to avoid not only all evil doing, but even the lightest suspicion thereof. And he was accounted a saint in the judgements of his very enemies, if he had such.'

It was said that whenever he met a poor boy on the road he would ask him questions and if pleased with the answers would there and then provide for his education; and in this way he was responsible for many famous scholars like Bishop George Carleton of Chichester or Hugh Broughton. His generosity was certainly on a princely scale. No poor parishioner could lose an animal without having it promptly replaced; and it only needed a bad harvest for the farmers to be remitted their tithes; while when on a journey Gilpin frequently gave away all his loose cash and much of his clothing besides. Annually he made progresses through the wilder parts of Yorkshire and Northumberland, such as Redesdale and Tynedale, preaching and relieving the necessities of the poor; 'where', he remarked, 'the people sat in the darkness of ignorance, and shadow of death'. Here he was immensely popular; and once when his horses were stolen the whole countryside was up in arms. The thief himself, directly he learnt the identity of his victim, promptly returned the animals; for, as he said, 'the devil would have seized him immediately, if he had taken them off, when he found they belonged to Mr Gilpin'.

The energetic and puritanical Gilpin was horrified at 'the ignorance, superstition and vice' of many of the neighbouring clergy; and in a sermon preached before the Bishop of Durham himself, boldly denounced their corruption. He then went on: 'Let not your lordship say, that these crimes have been committed by others, without your knowledge; for whatever either yourself shall do in person, or suffer through your connivance to be done by others, is wholly your own. Therefore in the presence of God, angels and men, I pronounce you to be the author of all these evils. Yea, and in that strict day of general account, I will be a witness to testify against you, that all these things have come to your knowledge by my means; and all these men shall bear witness thereof, who have heard me speak to you this day'. Far from being offended, however, at this out-spoken rebuke, Bishop Barnes took the first opportunity of seizing the preacher's hand and exclaiming: 'Father Gilpin, I acknowledge you are fitter to be the Bishop of Durham, than I am to be parson of your church . . . I know you have enemies; but while I live Bishop of Durham, be secure: none of them shall cause you any further trouble'. And Lord Burleigh, after spending a night under his roof, remarked to his companions on leaving: 'There is the enjoyment of life, indeed! Who can blame that man for refusing a bishopric? What doth he want to make him greater or happier or more useful to mankind?'[2]

Another famous Elizabethan divine was Alexander Nowell, for long Dean of St Paul's and the author of three catechisms, of which 'the small' is practically that of the Prayer Book today. At one time he was also the country parson of the beautiful little Hertfordshire village of Much Hadham, where, apparently, he spent much of his leisure fishing. This recreation is thirsty work, and Nowell used regularly to carry with him to the River Ash sundry bottles of ale. One of these, according to Fuller, was once left behind by mistake in the long grass, where it was rediscovered some days later and drained. The taste was found to have greatly improved, which first set Nowell thinking and then experimenting, with the pleasing result that he became the inventor of bottled beer. His character was summed up by a contemporary as follows: 'A man of most angelical life and deep learning: a great defender of justification by faith alone, and yet a great preacher of good works . . . a great honourer of the marriage of the clergy, and yet who lived and died single himself'.[3]

The tradition that a country parson is also a scholar was certainly nobly upheld in Elizabethan times by Anglican and Puritan alike in the persons of such men as Nicholas Fuller, Richard Mulcaster, John White, William Harrison, Henry Copinger, William Morgan, and above all Richard Hooker. Nicholas Fuller was Rector of Allington near Salisbury towards the close of Elizabeth's reign; a writer on the Scriptures, whose most important work was his *Miscellaneorum Theologicorum*. Fuller's parish and income indeed were both very small, and he never received any preferment; yet, as his biographer remarked of him, 'a contented mind extendeth the smallest parish into a diocese, and improveth the least benefice into a bishopric'.[4] Richard Mulcaster did better for himself. A fine scholar and an accomplished musician, he was headmaster first at Merchant Taylors' and then of St Paul's School before retiring to the country rectory of Stanford Rivers, Essex, in 1598, where his learned type of preaching was described by his scripture-obsessed Puritan enemies as being at once 'weak and unprofitable'.[5] John White, Rector of Barsham in Suffolk at the turn of the century, would have been a scholar more to the nonconformists' taste, with his strong views on the doctrines of election, predestination, and damnation, which, as we have already seen, he preached at great length and in uncompromising terms. He published in 1608 *The Way to the True Church*, at once a defence of extreme Protestantism and a virulent attack on Catholicism, but also an exceedingly able piece of religious controversy.[6]

Another Puritan country parson, albeit of milder and broader views, was William Harrison, Rector of Radwinter and the author of that delightful book *A Description of England*, which he dedicated to his patron, Lord Cobham. Apart from Radwinter, which he held from 1559 to his death in 1593, Harrison was also incumbent for a time of Wimbish, another Essex benefice, and in 1586 became a Canon of Windsor. As a country parson he earned some £40 a year, a comfortable maintenance enough when the cost of living was relatively cheap. He tells us, for example, how his wife and her maid brewed him two hundred gallons of beer for twenty shillings. Possibly William was a bit of a trial to his wife Marion (nee Isebrande) since he was always something of a ladies' man.

> 'To their faults a little blind,
> And to their virtues very kind.'

'Eve will be Eve', he once remarked philosophically, 'tho' Adam would saie naie'. However, much could be forgiven a man who loved and tended his garden so carefully. 'For mine own part, good reader', he wrote, 'let me boast a little of my garden, which is but small, and the whole Area thereof little above 300 foot of ground, such hath bene my good lucke in purchase of the varietie of simples, that notwithstanding my small abilitie, there are verie neere three hundred of one sort and other conteined therein, no one of them being common or usuallie to bee had'. He was a tender and conscientious pastor of his little flock in Radwinter, and when he died he did not forget them 'To the poor of Radwinter', states his Will, '40s'. At Radwinter too he 'workt away' at his *Chronologie*, collected Roman coins, and fought with 'the rascally' Essex lawyers. But he wrote *A Description of England* in London! Here he drew a sad picture of the conditions under which many of the clergy had to live, and the low social status and ignorance of the ministers themselves. He concluded: 'The generall contempt of the ministrie, and small consideration of their former paines taken, whereby lesse and lesse hope of competent maintenance by preaching the word is likelie to insue. Wherefore the greatest part of the more excellent wits choose rather to imploy their studies unto physike and the lawes, utterlie giving over the study of the scriptures, for feare least they should in time not get their bread by the same'.[7]

Henry Copinger, 'the painful parson of Lavenham' in Suffolk for forty-five years, was likewise a staunch upholder of the Church's rights. He flatly declined to accept Lavenham when first presented to it by the Earl of Oxford, since his patron had made his appointment conditional on the new Rector's requiring no tithes from the Earl's park, which incidentally comprised half the acreage of the parish! Eventually the Earl gave way. 'Well', he conceded sulkily, 'if you be of that mind, then take the tithes. I scorn that my estate should swell with church goods'. However, the battle had to be fought all over again with the agent of the next earl, who was a minor; and cost the Rector some £16,000 on law-suits. He won and saved the Church's possessions, although at considerable personal loss, 'being zealous in God's cause, but remiss in his own'. At Lavenham, we are told, there were some nine hundred communicants during Copinger's incumbency, all of whom looked to their Rector for help and guidance. He possessed a beautiful voice and a plentiful purse; and when he died he left a lump sum of twenty pounds in money and ten pounds per annum to the poor of the town. He lies buried in the chancel of the parish church.[8]

In the person of William Morgan, the Elizabethan Rector of a remote country parish in the diocese of St Asaph, we encounter Welsh biblical scholarship at its best. Here in his little country parsonage he struggled for ten years to translate the Bible into Welsh from the Greek and Hebrew texts, aided by the Latin Vulgate and the English Geneva Bible. 'Both in magnitude and quality', wrote an admirer, 'his work stands unequalled in the history of the Welsh Bible if not of Welsh scholarship. . . . Morgan's Welsh Bible preserved the Welsh language as a literary medium for all time'.[9] This magnum opus earned him a chaplaincy to Archbishop Whitgift, and subsequently the sees of Llandaff and St Asaph.

But when all is said and done the best known country parson in Elizabeth's reign is undoubtedly Richard Hooker, thanks to his kindly biographer Isaak Walton; although as Professor Sisson has recently taught us we must treat that fisherman's narrative with considerable caution. The gentle judicious scholar, whose great work *The Ecclesiastical Polity* cemented the foundations of the Elizabethan Settlement, married, one was long led to believe, a shrew of a wife, Joan Churchman, who 'brought him neither beauty nor portion: and for her conditions, they were too like that wife's, which is by Solomon compared to a dripping house'. In fact Hooker's marriage was just as judicious as his writings; for, while Master of the Temple in 1588, he married the daughter of a well-known family of Merchant Taylors, and received with her a dowry of £700. Joan's father, John Churchman, became Master of the Company in 1594; and it is highly probable that the Hookers lived with the Churchmans until such time as Richard was appointed in 1595 to the country benefice of Bishop's Bourne in Kent, where he remained until his death in 1600. As we have already seen it was most unlikely that he ever resided at Drayton-Beauchamp in Buckinghamshire. At Bishop's Bourne Hooker received many visitors, who were attracted both by his fame as a scholar and by the holiness of his life. He preached and catechized every Sunday, appealing always to the reason rather than the fears or emotions of his congregation; and was particularly careful to observe all the fasts and festivals of the Church. Every ember day he took 'from the parish clerk the key of the church door, into which place he retired . . . and locked himself up for many hours, and did the like most Fridays and other days of fasting'. He diligently visited the sick even when 'unsent for'; celebrated the Holy Communion frequently, and studied so constantly that he undermined his health. Walton thus described him during these last years: 'Usually girt in a coarse gown or canonical coat; of a mean stature, and stooping, yet more lowly in the thoughts of his soul; his body worn out, not with age, but study and holy mortifications; his face full of heat pimples, begot by his inactivity and sedentiary life . . . and was of so mild and humble a nature, that his poor parish clerk and he did ever talk but with both their hats on, or both off, at the same time'. Hooker left an estate worth £1092 9s. 2d., which, despite Walton's insinuations regarding her shrewishness and extravagance, was largely left to Joan as residuary legatee and sole executrix. Richard referred to her in his Will as 'well-beloved', and to his father-in-law, who was one of the overseers of that Will, as 'well-beloved father'. The legend of the unattractive scold foisted by scheming parents onto an innocent young scholar was probably the work of two of Hooker's Oxford pupils, Edwin Sandys and George Cranmer, who appear to have strongly disapproved of Joan and her family. Perhaps the fact that Joan herself married again within six months of Richard's death, that her father went bankrupt, and her two daughters engaged in litigation with Sandys, had something to do with this hostility which took in not only Walton but Fuller as well![10]

The first half of the seventeenth century was equally rich in the scholar-parson and the saint, both Puritan and Anglican, the sinner and the dunce; but added the poet and the diarist.

A prominent figure among country incumbents in James I's reign was Jeremiah Dyke, Vicar of Epping. With puritanical leanings, he was yet essentially 'one of a cheerful spirit . . . a gracious heart, and was profitable in his ministry'. He was also described as 'richly furnished with divine grace' and 'eminently useful in his ministry'. Dyke was no nonconformist bigot and quietly submitted to Canon Law, for the sake of both peace and uniformity, which his conscience told him justified the use of much that he personally disapproved of. He died 'piously' in 1620 and was buried in his church. A theologian of some repute, he wrote and published several learned works, of which the best known was a treatise on the Lord's Supper entitled *The Worthy Communicant*, besides piloting through the press the posthumous but controversial writings of his brother, Daniel.

Daniel Dyke, who was at one time minister at Coggeshall and later at St Albans, had been suspended and eventually deprived by Bishop Aylmer of London for his strong Puritan opinions. Among his numerous offences was the refusal to proceed from the diaconate to the priesthood, or to wear the surplice. Lord Burleigh interceded for him in vain; and Dyke died, still unrestored to his benefice, in 1614. His works were much admired, particularly *Mystery of Self-deceiving*. 'It is a book', wrote Fuller, 'that will be owned for a truth, while men have any badness in them; and will be owned as a treasure, while they have any goodness in them'. Jeremiah, it is worth recording, left an estate worth more than six hundred pounds, to which no doubt book-royalties had substantially contributed; nevertheless this was a welcome indication that some of the parochial clergy were now able to save money. His son, another Daniel, appears to have taken after his Uncle, for he became one of Oliver Cromwell's chaplains, Vicar of Much Hadham, from which the royalist Thomas Paske had been evicted, and finally a 'Trier' in 1655.[11]

Other early seventeenth-century Puritan country parsons catch the eye: Robert Bolton, the learned Oxford lecturer in natural and moral philosophy, who was presented in 1609 to the rectory of Broughton, Northamptonshire, by Sir Augustine Nichols, a justice of the common pleas, was a reformed rake. One who had 'loved plays and cards, was a horrible swearer, sabbath-breaker, and familiar associate of the wicked'; and had called the famous Puritan, William Perkins, 'a barren empty fellow, and a very mean scholar'. But, after nearly succumbing to the wiles of Rome, Bolton was 'converted' by Thomas Peacock in his thirty-fifth year. At Broughton, where he preached powerfully twice a Sunday besides catechizing the youth of the parish, he rapidly acquired the reputation of being 'a most authoritative and awakening' preacher who had been endowed 'with the most masculine and oratorical style of any in his time'. He prayed six times daily: twice by himself, twice with his family and twice with his wife. Like Jeremiah Dyke he had the good sense to avoid any clash with the ecclesiastical authorities and kept just within the letter of Canon Law. Nevertheless he was an ardent Protestant, who never preached a sermon to his people until he had first tried it over in private to himself; and on his deathbed thanked God 'for His wonderful mercy, in plucking him as a brand from the fire, and in blessing his ministry to the conversion of so many souls'. Eachard wrote of him as 'a great and shining light of the puritan party . . . justly celebrated for his singular learning and piety'. Bolton wrote numerous books, which were greatly admired and sought after by the nonconformist faction.[12]

Another thorough-going Puritan divine of this period was John Carter, Vicar first of Bramford and later Rector of Belstead in Suffolk, where he was sorely persecuted by Bishop Wren. At his ordination Carter had been asked whether he had read the Bible through, to which he made the devastating reply: 'I have read the Old Testament twice through in Hebrew, and the New Testament often through in Greek'. His income, despite the efforts made by his parishioners to improve it, rarely rose above £20 per annum; but as he always said 'he sought not *theirs* but *them* and so was content'. A man of wit as well as of learning, several of his sayings have been preserved. A typical one was his reply to a poor man who had complained: 'I work hard, and fare hard, and yet I cannot thrive'. Carter retorted: 'yet still you want one thing. You must work hard, and fare hard, and pray hard, and then you will be sure to thrive'. He died on 22 February 1634 in the eightieth year of his age. 'He was a man', wrote his biographer, 'of great learning and piety, an orthodox and peaceable divine, and an avowed enemy of Popery and Arminianism'. Among other works he published *A Commentary of Christ's Sermon upon the Mount* and two Catechisms.[13]

A good final example of the typical Puritan country parson is that of Hugh Clark, Vicar of Oundle. The people there he found lived 'in the constant profanation of the Lord's day by Whitsun-ales, morris-dancing and other ungodly sports'; and when he reproved them severely in a series of strongly-worded sermons he went in danger of his life. 'A lusty young man' visited him one morning with a dagger intent on his murder, but after a heart to heart talk with his Vicar changed his mind and confessed his guilt. 'I came hither', he said, 'with a full resolution to stab you, but God has prevented me. This was occasioned by your terrifying sermon yesterday'. Gradually Clark won his parishioners' hearts and changed their mode of life. From Oundle he proceeded to Wolston in Warwickshire, where he incurred the enmity of Bishop Overton. The story goes that the Bishop came one Sunday morning to Wolston to hear Clark preach. The Vicar ignored his presence and 'dispensed the word of life with his usual zeal and fervency'; whereupon Dr Overton, apparently, could hardly sit in his seat he was so annoyed and 'shifted from place to place, as if he sat upon thorns'. Observing his distress, but completely ignorant of the cause, one of the churchwardens brought him a cushion to sit on, and then another to recline upon, 'but still he appeared uncommonly restless'. Eventually his lordship departed in a rage, after informing the congregation :'This is indeed a hot fellow, but I will cool him'. He began by suspending Clark from preaching, whereupon the latter expounded the Scriptures; and forbidden to expound, he took to catechizing. At last the Vicar was excommunicated, arrested, and imprisoned; he then appealed to the Archbishop of Canterbury, who curiously enough took Clark's side and compelled the Bishop to acknowledge publicly that he was in the wrong. Henceforth Clark and his Bishop became very good friends, and during the former's forty-four-year pastorate at Wolston he incurred no further penalties; although he continued his 'zealous' sermons twice a Sunday at both the parish church and the chapel of ease. He died in 1634, after a long and painful illness, during his sixty-first year.[14]

Ill-health certainly dogged the footsteps of all too many country parsons, whose lives, if not exactly brutish and beastly, were often painful and short. Nicholas Byfield, the incumbent of Isleworth in Middlesex, was a famous preacher who regularly and conscientiously delivered a sermon twice every Sunday for fifteen years, besides catechizing each Wednesday and Friday, until some five weeks before his death, despite agonizing tortures from the stone. 'And', wrote a contemporary, 'having groaned for several years under the most excruciating pain, it brought him at length to his grave, in the year 1622'. How agonizing this pain must have been can be estimated from the fact that a post-mortem revealed a stone in his bladder weighing more than thirty-three ounces and measuring thirteen inches each way. 'It was', Fuller solemnly recorded, 'of a solid substance to look upon, like a flint'.[15] Another sufferer from the same cause was Jeremiah

Whitaker, Rector of Stretton in Rutland, who used to officiate 'afflicted with most racking pains'. He died in 1654 aged fifty-five, and when his body was opened 'his kidnies were full of ulcers, and one of them swelled to an enormous size and filled with purulent matter. In the neck of the bladder they found a stone about an inch and half long, and an inch broad, weighing about two ounces'.[16] The stone was no respecter of persons, for the famous Dr Henry Hammond, Rector of Penshurst, Kent, also died of it; whose torments are thus described: 'But now through the long suppression of Urine, the bloud being grown Thin and Serious, and withal, Eager and Tumultuous, through the mixture of Heterrogeneous parts; this excellent person fell to a violent bleeding . . . and found no ease, but that the pain of the Humors stoppage relieved the Stone, the Lethargy that, and the Flux of Bloud the Lethargy; which variety of tortures, exercised not only his patience, but his thankfulness too; crying out in his greatest extreamities, "Blessed be God, blessed be God" '.[17]

As the seventeenth century went on, of course, a more high church or Arminian parson began to appear in many country parishes, where he often had to contend with a Protestant underworld. William Sclater, for example, early in James I's reign encountered considerable opposition from his puritanical parishioners at Pitminster in Somerset. 'Here', wrote Fuller, 'he met with manifold and expensive vexations, even to the jeopardy of his life; but, by the goodness of God, his own innocency and courage, with the favour of his diocesan, he came off with no less honour to himself than confusion to his adversaries'. Sclater, who died in 1627, has left behind him a remarkable treatise, based doubtless on his own experiences, entitled: *The Ministers Portion*.[18]

The two outstanding names among Laudian country clergy are those of George Herbert and Nicholas Ferrar. Herbert, well-born and well-connected, a favourite of James I, seemed destined for a brilliant career at Court. But the death of the King and two of his most powerful friends, the Duke of Richmond and the Marquis of Hamilton, together with his own ill-health, turned his eyes in another direction. His mother wished him to enter the Church, and against the advice of his friends, who pointed out the mean social status of the average parson, Herbert decided to do so. 'The domestic servants of the King of Heaven', he declared, 'should be of the noblest families on earth. And though the iniquity of the late times have made clergymen meanly valued, and the sacred name of priest contemptible; yet I will labour to make it honourable, by consecrating all my learning, and all my poor abilities to advance the glory of that God that gave them'. Eventually, encouraged by William Laud himself, Herbert accepted the rectory of Bemerton near Salisbury. At his induction he shut himself alone into

K

Bermerton church, prostrated himself upon the ground and 'set some rules to himself, for the future management of his life; and then and there made a vow to labour to keep them'. The blue-blooded courtier, in fact, had become lost in the humble pastor. 'A priest's wife', he told Mrs Herbert, 'can challenge no precedent or place, but that which she purchases by her obliging humility'. Both husband and wife laboured unceasingly during their all too short spell at Bemerton. Herbert, who also held the prebend of Layton Ecclesia, rebuilt with the aid of Nicholas Ferrar and the goldsmith Arthur Woodnoth the parish church of Layton Ecclesia; reconstructed his own parsonage; and restored Bemerton church and the little chapel that stood by his house; all by means of his own and personal friends' contributions. To the poor and the sick he was an ever present help in trouble. Over the mantelpiece in his hall he engraved the following lines:

> *To my Successor*
> 'If thou chance for to find
> A new house to thy mind,
> And built without thy cost;
> Be good to the poor,
> As God gives thee store,
> And then my labour's not lost.'

The Rector of Bemerton preached simple gospel sermons of half-an-hour's duration, expounded the meaning and value of the Prayer Book services, spoke of the need for the Church's festivals and fast-days, approved the reverential attitudes of kneeling for prayer and standing to worship, and carefully adopted all those ceremonies commanded by lawful authority. Twice every day he and his whole family attended in the chapel for the daily offices 'at the canonical hours of ten and four, and then and there he lifted up pure and charitable hands to God in the midst of the congregation'. For, ere long, he had induced most of his parishioners and many of the neighbouring gentry to join him in these devotions. 'Some of the meaner sort of the parish', wrote Walton, 'did so love and reverence Mr Herbert, that they would let their plough rest when Mr Herbert's saints-bell rung to prayers, that they might also offer their devotions to God with him; and would then return back to their plough'. Private devotions and family prayers likewise took up a substantial part of each day's routine. Herbert's remedies for the religious ills of his time were startlingly akin to much that is preached today: first, the urgent need for catechizing the children and teaching the faith to the ignorant; and secondly a wholehearted and widespread display of practical Christian living by professing churchmen and churchwomen themselves. The story of how on his way to a musical party at Salisbury, Herbert helped a poor man to unload and then re-load a fallen horse, eventually arriving covered in dirt and sweat, to the manifest disgust of his friends, was a typical instance of his own behaviour in this respect. 'Though I do not wish for the like occasion every day', he told them, 'yet let me tell you, I would not willingly pass one day of my life without comforting a sad soul or showing mercy'. A tenth of his income he handed over to his wife for charity; but quite apart from this tithing of himself, he was so bountiful that it was freely prophesied that he would be ruined. He replied that he had no family and his wife already possessed 'a competent maintenance secured her'.

Holy living, alas, soon gave place to holy dying; for his health, which had never been robust, gave way under the strain of his manifold labours. On his death-bed, however, he compiled the famous book of poems, *The Temple; or Sacred Poems and Private Ejaculations*, which together with *A Priest to the Temple, or the Country Parson His Character and Rule of Holy Life* constitute his claim to immortality as an author and poet. To his friend, Nicholas Ferrar, he entrusted the publication of the poems, which contained the celebrated lines expressing his growing fears for the Church of England:

> 'Religion stands a tiptoe in our land
> Ready to pass to the American strand'.

The Country Parson, wherein Herbert described the parson as 'the deputy of Christ for the reducing of man to the obedience of God', and affirmed that 'out of this character of the priesthood may be plainly gathered both the dignity thereof and the duty' was published posthumously by Barnabas Oley in 1652. It sought to provide 'a mark to aim at' for his brother clergy, which few showed any inclination to follow.[19]

Just as George Herbert had set the standard for the ordinary country incumbent, so his great ally, Nicholas Ferrar, sought to revive the spirit of the religious community at his home in Little Gidding. This neo-monastic experiment aroused at once some applause and a great deal of bitter criticism, leading eventually to its dissolution. Nicholas Ferrar, like George Herbert, had played an active and distinguished part in the world before he retired with his family to Little Gidding. His father, who was a prosperous London merchant, gave him a good education; and Nicholas became a fellow of Clare College, Cambridge, travelled extensively on the continent, and returned in 1618 to join the Virginia Company, in which the whole Ferrar family was then deeply interested. Here he worked hard, and his ability and industry quickly won him the position of deputy-treasurer. He also entered Parliament, largely in order to be able to state the Company's case against the pronounced and growing hostility of the King.

'In the five brief years since his return from abroad', writes his most recent biographer, 'Nicholas' rise to eminence . . . had been nothing short of meteoric. He had shown that he possessed administrative abilities of the very first order; he had shown that he could assume the highest responsibilities and direct great issues with wisdom and skill; he had been brought in contact with most of the leading men of the time and had impressed every one of them by his talent and his superb judgment. The King himself had noted and commented on his abilities; in the involved and difficult negotiations between the Privy Council and the Virginia Company Nicholas had behaved not only with discretion and tact, but in a manner that had made a profound impression on the Councillors. We know that he was actually offered his choice of two important posts in government service: either a clerkship to the Privy Council or the British embassy in Savoy. These offers he had refused and had at the time professed to two of his greatest friends, and on their promise of secrecy, his solemn determination to enter upon a life of religious retirement, as soon as his present duties permitted.'[20]

The plague of 1625 hastened his decision. Nicholas took deacon's orders, although he never proceeded to the priesthood; and once the church and manor house at Little Gidding had been cleansed and restored, the whole Ferrar family, some thirty of them in all, under the nominal headship of old Mrs Ferrar, but with Nicholas as its guiding and burning light, moved in. There they built up a regular and never ceasing round of prayer, worship, study, manual labour, charitable works, and recreation, which continued until Nicholas's death and the sacking of the house and church by the Puritans. The friendship of William Laud and Bishop Williams of Lincoln, the patronage of King Charles himself, and the host of friends and admirers who visited Little Gidding, all helped to create a legend that aroused the bitterest antagonism among the Puritans, who referred to this little community in a widely circulated pamphlet as 'The Arminian Nunnery . . . the late erected Monasticall Place'. In point of fact the family group at Little Gidding was never a monastery; but simply an entire family devoting its life to the worship and service of God in a regular and orderly way. No vows were either demanded or taken. There were always, too, the ordinary household duties to perform: bringing up the children, looking after the garden, preparing food, making and mending clothes. The Ferrars were, of course, a relatively well-to-do family; for such an existence would not have been possible if they had had seriously to earn their own living. However, their income was supplemented to a certain extent by taking in paying pupils and paying guests.

What of Nicholas himself? He was very industrious, working eighteen hours out of the twenty-four, but never long at any one occupation. A strong believer, despite his own delicate constitution, in bringing the body under subjection by stern discipline, he used regularly to conduct his voluminous correspondence either standing or kneeling; he fasted strictly and never allowed himself more than four hours' sleep, stretched on a board with a white bearskin beneath him and wrapped in a black frieze gown; while on the three nights every week that he 'watched', he took no sleep at all. Nicholas was the born organizer and civil servant: patient, accurate, and tireless; carrying through his purposes without fuss or hurry, but always smoothly and efficiently. He was the acknowledged leader at Little Gidding; yet he never played the tyrant, and whether as spiritual director or secular organizer he got his way by means of persuasion or the force of his personality, never by compulsion or threats. A great believer in simplicity and commonsense, whether in medicine or religion, his advice was always down to earth. For instance, he told his great friend, Arthur Woodnoth the goldsmith, to walk more and eat less in order to get his weight down; and he laid emphasis on the need for a scriptural as well as a sacramental type of worship. Hence his great love for the Gospels, the Psalter, and the Prayer Book, and opposition to the heady wine of a formless Puritanism.

Some of the manual work done at Little Gidding was of superb craftsmanship, as for example in the construction of their concordances. Charles I was, indeed, so pleased with their Concordance of the Gospels that he commissioned a similar one for himself. This was splendidly bound in crimson leather, tooled in gilt, and was presented to the King by John Cosin on behalf of the Ferrars. Turning over the pages Charles cried out in delight: 'How happy a King were I if I had many more such workmen and women in my Kingdom'. Later, through the agency of Archbishop Laud, he asked for a Harmony of the Books of Kings and Chronicles. When this arrived, he remarked to those around him: 'My Lords, this is a jewel in all respects, to be continually worn on a King's breast and in his heart'.

In connection with Nicholas Ferrar, the deacon of Little Gidding, one must needs mention, if only in passing, the names of two faithful country priests who helped him in his work. The Rector of Steeple Gidding, David Stevens, was an absentee; and it was Luke Grosse, Vicar of Great Gidding and curate at Steeple Gidding, who used to come down Sunday after Sunday with his congregation to preach at Matins in Little Gidding church. Once a month he also celebrated communion there; and regularly the whole Ferrar household crossed the fields to Steeple Gidding for Sunday Evensong. Luke Grosse attended Nicholas on his death-bed, heard his confession, and gave him the sacrament.

Joshua Mapletoft, who was Nicholas's brother-in-law, was rector of Margaretting in Essex; a quiet, humble, not over-intelligent man, but

one that worshipped the very ground on which Nicholas trod, and
strove to imitate him in all things. Margaretting vicarage became a kind
of second Little Gidding; and eventually four out of his five children
joined the Ferrar household. But the patient, gentle, unambitious
Joshua possessed the courage of an early Christian martyr. He endured
a fearsome and almost incredibly painful operation with tremendous
courage and cheerfulness; and although he never really recovered from
it, lingered on for another two years. During these years he set himself
to examine 'the secret places of his heart' and rededicated himself completely anew to God's service. He trained his own and the village
children in the learning of the psalms by heart, strove to secure the
restoration of impropriate tithes and glebe lands to his church, and was
one of the first Essex incumbents to inaugurate a regular monthly
communion.

From the semi-cloistered devotions of the Ferrar family we now
turn to the semi-pagan Robert Herrick, Vicar of Dean Prior from 1629
to 1647, and again from 1662 to 1674. Herrick rejoiced in the lush
beauty and fruitfulness of Devonshire, although he always professed
to be forever pinning for his 'beloved Westminster'. As a rural poet
he was, indeed, of the earth earthy, and sang of the pagan folk-lore and
folk-ritual of his rustic parishioners. Yet, as Rose Macaulay once
pointed out in *They were Defeated*, he never shared the savage cruelties
that accompanied them, such as witch-hunting or bear-baiting. He
referred, in fact, to his people as being 'currish; churlish as the seas;
And rude almost as rudest savages'. Nevertheless their church wakes
and ales, morris dances and harvest homes were the very breath of life
to a parson like Herrick. He wrote of the Church's feasts:

> For Sports for Pagentrie and Playes,
> Thou hast thy Eves and Holydayes . . .
> Thy Wakes, thy Quintels, here thou hast,
> Thy May-poles too with Garlands grac't:
> Thy Morris-dance; thy Whitsun-ale;
> Thy Sheering-feast, which never faile.
> Thy Harvest home; thy Wassaile bowle,
> That's tost up after Fox i' th'Hole;
> Thy Mummeries: thy Twelfe-tide Kings
> And Queenes: thy Christmas revellings.

And, despite his hankerings after the London taverns, and professed
discontent with 'Lothed' and 'dull Devonshire', he was really happy
enough in his country living, isolated as it undoubtedly was. He threw
himself whole-heartedly into farming his ninety-three-acre glebe,
conscientiously if not very fervently served his beautiful little church,
lovingly tended his flower-garden, and lived comfortably but frugally

in his rustic parsonage, where Prudence Baldwin, his faithful maid,
looked after him. After the latter's death he wrote:

> 'In this little Urne is laid
> Prewdence Baldwin (once my maid)
> From whose happy spark here let
> Spring the purple violet.'

These lines sum up Herrick's own attitude towards religion. A kindly
man, who fed the poor and possessed in considerable measure the
great virtues of thankfulness, contentment, and stoicism, he was yet
utterly lacking in any deep spiritual powers or experience. 'He was no
saint', writes a modern essayist, 'but neither does he seem particularly
aware of being a sinner. It was as an artist that his conscience was most
exacting'.[21] Contentment was his abiding companion:

> Lord, Thou hast given me a cell
>   Wherein to dwell.
> A little House whose humble roof
>   Is weather proof;
> Under the spars of which I lie
>   Both soft and dry.
>
> Like as my Parlour, so my Hall
>   And Kitchin's small:
> A little Butterie, and therein
>   A little Byn,
> Which keeps my little loafe of Bread
>   Un chipt't, unflead:
> Some little sticks of Thorne or Briar
>   Make me a fire,
> Close by whose living coale I sit,
>   And glow like it.

But if Herrick was no saint, the next parson on our list, the Reverend
Edward Barbet, Vicar of Chislet in Kent, was from all accounts a
notable sinner. However, the picture that has come down to us in the
petition sent to Sir Edward Dering by his enraged puritanical parishioners is hardly an objective or impartial one. Barbet was one of Laud's
nominees, and as such was ranked with the unpopular high church
party. He is described as an erstwhile country gentleman, who, after
dissipating the greater part of his estate on riotous living, and having
seen the inside of a prison for more than a year, 'made composition
with his creditors' and took orders 'for his better mayntenance and
livelyhood'. At Chislet, apparently, his ministry was a cross between
the scandalous and ludicrous. 'Touching his readinge of Divine

Service', wrote his enemies, 'he reads soe false, and with such ill gesture, and ridiculous behaviour, laughing when some women come into Church, and soe careless in readinge, that sometimes he reads the Ten Commandments twice over, at morning Prayer, besides many other slips, mistakings, and negligences, not fittinge for a minister of God's work'. He was further accused of being an unlearned and ignorant man who had 'never studyed Divinity' and preached 'weake' sermons, while denying the use of his pulpit to abler men. 'It is well-knowne', they continued, 'that hee is a common lyer, a notorious swearer, a foule, obscene, and bawdy speaker of Ribaldry, utteringe sometimes such words as are not to be spoken by any modest man, nor to be heard by any Christian eares. And hee is also of an incontinent life; and hath affirmed that marriage was a superficial ceremony, and that yt was but the mumblinge of a Preist'.[22]

We now come to the seventeenth-century clerical diarists amongst country parsons: John Rous was Rector of Santon Downham in Suffolk from 1625 to 1642, during which period he kept a journal of sorts. This was very largely filled with accounts of political or military events, trials, proclamations, and petitions; and few personal details are recorded. Rous, who lived for many years with his father at Weeting parsonage, was twice married and had several daughters, although we learn little enough about them from the diary. However, there are comments on the weather, the crops and prices, besides a collection of satirical verses and notes on local crimes and extraordinary occurrences. The Rector never actually resided at Santon Downham. He remained until his father's death at Weeting acting as his amanuensis; and then moved to Brandon, 'where in a particular building, called "the minister's house", several of the clergy of the adjacent rural parishes took up their abode'. Interested in politics and religious controversy, he was himself very much a middle-of-the-road man, who first supported the King and then later veered over to the Parliament, but was never a very warm partisan of either side. Rous was something of a scholar, judging from his Latin and French quotations, knowledgeable in country matters like farming or the weather, and an incurable gossip. A good example of this last is to be found in the market-tale of William Utting, the toad-eater: 'In October 1629', wrote the Rector, 'I having been at Wickham Market . . . in our returne . . . I fell into the company of one Paine, a shopkeeper in Laxfield, of whom, after much talke about Mr Skinner and my oulde acquaintance at Laxfield and Dennington, I inquired of him if William Utting the toade-eater . . . did not once keepe at Laxfield; he tould me yes, and said he had seene him eate a toade, nay two. A man in whose house he kept went to him . . . and after salutation, tould him that a friend of his would give a groate to see him eate a toade (thus was the way to see it): he accepted the offer, and went and fetched in, from under blockes, 2 toades, and rubbing off the earth ... he swallowed them downe, but presently he cast them up into his hands, and after some pawse, "Nay", saith he, "I will not loose my groate", so taking that which came up last (saith he) "thou wentest in first before and shalt soe do againe". When both then were downe, his stomacke held them, and he had his groate. This said Paine'. If Rous was living today he would undoubtedly have been a detective-story fan; for no-one was fonder than he of recording local tales of murder, suicide, or fatal accidents; and from his frequent mention of Quarter Sessions and Assizes it is highly probable that he was himself a Justice of the Peace.

The obscurity of Santon Downham must at times have irked a parson whose scholarship and wide interests in religious and political controversy fitted him for a more active role in the Church; and his sense of frustration seemingly found an outlet in some lines inserted into the diary during 1641, entitled *The Scholler's Lament:*

> Into some country village
>   Nowe I must goe,
> Where neither tithe nor tillage
>   The greedy patron
>   And coached matron
> Sweare to the Church they owe;
> But if I preach and pray too on the suddaine,
> And confute the Pope too, extempore without studying
>   I've tenne poundes a yeere, besides my Sunday
>   pudding.
>   Alas, pore scholler!
> Whether wilt thou goe?[23]

Giles Moore, who was Rector of Horsted Keynes, Sussex, in 1655, kept an interesting account book, which he headed with the words: 'Wee reckon our expenses but not our sins; wee account what wee expend but not where wee offend'. He recorded some interesting prices: 'For 3 yards and ¾ of scarlet serge', he noted, 'of which I made the library cupboard carpet besydes my wastcoate made thereof', he paid 15s. He bought beef at 1s. 10d. a stone; six months' 'barbouring' cost 7s. 6d.; being blooded 1s.; a hog 30s.; 2 quarts of sack 4s.; and a quart of claret 1s. On the other hand 'a payre of silk stockings' fetched a guinea, and a 'shaggy demi castor hat' 16s. 6d. He paid his doctor at the following rates: 'For the advising about the turning about of my neck £1. For 2 dozen of pills 3s. and for a pint of sack 1s. His direction is that I am to take 3 pills over night and anything warm in the morning once in two days and if I am no better I am to use a large blyster behind the shoulder blade: to do it again in a fortnight and then afterwards to shave my head'. Sometimes Moore engaged in barter. 'I sent to Mr Hely a ribspare and hoggs pudding for which he returned me a box of pills and sermons . . . I sent Mistresse Michelbourne a galon of rose water and 1 quarter of damasks, she sending me back by the messenger 3 dozen of pigeons'. He made various trips to the Isle of Wight, Chichester, and London; to the last of which he took with him his god-daughter, Mat. But we hear nothing about these expeditions from the diary, excepting his purchases and expenses. The Rector certainly believed in getting his money's worth. For instance he had to pay £1 10s. for Mat's board and lodging for six weeks at 'Mistress Chalmers'; but during that time Mat 'made mee shirts and bands'. She was later rewarded with five shillings 'to buy a hood at the faire'. 24

The diary of Ralph Josselin, the puritanical Vicar of Earls Colne, Essex, is a much more intimate and hence more interesting document. Josselin was born at Bishop's Stortford: 'God fittinge mee for a scholler and giving me a spirit for the same, from which nothing would divert mee'. After taking his degree at Jesus College, Cambridge, and receiving no more than £20 from his late father's estate, Ralph was at one time almost completely destitute; but his uncle Benton in Norfolk 'entertayned mee with love and pity and offered mee to stay a while with him; here was providence, abroad I had none, money none, and friends were not so kinde as I expected'. Eventually he became an usher, first at Deane, Bedfordshire, and later at Olney, where he was ordained. Here as a curate he lived at the parsonage and earned £14 per annum. 'I lived with them [Mr Gifford, the incumbent and his family]', he wrote, 'very comfortably and contentedly; wee used Shovelboard for our recreation of which I grew weary presently'.

Josselin was the typical Puritan combining thrift and piety with a shrewd business capacity for making money. Steadily he rose up the clerical ladder. From Olney he migrated to a curacy at Cranham in Essex, where 'ye minister allowing £24 per annum and my uncle my diett of £10 and the Towne £10 more'; was shortly afterward offered a lectureship in Hornchurch worth £80 a year; and finally accepted the living of Earls Colne during 1640, to which he was presented by Richard Harlakenden, Cromwell's friend. There he remained for the rest of his long life. The income was reputed to be worth £80 per annum, although the *Valor Ecclesiasticus* valued it at only £8 10s. 8d.; but Josselin often had great difficulty in making his parishioners pay up, and was forever threatening to leave them unless they did so. In various ways: by legacies from relations, profits from his farm, his salary as a schoolmaster and army chaplaincy during the Civil War, and a parliamentary augmentation of his living, he gradually amassed a considerable fortune and left his family well off. An ardent supporter of Parliament, he cheerfully obeyed its commands and played an active part in its defence. 'This Michaelmas [1641]', he recorded in his diary, 'upon an order of the House of Commons to that purpose, wee tooke downe all images and pictures and such like glasses'. He went to London and 'provided for myselfe Sword, Halbert, Powder and Match'; then returning to Earle Colne, 'I endeavoured to encourage others to go forth'. At a later stage as an army chaplain in Colonel Harlakenden's regiment Josslin himself saw active service.

His puritanical beliefs are clearly expressed in such passages as the following: 'Visited a sicke man one Guy Penhacke who was much troubled in his mind upon his life: he had strong temptacons from Sathan. I urged him to a Covent with God to bee a new man if he recovered'; or 'Stung I was with a bee on my nose. I presently pluckt out ye sting and layd on honey, so that my face swelled not; thus divine providence reaches to the lowest things. Lett not sin oh Lord that dreadful sting bee able to poyson mee'. All things Laudian, on the other hand, were anathema to him: 'I made a serious exhortation to lay aside ye jollity and vanity of ye time custome hath wedded us unto, and to keep the Sabbath better which is the only Lds day we are commanded to observe'. The Archbishop's own execution and the supersession of the Prayer Book by the Directory both rejoiced his heart. On 10 January 1644/5, he wrote: 'The Arch Bp, yt grand enemy of the pouer of godlynes, that great stickler for all outward pompe in the service of God, left his head at Tower hill London, by ordinance of parliamt'; and two months later on 23 March he recorded: 'This weeke I saw ye Directory and an Ordnance of Parliament to take away ye heavy burthen of ye booke of Common prayer in all parts of the same'. Josselin appears to have been a kindly soul much beloved of his parishioners, who showed their appreciation of his services and long sermons by sending him gifts in kind. 'One sends me', he noted, 'a parcel of plums and sugar, another a fatt goose, another a capon and cheese'. Out of the goodness of his heart, although he personally disapproved of the sect, the Vicar secured the release of one of his parishioners, an anabaptist, who had been pressed for a soldier. On another occasion he saved a poor simple soul accused of witchcraft. 'One J. Biford', he wrote, in August 1656, 'was clamoured on as a witch, and Mr C. thought his child ill by it; I could no way apprehend it, I tooke ye fellow along into the feild and dealt wity him solemnly, and I conceive ye poore wretch is innocent as to that evill'. Apart from his absorbing and very active interest in the fortunes of the Puritan and parliamentary forces—an interest for which he suffered grievously when Goring and his cavaliers sacked Earls Colne in 1648: 'June 12. On Monday morning', the diary tells us, 'the enemy came to Colne, and were resisted by our towne men. No part of Essex gave them so much opposition as wee did; they plundered us, and mee in particular, of all that was portable, except brasse, pewter, and bedding'—Josselin is revealed by the diary as an affectionate family man, something of a scholar, and a countryman with a keen eye for the weather and the changing seasons. He rose early in the morning in order to study Hebrew by candle-light, was always a voracious reader, and even engaged himself upon 'a reconciler of Scriptures'. He also noted carefully the constantly rising prices of foodstuffs: 'On September 26th, 1645', he commented, 'things are at that rate as never was in our days: wheat 8s., malt 4s., beefe 3d. (per lb), butter 6½d., cheese 4d., candle 7d., currants 9d., sugar 18d., and everything whatsoever deare'. His religious principles were simple but very firm; and his faith in God's goodness was absolute, despite much affliction. 'This day', he wrote on 2 February 1648, 'my deare babe Ralph quietly fell asleepe, and is at rest with the Lord; the Lord in mercy sanctifie his hand unto mee and doe mee good by it and teach mee how to walke more closely with him'. He sought diligently in his own mind to account for 'this correction'; and discovered reasons in his 'unseasonable playing of chesss', 'vanieite in my thoughts', and above all because he had served 'divers lusts too much in thought and in actions, whereas both body and soule should bee the Lords who hath called mee to holynes'.

The Vicar was a tireless preacher; once at least he preached for three hours, and on 5 October 1650 had the honour of delivering a sermon in St Paul's Cathedral 'by order from ye Ld Mayor'. Presbyterian-minded himself, he did not approve of the various sectaries, particularly the Quakers. 'Sad are the fits at Coxall [Coggeshall]', he remarked, 'like the pow-wowing among the Indies'; nor did he like the rule of the Major Generals. He was, in fact, at heart a convinced monarchist and deeply lamented the execution of Charles I. 'I was much troubled', he confided to his journal, 'with the blacke providence of putting the King to death'. The passing of Oliver Cromwell was noted with indifference, and he greatly rejoiced at the return of the Stuarts.[25]

Autobiographies abound in the seventeenth-century. Two written by Puritan divines, Henry Newcome and Richard Baxter, concern us briefly here.

Henry Newcome, who was born in 1627, the son and brother of Anglican parsons, was himself educated at St John's College, Cambridge, but was never episcopally ordained. He first preached and taught at Congleton in Cheshire during 1647; but after his marriage the following year moved to Goosetree and then to the rectory of Gawsworth. Newcome thus describes his presbyterian form of ordination: 'On the 22nd of August this very year [1648], I was ordained at Sandbach, I did not think of it, but casually asking Mr Ley whether there would be an ordination or no, he told me there would, and asked me whether I would be ordained? I thought of it, and so entered upon examination. God gave me favour in their eyes, and, though young, they passed me, and I was solemnly set apart that day. Old Mr Langley preached, and Mr Ley managed the ordination'. As a Presbyterian minister he now played his full part in striving to put that system into operation in both his parish and neighbourhood, often in face of strong opposition from the sects. The sacrament at Gawsworth was only given to those who 'came willingly to be examined'; many of his parishioners and neighbours were 'affected with the Word, and began to make a very hopeful profession'; and Newcome was 'mightily concerned at peoples' swearing petty oaths, or taking the name of God in vain'. The Rector too had a habit of putting certain questions to himself daily in order to establish his spiritual state. 'What wouldst thou fain have?' he asked himself in conclusion, and replied: 'Grace to delight in God'. He took a very active interest in the local classis and preached for it 'at the Knutsford exercise'; but when he found on 17 January 1653/4, that he had been left out from those ministers who were to assist at the ordination of Mr Edge, 'the baseness of my heart was such that I had great tugging with myself'. Like Josselin he was much concerned at the rising prices; 'We gave sixteen shilling a hoop for wheat', he wrote, 'ten shillings for barley, between fifty shillings and three pounds for a load of malt, and so it put us behind for clothes'.

Newcombe was no Cromwellian. He sincerely mourned the King's death. 'This January 30th [1649]', he recorded sorrowfully, 'was his majesty Charles the First beheaded, which news came to us when I lived at Goosetree, and a general sadness it put upon us all. It dejected me much, I remember, the horridness of the fact, and much indisposed me for the service of the Sabbath next after the news came'. He refused to publish the Army's Declaration in his church following the expulsion of the Rump Parliament. 'I found my heart', he said, 'after reproached me not'. And he rejoiced 'in the preservation of his majesty' after the defeat at Worcester. Finally, as we have already seen, he preached the thanksgiving sermon at Manchester for the Restoration, taking as his text: 'They sent unto the king, saying, Return and all thy servants' (II.Sam.XIX.14). Newcome was certainly a very busy man. For quite apart from his normal parish work and his activities in relation to the classis, he also delivered a monthly lecture at Marton and undertook exacting preaching tours in the locality. Gawsworth, however, did not provide him with a 'maintenance'; and so after much heart-burning and endless trouble in securing a suitable successor, he went as an assistant curate to Manchester under Mr Heyricke, where he was certain of £94 per annum and had received a promise from the congregation to make it up to £120, which indeed they did. It is sad to think that in return for all his loyalty to the House of Stuart he was one of the Bartholomew martyrs. In 1672 he obtained a licence to preach and continued to do so until his death during 1695.[26]

Richard Baxter, a much better known figure, tells us in his autobiography something of his early childhood and later ministry at Kidderminster. He was born in 1615 in Shropshire and was brought up in the wake of the Laudian reaction. 'We lived in a country', he wrote, 'that had but little preaching at all. In the village where I was born there were four readers successively in six years' time, ignorant men, and two of them immoral in their lives, who were all my schoolmasters.' These readers, Baxter went on to say, whipped the boys when they were drunk and gabbled through the church service of a Sunday morning in order to allow as much time as possible for Sunday sports. 'The rest of the day even till dark night almost, except eating-time, was spent in dancing under a maypole and a great tree not far from my father's door.' Richard's father was a strict Puritan and while the majority of the villagers danced, led by tabor and pipe, he and a few more prayed and read their Bibles. At first Richard himself was attracted by the dancing, but, he declared, 'when I heard them call my father Puritan it did much to cure me and alienate me from them; for I considered that my father's exercise of reading the Scripture was better than theirs, and would surely be better thought on by all men at the last'.

After ordination Baxter went to Bridgnorth, where apparently the Laudian writ did not run. Here were six parishes, two in the town and four others in the countryside, all under Parson William Madstard, who was 'privileged from all episcopal jurisdiction except the archbishop's triennial visitation'. Consequently Baxter's scruples and conscience were not unduly troubled. 'I often read the Common Prayer before I preached', he recorded, 'both on the Lords days and Holy days, but I never administered the Lord's Supper, nor ever baptised any child with the sign of the cross, nor ever wore the surplice, nor was ever put to appear at any bishop's court'. However, he and his fellow Puritan clergy were roused to wrath by the Et caetera Oath and decided to take the offensive: 'For now our drowsy mindlessness of that subject was shaken off by their violence; and we that thought it best to follow our business and live in quietness and let the bishops alone, were roused by the terrors of an oath to look about us and understand what we did'. This he certainly did during his famous and well-known ministry at Kidderminster by preaching, catechizing, and conference. A strict discipline, enforced by excommunication, was also practised throughout the town during his incumbency. 'The congregation was usually full', he wrote, 'so that we were fain to build five galleries after my coming thither, the church itself being very capacious, and most commodious and convenient that ever I was in. Our private meetings also were full. On the Lords-days there was no disorder to be seen in the streets, but you might hear an hundred families singing psalms and repeating sermons as you passed through the streets'.[27]

All too many of the clergy, as we have already seen, suffered in one form or another, from one side or the other, during the Civil Wars.

John White, Rector of Dorchester in Dorset for forty years, was a moderate Puritan, who nevertheless had been prosecuted before the High Commission 'for preaching against Arminianism and the popish ceremonies'. It was his boast, indeed, that in the course of his ministry he had expounded the Scriptures all over once and half over again, while a beggar could not be found in his town. Deeply respected and loved by his parishioners, who called him 'the patriarch of Dorchester', he yet found when civil war broke out that 'factions and fond opinions' had crept into his little flock. A troop of Rupert's horse plundered his rectory and carried off his library, while he himself was compelled to fly to London. There, in 1645, he took the place of the sequestered Dr Featley in Lambeth parish church and also 'was appointed to have the care and use of the doctor's library, until the doctor should be able to procure his'. This seemed a fair tit for tat; but the old man could not rest content until he had returned to his beloved Dorchester, after refusing in 1647 the Wardenship of New College. Alas, times had changed, and he found his influence and prestige had sadly waned in his own country. He died broken-hearted in 1650.[28]

Neutrality was no safeguard. John Dod, Vicar of Fawsley in Northamptonshire, described himself as 'a passive nonconformist'; and had on several occasions defended the bishops against the attacks of Puritan extremists. Furthermore as a good decalogist he believed in obeying 'lawful authority'. All this did not save him from the attentions of the cavaliers, who plundered him three times. At their first appearance they threatened to take his life, to which Dod replied: 'If you do, you will send me to heaven, where I long to be'. Their second arrival found him confined to his bed by sickness; but this did not prevent them from cutting away the bed curtains and stealing the pillows from under his head. The third time he was sitting by the parlour fire when one of the plunderers carried down the sheets from his bedroom and left them there, while he went in search of more loot. The Vicar promptly concealed the best pair under the cushion on which he was seated and thus, as he chuckled to himself after their departure, 'plundered the plunderers'. Dod, who 'loved all who loved Christ', was described by Granger in his *Biographical History* as one whose 'learning was excelled by few and his unaffected piety by none'. His 'sayings' were, apparently, pasted up on the walls of cottages in his neighbourhood; and one old woman actually declared 'that she would have gone distracted for the loss of her husband, if she had been

ECCLESIA ANGLICANA.

The looting of a parsonage (1648)

without Mr Dod's sayings in her house'. He published among other works: *The Patrimony of Christian Children*, *An Exposition of the Ten Commandments*, and *Ten Sermons to fit Men for the Worthy Receiving of the Lord's Supper*.[29]

When Jeremy Taylor was taken prisoner by the Roundheads at Cardigan Castle in February 1645/6, his captors alluded to him as 'a most spruce neat formalist, a very ginger-bread Idoll, an Arminian in print'. Taylor, who was Rector of Uppingham from 1638 to 1642, was certainly a notable Laudian. Barlow referred to him in 1641 as one of those who 'were forcing the Church of England into the extremes of doctrine not allowed by law'. As soon as Civil War broke out he joined the King at Oxford, became an army chaplain, was captured at Cardigan Castle, and eventually took refuge with the Vaughan family at Golden Grove. Here much of his splendid prose was written, including the two treatises on *Holy Living* and *Holy Dying*. Yet although so many of his books and sermons are classics very little is known about his personal life. For a short period he was incarcerated in Chepstow Castle; but he had found his way back into the ministry in London before the Restoration, when he began his brief and brilliant career in Ireland.[30]

Another literary, musical, and Laudian parson, but of a slightly earlier generation than Taylor's, was Charles Butler, Vicar of Wotton St Lawrence in Hampshire. 'He was of the true Laudian school', writes a correspondent. 'Things in his church were decently ordered, the altar being overspread with a rich carpet falling on all sides in lovely folds, and fenced off in the chancel by Communion rails. He wore, too, a "clean surplice", and had new service books provided.'[31] Butler lived and worked for forty-seven years at Wootton St Lawrence in a wretched little thatched vicarage that a friend declared was unworthy of so fine a scholar. The Vicar was certainly a man of many parts. He wrote an English Grammar, *The Principles of Music*, and his ever famous book on bees, *The Feminine Monarchy*. Butler, who has been called the father of British bee-keeping, was the first to discover that bees were feminine, while the drones were male; but remained ignorant until the day of his death that the Queen was the mother and slave of the swarm instead of the ruler of the hive. Undoubtedly he made it pay. From the profits of his hives he gave his daughter, whom he called his 'sweet honey girl', a marriage portion of four hundred pounds. Butler was described by Fuller as a pious, painstaking, and learned clergyman, who performed his parish duties most conscientiously. Communion was celebrated once a quarter, when the Vicar personally went round all the hamlets attached to his parish, thus insuring that none should lack the opportunity of partaking of the sacrament. The churchwardens' accounts show that the poor were relieved and the church kept in good repair during his long incumbency. For the latter purpose he did not scruple to encourage wakes and church ales. Butler's last written words reflect the regular tenor of his ways: 'Live soberly, righteously and holily; holily in respect to God, righteously in respect of our neighbour; soberly in respect of ourselves'. Even the Round-heads could respect such a parson and allowed him to remain un-molested in his living.

The last but by no means least character in this our gallery of country parsons, is that worthy historian Thomas Fuller himself. Fuller, the son of a Rector of St Peter's Aldwincle in Northampton-shire, had been educated at Queen's College, Cambridge and Sydney Sussex and became curate of St Benet's. His uncle, Bishop Davenant of Salisbury, then presented him to a prebend in his cathedral and the valuable Dorset living of Broadwindsor, a straggling country parish some seven miles long and four wide. Here he was well liked; and there is a tradition to the effect that he used to preach from the church steps in summertime to a congregation so large that no room could be found for it in the church itself.

Fuller was as homely and knowledgeable a countryman, despite his donnish training, as any of his parishioners. He dwelt in a cottage, farmed his own glebe, and collected local proverbs. At Broadwindsor he wrote his first book, *The Holy State*, with its sketches of the faithful minister and the good wife. The minister, he said, 'endeavours to get the general love and goodwill of his parish . . . otherwise he may preach his own heart out, before he preacheth anything into theirs. . . . He shall sooner get their good will by walking uprightly than by crouching and creeping.' The good wife, whose portrait was doubtless

L

based on his own wife, Ellen Groves, is described as a prudent house-
wife, a good mother, her demeanour meek towards her husband and
modest to the rest of the world, dressed respectably but not expen-
sively, and above all never giving away her husband's secrets, if indeed
she is ever entrusted with them. For Fuller added as a postscript: 'he
knows little who will tell his wife all he knows'. The good life, he
maintained, was to live under a good king; but although always a
royalist he was no Laudian or Puritan; approving neither 'popish
practices' nor Calvinist austerity. His inclination was to pray with
the saints, but play with the sinners.

Before Civil War broke out Fuller had left Broadwindsor for the
Savoy Chapel, although he still retained the former living. It was, of
course, sequestered by parliament; but John Pinney, the intruding
minister, who had the reputation of being at once a gentleman-scholar
and a 'charming preacher', appears to have so commended himself to
the ex-vicar that eventually Fuller resigned in his favour. He himself
remained in London until August 1643 when he finally declined to take
a parliamentary oath repudiating the King's cause and fled to Oxford,
where he immediately offended the royalist extremists by advocating
making peace on honourable terms. Oxford, in fact, became too hot to
hold him; so he joined Hopton's Army in the west as an Army chaplain,
and took refuge after that general's defeat in Basing House, the splendid
library of which enabled him to go on making notes for *The Church
History of Britain* and *The History of the Worthies of England*. The
hot-tempered chaplain was much put out when his studies were
interrupted by Waller's cannon; and he told the garrison, in most
unbecoming language, how to deal 'with those howling wolves that
threatened his peace'. He then moved to Exeter as chaplain to the
infant princess Henrietta; and there helped to draw up favourable
terms for the surrender of the city. These Exeter Articles later
exempted him from having to subscribe to the Solemn Leage and
Covenant. For a while he became a wandering scholar; but once again
settled in London until complaints were made in the House of Commons that malignant ministers in various parts of the metropolis were
illegally using the Prayer Book. Fuller was one of them; for although in
many respects a moderate Puritan he was also a Church of England
man, who loved her liturgy. Nevertheless it was not long before this
broad-church divine found a suitable niche in the new regime. The
Earl of Carlisle presented him to the living of Waltham Abbey in
1649. There most of the parish work was performed by the curate,
Nathaniel Hatley, while the Vicar used his ample leisure for study and
writing. He certainly remained on the very best of terms with the local
parliamentary committee, as later with the Triers. There is an amusing
story that when he appeared before the latter searching questions were

asked and a delicate situation arose, which Fuller handled with his somewhat boisterous good-humour. 'Sir', he said to John How, 'you may
observe that I am a pretty corpulent man, and I am to go through a
passage that is very straight: I beg you would be so good as to give me
a shove and help me through'. The historian, alas, was not always so
tactful. His patron, the Earl of Carlisle, had been greatly amused by
some verses Fuller had written on a scold, and asked for a copy. The
author replied: 'What need of that, my Lord? you have the original'.
Such plain speaking lead to the resignation of Waltham Abbey and
the acceptance instead of Cranford in Middlesex. During this period in
the country Fuller had access to the libraries of the Earls of Middlesex
and Bath, and completed *The Church History of Britain*, which was
published while he still lived at Waltham Abbey.

In 1651 the historian re-appeared in London as a lecturer at St
Clement Dane, where Pepys became one of his admirers; and he
played an active part, in association with General Monk, in bringing
about the Restoration. Only his sudden and most unexpected death
deprived him of the bishopric he so richly deserved. His *History of the
Worthies of England* was published posthumously in 1662.

Tom Fuller was essentially of the school of the Elizabethan Hooker,
rather than that of the Jacobean Laud. 'A broad-chested soul', he
believed firmly in the humanities, tolerated all the sects, apart from the
Quakers, and was not interested in party labels. 'For those who en-
deavour', he wrote, 'to make the way to heaven narrower than God
hath made it, by prohibiting what he permits, do in event make the way
to hell wider, accasioning the committing of such sins, which God
hath forbidden'.[32]

NOTES

[1] He refused because 'he had so much kindred about Carlisle at whom he
must either connive in many things, not without hurt to himself; or else
deny them, not without offence to them'. Fuller, *Church History*, Vol. II,
p. 521.

[2] Fuller, *Church History*, Vol. III, p. 107; *The History of the Worthies of
England*, Vol. III, p. 308, Brook, *Lives of the Puritans*, Vol. I, pp. 242–62.

[3] Fuller, *Church History*, Vol. III, p. 184; Addison, *English Country
Parson*, p. 32; *Nowell's Catechism* (Parker Society) pp. i–ix.

[4] Fuller, *Worthies*, Vol. II, p. 19.

[5] D.N.B.

[6] D.N.B.; Mitchell, *English Pulpit Oratory*, pp. 198–9.

[7] *Harrison's Description of England*, Vol. I, p. 37.

[8] Fuller, *Church History*, Vol. III, p. 347.

[9] Quoted from *The Times*, 26 August 1954.

L*

[10] See Isaak Walton, *The Life of Mr Richard Hooker*. C. J. Sisson, *The Judicious Marriage of Mr Hooker and the Birth of the Laws of Ecclesiastical Polity*. Shirley, *Richard Hooker and Contemporary Political Ideas*.

[11] Addison, *English Country Parson*, pp. 45–7. Fuller, *Worthies*, Vol. I, p. 55. Brook, *Lives of the Puritans*, Vol. II, pp. 235–7; 259.

It should be noted that a clergyman of the same name, but a different person, became Vicar of Stansted Abbots in 1640, and of Great Parndon in 1645.

[12] Brook, *Lives of the Puritans*, Vol. II, pp. 390–5. Fuller, *Worthies*, Vol. II, p. 207. D.N.B. Haller, *Rise of Puritanism*, p. 110.

[13] Brook, *Lives of the Puritans*, Vol. II, pp. 409–12. Haller, *Rise of Puritanism*, pp. 62 and 67.

[14] Brook, *Lives of the Puritans*, Vol. II, pp. 412–15. Haller, *Rise of Puritanism*, p. 102.

[15] Fuller, *Worthies*, Vol. III, p. 286. Dr W. Gouge wrote: 'There were many eyewitnesses besides myself'.

[16] Brook, *Lives of the Puritans*, Vol. III, pp. 190–6.

[17] Lloyd, *Memoirs*, pp. 388–9. Haller, *Rise of Puritanism*, p. 108.

[18] Fuller, *Worthies*, Vol. I, p. 171.

[19] Walton, *The Life of Mr George Herbert*. Margaret Bottrall, *George Herbert. George Herbert's Country Parson*, ed. G. M. Forbes.

John Aubrey wrote of his funeral: 'he was buryed (according to his owne desire) with the singing service for the buriall of the dead, by the singing men of Salisbury . . . he lyes in the chancell, under no large, nor yet very good, marble grave-stone, without any inscription'.

[20] A. L. Maycock, *Nicholas Ferrar of Little Gidding*, p. 104.

[21] *Church Quarterly Review*, July–September, 1955. Basil Willey, *Robert Herrick*, p. 254.

[22] *Proceedings, . . . County of Kent*, pp. 176 and 177.

[23] *Diary of John Rous*, (Camden Society).

[24] See, *Sussex Archaeological Collections*, Vol. I, 1853; also Arthur Ponsonby, *English Diaries*, pp. 125–7.

[25] *The Diary of the Rev. Ralph Josselin*, (Camden Society).

[26] *Autobiography of Henry Newcome*, (Chetham Society), Vol. I.

[27] *Autobiography of Richard Baxter*, ed. Lloyd Thomas.

[28] Fuller, *Worthies*, Vol. III, p. 25. Brook, *Lives of the Puritans*, Vol. III, pp. 88–90.

[29] Fuller, *Church History*, Vol. III, p. 539. Lloyd, *Memoirs*, pp. 129–37. Brook, *Lives of the Puritans*, Vol. III, pp. 1–6. Haller, *Rise of Puritanism*, pp. 56–62.

[30] Matthews, *Walker Revised*, p. 302. See also C. J. Stranks, *The Life and Writings of Jeremy Taylor*.

[31] *The Church Times*, 17 September 1954.

[32] See W. Addison, *Worthy Dr Fuller*, p. 280. Lloyd, *Memoirs*, pp. 523–4.

APPENDIX A

Church Registers

The story of Parish Registers in England began with Thomas Cromwell's injunction of 29 September 1538: 'The curate of every parish church', it ran, 'shall keep one book or register, which book he shall every Sunday take forth and in the presence of the churchwardens or one of them, write and record in the same of all the weddings, christenings and burials made the whole week before; and for every time the same shall be omitted, shall forfeit to the said church iiis and iiiid'. Some fifty-nine years later, on 25 October 1597, Convocation, with the Queen's approval, prescribed further and detailed regulations on this subject that eventually became embodied in the 70th Canon of 1604. These demanded that every minister at his institution should subscribe as follows: 'I shall keep the register-book according to the queen's majesty's instructions'. Every parish had now to provide itself with a parchment book, into which the entries from the old paper books should first be copied; each page being signed by the incumbent and his churchwardens. This parchment book was to be kept in a 'sure coffer with three locks', of which the minister and churchwardens all held keys. Furthermore a copy of each year's entries had to be sent to the bishop after Easter to be preserved in the episcopal archives.

The Directory of Public Worship, which superseded the Prayer Book in 1645, ordered that a register book of vellum be provided in each parish, where not only baptisms, marriages, and deaths were to be recorded, but births as well. The clergy, however, retained the custody of them until the Marriage and Registration Act was passed by the Praise-God Barebones Parliament in 1653. By this Act the registers were handed over to laymen, who were elected by the householders in a parish and called 'parish registers'. Here, for example, is the memorandum recording the appointment of the first parish register at Gainsborough in Lincolnshire:

'September 18th, 1653, Francis Crance of Gainsborough was, according to the direction of the Act of Parliament, August 24th, 1653, for Registring of Marriages, Births and Burials, chosen by the greater part of the Inhabitants and householders of Gainsborough to be the Parish Register, who was September 23rd sworne and approved of by

Chris. Wraye,
Justice of Peace for Gainsborough in the County of Lincolnshire.'

These men were responsible for entering all banns, marriages, births, and burials; but not, apparently, baptisms.

But apart from the interlude of the Commonwealth and Protectorate, the 70th Canon has remained in force, and the clergy kept the registers under its authority until the passing of Rose's Act in 1812.[1]

NOTE

[1] R. E. Chester Waters, *Parish Registers in England*, pp. 6–9. Cardwell, *Synodalia*, Vol. I, pp. 160, 204, 286. Cardwell, *Documentary Annals*, Vol. I, pp. 11, 44, 183, 211, 296, 323. Vol. II, p. 304. J. Gurnhill, *A Monograph on the Gainsborough Parish Registers*, p. 31.

APPENDIX B

Clerical Wills and Estates

Throughout the period covered by this book the standard of living of some country parsons was steadily rising; and this is amply confirmed by clerical wills and inventories of estates. In 1550 Hugh Collinson, Vicar of Kirton-in-Lindsey, Lincolnshire, drew up his Will as follows; 'Hewe Collynson, priest, Soul to God, body to be buried in choir of parish church of Kirton Lindsey. To high altar in same 8*d.*, to same altar an altar cloth of diapar "yf yt may be occupied uppon the same altar accordyng to my will", if not, it shall remain to my friends. To our Lady work of Lincoln xiid. To Hewe Collynson my kinsman 11 sheep, i.e. 4 yowes & 4 lambs, 3 wethers; 3 hogs & two silver spoons. To Margaret his daughter one yowe and a lamb. To Robert Collynson my kinsman one shop upon the hill after the decease of his father, to him and his heirs and assigns and if he sell it, he is to sell it to some of his brethren before any other man. To same Robert Collynson one "brewyng ledde". To Jennet Collynson my brother's daughter a chair and one linen sheet. To Agnes Collynson my brother's daughter one table centre, a chair and one linen sheet. To Alys Ward one short gown. To Richard Tayler her son one yowe and a lamb. To Robert Dawson my brother's servant one yowe and a lamb. To Agnes Tayler to buy her a cupboard 3*s.* 8*d.* To Richard Collynson my brother's son dwelling in Norfolk two silver spoons. To Phillip Collynson my brother's son my bedding which I lie in and all my books. Residue to my brother John Collynson, sole executor'[1]. Whatever the residue may have consisted of, Hugh Collinson's personal possessions appear to have been small and scanty. Similarly the will of Robert Garton, Rector of Algarkirk, who died in 1542, is likewise short and simple. The largest beneficiary was his sister who received forty shillings; few clothes are mentioned, 'my whyt amblyng horse' and 'my downde maer', some books, bed-covers and surplices.

It is a very different matter, however, the further we probe into the seventeenth century. Thomas Wrightson, Vicar of Winthorpe in the same county, died in 1653. 'To John Wrightson my brother', he declared, 'forty ewes, wethers and hogs; the ground I have of Thomas Gusse during the time I have it by lease. To John Wrightson, my kinsman, 10s., at 21 years. To James Wrightson, son of James Wrightson, 40s. at 21 years. To Marie Wrightson, daughter of James Wrightson, 40s at 21 years. To Alice Buyerley, wife of William Buyerley, £3. To John Pickeringe, my kinsman, £4. To Ann Pickeringe, my kinswoman, £5. To William Slight, 20s. To Robert Slight, 10s. To James Wrightson, my brother, 10s. To Richard Pickeringe, 20s. To Marie Younge, John Younge, and William Younge children of William Younge, of Crofte, 20s apiece at 21 years. To Elizabeth Tokin, my kinswoman, 5s. To the poor of our parish, 5s. To Elizabeth, my wife, whom I make executrix, the rest of my goods'.[2] Ready money is evidently now much more plentiful; and from inventories of clerical estates of the same period we find that furnishings and personal effects are also much more abundant. Isaac Allen, Rector of Prestwich, in Lancashire, possessed a large store of such items as bedding, chairs, stools, tables, beds, cushions, fire-irons, 'one hundred and fiftye books', cupboards, 'eight pewter dishes and two flagons', 'two dosen and a halfe of trenchers', many kitchen utensils, three hogsheads in the cellar and brewing instruments in the brewhouse. He evidently employed a considerable staff of servants and was well equipped for farming his forty-acre glebe and for cheese-making.[3] His house was big and roomy, well furnished with every seventeenth-century convenience and plenty of everything to eat and drink. Here was no peasant or poor scholar, but a prosperous gentleman-farmer, cultured, educated, fastidious.

NOTES

[1] *Kirton Lindsey Subdecanal Court Wills*, Vol. II, p. 20.
[2] *Abstracts of Lincolnshire Wills*, p. 236.
[3] Bodleian Library MS. J. W. c.5.fol.288. Quoted from Tatham, *Puritans in Power*, pp. 264–7.

Select Bibliography

PRIMARY SOURCES (UNPUBLISHED)

Newton, W. R., *The Church in Worcestershire*, 1617–1645. An unpublished thesis based on the *Liber Decani et Canonicorum Ecclesiae Cathedralis Wignorniensis.*

The Peterborough Diocesan Records (Lamport Hall MSS). *Church Survey Books.*

PRIMARY SOURCES (PUBLISHED)

Anglo-Catholic Library of Theology:
The Works of William Laud, 7 vols., 1847–60.

Camden Society Publications:
Diary of John Rous, ed. M. A. E. Green, 1856.
Diary of the Revd. Ralph Josselin, ed. E. Hockliffe, 1908.
Letters written by John Chamberlain during the reign of Queen Elizabeth, ed. S. Williams, 1861.
Presbyterian Movement in the Reign of Queen Elizabeth as Illustrated by the Minute Book of the Dedham Classis. 1582–1589, ed. R. G. Usher, 1905.
Proceedings, principally in the County of Kent, ed. L. B. Larking, 1862.
Reports of Cases in the Courts of Star Chamber and High Commission, ed. S. R. Gardiner, 1886.

Chetham Society Publication:
The Autobiography of Henry Newcombe, 2 vols., ed. R. Parkinson, 1852.

County Record Society Publications:
Bedfordshire. Vol. 33. *Elizabethan Churchwardens' Accounts*, ed. J. E. Farmiloe and R. Nixseaman, 1953.
Essex. Vol. 17. *English History from Essex Sources*, ed. A. C. Edwards, 2 vols., 1952.
Lincolnshire. Vol. 2. *Lincoln Episcopal Records in the Time of Thomas Cooper*, 1912.
Vol. 23. *The State of the Church in the Reigns of Elizabeth and James I*, ed. C. W. Foster, 1926.
Norfolk. Vol. 18. *Bishop Redman's Visitation, 1597*, ed. J. F. Williams, 1946. Vol. 24. *Norwich Chapter Books. 1566–1649*, ed. J. F. Williams and B. Cozens-Hardy, 1953.
Northamptonshire. Vol. I. *Quarter Sessions Records of the County of Northampton. 1630–1658*, ed. Joan Wake, 1921/2.
Oxfordshire. Vol. 10. *Oxfordshire Peculiars*, ed. S. A. Peyton, 1928.
Vol. 23. *The Archdeacon's Court 1584*, ed. E. R. Brinkworth, 2 vols., 1942–6.
Somerset. Vol. 43. *Collecteana II*, ed. T. F. Palmer, 1928.

Parker Society Publications:
  Archbishop Sandys, *Sermons and Miscellaneous Pieces*, 1841.
  Bullinger's Decades, 1845–50.
  Correspondence of Archbishop Parker, 1853.
  Fulke's Defence of Translations of the Bible, 1843.
  Fulke's Answers, 1848.
  Nowell's Catechism, 1853.
  Original Letters, 1537–1558, 1847.
  Remains of Archbishop Grindal, 1843.
  Works of Bishop Jewel, 1845–50.
  Works of Archbishop Whitgift, 1851–53.
  Zurich Letters, 1842-5.

Surtees Society Publication:
  Correspondence of John Cosin, 2 vols., 1869.

MISCELLANEOUS SOURCES

Addison, W. *The English Country Parson*, 1947.
  Worthy Dr Fuller, 1951.
Addleshaw, G. W., and F. Etchells, *The Architectural Settings of Anglican Worship*, 1948.
  The High Church Tradition, 1941.
Aubrey, John, *Brief Lives*, 2 vols., ed. Andrew Clark, 1898.

Baskerville, G., *English Monks and the Suppression of the Monasteries*, 1937.
Bewes, W. A., *Church Briefs*, 1896.
Bottrall, M., *George Herbert*, 1954.
Brook, B., *The Lives of the Puritans*, 3 vols., 1813.
Brooks, F. W., *The Social Position of the Parson in the Sixteenth Century*, 1947.

Calder, Isobel, *The Activities of the Puritan Faction of the Church of England: 1625–1633*, 1957.
Cardwell, E., *Documentary Annals*, 2 vols., 1839.
  Synodalia, 2 vols., 1842.
Clarke, W. K. Lowther, *Liturgy and Worship*, 1932.
Cross, F. L., and Walker, P. E., *Anglicanism*, 1935.

Davies, Horton, *The Worship of the English Puritans*, 1948.
Dowden, E., *Puritan and Anglican*, 1900.

Elton, G. R., *England under the Tudors*, 1955.

Frere, W. H., *The English Church in the Reigns of Elizabeth and James I*, 1904.
Frere, W. H., and Douglas, C. E., *Puritan Manifestoes*, 1907.
Frere, W. H., and Kennedy, W. M., *Visitation Articles and Injunctions of the Period of the Reformation*, 3 vols., (Alcuin Club Collections), 1910.
Fuller, T., *The Church History of Britain*, 3 vols., ed. J. Nichols, 1868.
  The History of the Worthies of England, 3 vols., ed. P. A. Nuttall, 1840.

Gee, H., *The Elizabethan Clergy*, 1898.
  The Elizabethan Prayer Book, 1902.

Gibbon, A., *Valuations in the Diocese of Lincoln in 1524.*
Gooch, G. P., *Political Thought from Bacon to Halifax,* 1927.
Gurnhill, J., *A Monograph on the Gainsborough Parish Registers,* 1890.

Haller, W., *The Rise of Puritanism,* 1938.
    Liberty and Reformation in the Puritan Revolution, 1955.
Heylin, P., *Cyprianus Anglicus,* 1668.
Hood, C. M., *Sequestered Loyalists and Bartholomew Sufferers,* 1922.

Kennedy, W. M., *Elizabethan Episcopal Administration,* 3 vols., (Alcuin Club
    Collections), 1924.
Ketton Cremer, R. W., *A Norfolk Gallery,* 1948.

Lloyd, David, *Memoirs, Actions, Sufferings and Deaths of those that suffered
    for the Protestant Religion in our late Intestine Wars,* 1668.

Magee, Brian, *The English Recusants,* 1938.
Marsden, J. B., *The History of the Early Puritans,* 1860.
Mason, R. H., *The History of Norfolk,* 1884.
Matthews, A. G., *Calamy Revised,* 1934.
    Walker Revised, 1948.
Maycock, A. L., *Nicholas Ferrar of Little Gidding,* 1938.
Mitchell, W. F., *English Pulpit Oratory from Andrewes to Tillotson,* 1932.
Montague, Richard, *Visitation Articles for the Diocese of Norwich, 1638.*

Neal, Daniel, *The History of the Puritans,* 5 vols., 1822.

Ponsonby Arthur, *English Diaries,* 1923.
    More English Diaries, 1927.
Powicke, F. M., *The Reformation in England,* 1942.
Prothero, G. W., *Select Statutes . . . reigns of Elizabeth and James I,* 1906.
Prynne, W., *Canterburies Doome,* 1644.

Richardson, C. F., *English Preachers and Preaching, 1640–1670,* 1928.
Roberts, B. Drew, *Mitre and Musket,* 1938.

Salzman, L. F., *England in Tudor Times,* 1926.
Selden, J., *Table Talk,* 1689.
Shaw, W. A., *A History of the English Church during the Civil Wars and
    under the Commonwealth,* 2 vols., 1900.
Shirley, F. G., *Richard Hooker and Contemporary Political Ideas,* 1949.
Sisson, C. J., *The Judicious Marriage of Mr Hooker and the Birth of the
    Laws of Ecclesiastical Polity,* 1940.
Soden, G., *Godfrey Goodman,* 1953.
Stranks, C. J., *The Life and Writings of Jeremy Taylor,* 1952.
Strype, John, *Annals of the Reformation,* 2 vols., 1824 edition.
    History of the Life and Acts of Edmund Grindal, 1821 edition.
    The Life and Acts of John Aylmer, 1821 edition.
    The Life and Acts of Matthew Parker, 1821 edition.
    The Life and Acts of John Whitgift, 1882 edition.
    Memorials of Thomas Cranmer, 1848 edition.
Sykes, N., *Old Priest and New Presbyter,* 1956.

Tate, W. E., *The Parish Chest*, 1946.
Tatham, G. B., *The Puritans in Power*, 1913.
Trevelyan, G. M., *English Social History*, 2nd edition, 1946.
Trevor-Roper, H. R., *Archbishop Laud*, 1940.
Trotter, E., *Seventeenth Century Life in the Country Parish*, 1919.

Usher, R. G., *The Reconstruction of the English Church*, 2 vols., 1910.

Venn, J. A., *The Foundations of Agricultural Economics*, 2nd edition, 1933.

Wakeman, H. O., *The Church and the Puritans*, 1894.
Walker, J., *Sufferings of the Clergy*, 1714.
Walton, Isaak, *The Lives of Mr Richard Hooker, Mr George Herbert, etc.*, 1895 edition.
Ware, S. L., *The Elizabethan Parish in its Ecclesiastical and Financial Aspect*, 1908.
Waters, R. E. Chester, *Parish Registers in England*, 1883.
Watt, M., *The History of the Parson's Wife*, 1943.
West, F. H., *Rude Forefathers*, 1949.
Whitaker, W. B., *Sunday in Tudor and Stuart Times*, 1933.
Woodhouse, H. F., *The Doctrine of the Church in Anglican Theology, 1547–1603*, 1954.

Abstracts of Lincolnshire Wills.
Annals of Evangelical Nonconformity in the County of Essex, ed. T. W. Davids, 1863.
Acts and Ordinances of the Interregnum, ed. C. H. Firth and R. S. Rait, 3 vols., 1911.
Autobiography of Richard Baxter, ed. J. M. Lloyd Thomas, 1925.
Book of the Valuations of the Ecclestiastical Preferments in England, A, 1680.
Calendar of State Papers Domestic: Charles I.
Documents Illustrative of English Church History, ed. H. Gee and Hardy, 1921.
George Herbert's Country Parson, ed. G. M. Forbes, 1949.
Harrison's Description of England in Shakespeare's Youth, 2 vols., ed. F. J. Furnival, 1877.
Journal of William Dowsing, ed. E. H. Evelyn White, 1885.
Journals of the House of Commons, Vols. I, II, III.
Kirton Lindsey Subdecanal Court Wills, 2 vols.
Lincoln Episcopal Visitations, ed. E. Peacock, 1884.
Records of Oundle Parish Church, ed. W. Richardson and S. C. Harries, 1954.
Tracts Ascribed to Richard Bancroft, ed. A. Peel, 1953.
Tudor Parish Documents of the Diocese of York, ed. J. S. Purvis, 1948.
Two Elizabethan Puritan Diaries by Richard Rogers and Samuel Ward, ed. M. M. Kappen, 1930.
Victoria County History of Worcestershire, Vol. II.
Viewe of the Clargie of Essex, London, 1610.

PERIODICALS

Essex Review, Vol. XV, 1906, 'Essex Churches: Notes contributed by R. H. Browne concerning the condition of some Essex Churches, furniture and graveyards in the sixteenth and seventeenth centuries'.

Essex Review, Vol. XXXII, 1923, 'Visitation of the Archdeaconry of Colchester. 1588'.

Essex Review, Vol. XLV. 1936, 'The Surplice in Essex'.

The Thirty-eighth Report of the Associated Architectural Societies, Vol. XVI, Part I, 1881, 'The Primary Visitation of the Diocese of Lincoln by Bishop Neile. A.D. 1614', ed. Rev. Precentor Venables.

The Fifty-fifth Report of the Associated Architectural Societies, Vol. XXIV, Part II, 1898, 'Institutions to Benefices in the Diocese of Lincoln, 1540–1570. Calendar No. 1', ed. C. W. Foster.

The Sixty-fifth Report of the Associated Architectural Societies, Vol. XXIX, Part II, 1908, 'Leicestershire: The Metropolitical Visitation of Archbishop Laud'.

Lincoln Architectural and Archaeological Society Reports and Papers, Vol. II, Part I, New Series, 1938, 'The Royalist Clergy of Lincolnshire', ed. J. W. F. Hill.

Norfolk and Norwich Archaeological Society, Vol. XXVIII, 'An Episcopal Visitation in 1593', ed. J. F. Williams.

Norfolk and Norwich Archaeological Society, Vol. XVIII, Part I, 'A List of the Clergy of Norfolk and their Status: 1592–3', H. W. Saunders.

Norfolk and Norwich Archaeological Society, Vol. X, Part I, 'The Condition of the Archdeaconry of Norwich in 1603'.

DICTIONARIES.

Dictionary of National Biography.

Index